The Lightning Phenomenon

Need for Awareness, Detection and Protection from Damage Caused by Lightning

The Lightning Phenomenon

Need for Awareness, Detection and Protection from Damage Caused by Lightning

Editors
Ravindra Arora
Chandima Gomes

CENTRE FOR SCIENCE & TECHNOLOGY OF THE NON-ALIGNED AND OTHER DEVELOPING COUNTRIES (NAM S&T CENTRE)

NATIONAL SCIENCE AND TECHNOLOGY COMMISSION (NASTEC), COLOMBO, SRI LANKA

2009
DAYA PUBLISHING HOUSE
Delhi - 110 035

ISBN10 81-7035-579-6
ISBN13 978-81-7035-579-3

Centre for Science and Technology of the Non-Aligned and Other Developing Countries (NAM S&T Centre)
Core-6A, 2nd Floor, India Habitat Centre, Lodhi Road,
New Delhi-110 003 (India)
Phone: +91-11-24644974, 24645134, Fax: +91-11-24644973
E-mail: namstct@gmail.com
Website: www.namstct.org

Published by : **Daya Publishing House**
1123/74, Deva Ram Park, Tri Nagar, Delhi - 110 035
Phone: 27383999, Fax: (011) 23260116
e-mail: dayabooks@vsnl.com
website: www.dayabooks.com
Showroom : 4760-61/23, Ansari Road, Darya Ganj
New Delhi - 110 002
Phone: 23245578, 23244987

Laser Typesetting : **Classic Computer Services**
Delhi - 110 035

Printed at : **Chawla Offset Printers**
Delhi - 110 052

Printed in India

Foreword

Lightning was striking the Earth long before human life began, and may even have played a crucial role in the evolution of life on our planet. Around the globe, lightning lights up the sky fifty to one hundred times per second, and while not every lightning bolt reaches the ground – about 75% of lightning discharges remain in the clouds–each year in the United States alone lightning hits the ground about twenty-five million times. The highest levels of lightning activity are observed in tropical and subtropical regions of the world. Lightning is a spectacular natural phenomenon, but it is also a severe hazard to human life and to various objects and systems. Although the lightning death rate in industrialized countries has decreased during the course of the twentieth century by a factor of 5 or more, there are still about 100 individuals killed annually in the United States and about 1000 injured. Worldwide, annually there are a few thousand lightning deaths and tens of thousands of lightning injuries, most of them in developing countries. Lightning initiates many forest fires, and over 30% of all electric power failures are lightning related. A lightning strike to an unprotected or inadequately protected object can be catastrophic.

There are generally two types of lightning protection: structural protection and surge protection. Basically, a structural lightning protection system (LPS) includes (1) air terminals, (2) down conductors, and (3) ground terminals. These three elements of the system must form a continuous conductive path (actually at least two paths) for lightning current, with all connections between the elements typically being accomplished by bolting or welding. The function of such a system is to intercept imminent lightning and safely direct its current to ground. The structural metal framework (including metal support posts) can play the role of down conductors if it is electrically continuous. Vertically driven rods are typically used as ground terminals, but sometimes the ground terminal is made of a buried horizontal loop conductor encircling the structure (also called a ring electrode). The latter type of grounding is beneficial in that it additionally serves to intercept ground surface or underground electrical arcs that may develop toward the structure from a nearby object (such as a tree) struck by lightning. The closer the structure approaches a Faraday cage (a metallic enclosure of sufficient thickness), the better its interior is protected from lightning effects. All metallic objects above or below the ground surface that are separated from LPS conductors by distances smaller than the so-called safety distance must be bonded to the LPS conductors. Surge protection serves to limit currents and voltages on electronic, power, and communication systems.

Timely warning of a lightning threat is crucial for personal safety. If thunderstorms are predicted in the area, it might be better not to plan or to postpone outdoor activities. Dark clouds should generally be viewed as potential lightning producers and as a signal to consider termination of outdoor activities. Any time that visual (flashes) or audible (thunder) indications of a thunderstorm exist, moving in or remaining in reasonably safe shelters, such as large buildings and all metal body cars, should be considered. The distance to the lightning can be estimated by counting the number of seconds between the flash and the thunder and dividing the result by 3 (to obtain kilometers). For example, if the time interval between the flash and the thunder is 30 s, the lightning is approximately at a distance of 10 km. A typical thunderstorm covers this distance in 15 minutes or so. However, many lightning discharges strike ground at more than one point, with separation between the strike points (produced within less than a second) being up to several kilometers. An AM-radio, tuned to the low end of the broadcast band (550 kHz), acts as a primitive lightning detector responding by periodic static "crashes" to electromagnetic radiation pulses produced by lightning discharges. Modern multiple-station lightning locating systems, such as the U.S. National Lightning Detection Network (NLDN), continuously provide information on the cloud-to-ground lightning activity in nearly real time in a number of countries, but insufficiently so in the third world.

The annual toll of lightning casualties can be reduced through public education, and serious lightning damage to various objects and systems can be often avoided when adequate lightning protection and warning systems are employed. In this regard, I applaud the recent contribution made by the International Roundtable on Lightning Protection in Colombo, Sri Lanka, May 22-25, 2007. The Forum was attended by 52 scientists from 12 countries, many of which experience both a high level of lightning activity and lack of technical expertise in solving lightning related-problems. I hope the Roundtable on Lightning Protection will become a regular event helping save human life and mitigate lightning effects on objects and systems.

Vladimir A. Rakov, *Ph.D., FIEEE, FAMS, FIET*
Professor and Co-Director of the International Center for Lightning Research and Testing
Chair of Electromagnetics and Energy Systems Division
Department of Electrical and Computer Engineering
University of Florida, Gainesville, FL, USA

Preface

The phenomenon of lightning is fascinating when observed from a distance. However, if it strikes nearby, it is most scary. That is why major population of the world considers it to be a curse from God. Every lightning strike is unique and peculiar in itself. In spite of so much of advancement in science and engineering and large number of scientists working on this phenomenon since several centuries, it has been a challenge for the mankind from the nature to explain every deleterious effect caused by lightning strikes. Damage to the life and property due to lightning continues all over the world. Even advanced countries, like the USA, suffer from heavy damage of life and property.

The phenomenon of 'lightning' is as old as this planet. NASA reported recently (2007) observation of the occurrence of lightning even on the planet Venus. A capacitor is formed by the dielectric in between two electrodes. Air is the cheapest and freely available dielectric on our earth. It is the most widely utilized dielectric by the power system network. Clouds, aerosols and pollution layers in the atmosphere carry electric charge generated by various processes, such as, UV and cosmic ray irradiation, friction by air currents and rapid movement of objects like aircrafts in the atmosphere. High electric field intensity giving rise to corona is also a source of electric charge in the atmosphere.

Electric charge is restful in the dielectrics but restless in the conductors. Accumulation of charge gives rise to potential. Electrically charged layers, mentioned above, develop high potential and behave like an electrode at high voltage. The mother earth, having a unique property of maintaining its potential to be at zero level, behaves like the other electrode of the capacitor formed by the atmospheric air as dielectric in between the two electrodes.

The charge resting in the thick layers has a tendency to segregate, forming concentrations of like polarity charges, the space charge. This process gives rise to further enhancement of the potential at the charged particle layers in the atmosphere.

When this static potential, which could be of either polarity, rises excessively, the electric field enhancement results in the failure of insulation properties of the air gap leading to a breakdown of the atmospheric air in between the cloud and the ground. This is nothing but the lightning strike seen as development of streamer and unstable leader in the atmosphere.

The people of the developing countries are thankful to NAM S&T Centre, New Delhi, India and National Science and Technology Commission (NASTEC), Colombo, Sri Lanka to have organized "The International Roundtable on Lightning Protection" at Colombo, Sri Lanka from 22nd to 25th May 2007. It was an exciting event. Experts and representatives from twelve countries were together for four days. Presentations of the papers were followed by lively discussions. It revealed the level of awareness, activities, protective measures and myths prevailing in these countries. It was concluded that the most important task is to educate and make aware the people at large to protect both, the life and property from the catastrophe caused by lightning.

The papers presented have been sorted out and categorized into four main chapters. There was a vast difference in the quality of individual papers presented at the Roundtable. However, even if a paper just revealed the poor state of affairs of activities and awareness in the field of lightning in a country, it has been included in the proceedings after vigorous correction work. This compilation provides a base for the awareness, research and protection activities required to be undertaken in most of the countries in this part of the world.

Ravindra Arora

Introduction

Lightning has always greatly fascinated, awed and frightened the humankind with its spectacular intense tree-like flashes. It was present on our planet Earth long before the evolution of life approximately 3 billion years ago and probably played a significant role in the production of organic molecules necessary for the creation of the life form. Lightning is caused by the build up of electrostatic charge in clouds. One region within the cloud builds up a positive charge and the other a negative charge. In this the bottom of the cloud usually ends up being negatively charged and the top positively charged. If the build up of charge becomes great enough, the negative charges may either leap to the positive side of another cloud, called as sheet lightning, or it may leap to the ground. The electrical discharge from a cloud travels the path of least impedance. After striking the ground, rather than going into the Earth, these discharges propagate outward from the strike points on the earth surface. Some facts about the lightning are that a bolt of lightning can travel at a speed of 45 km/s. It can reach temperatures approaching 28,000°C, hot enough to fuse soil or sand into glass channels. An average bolt of negative lightning carries a current of 40 kA, although some bolts can be up to 120 kA, and transfers a charge of 5 coulombs and 500 megajoules that is about one billion volts of electricity, which is enough to light a 100 watt light bulb for 3 months. Incidentally, lightning can be caused by violent forest fires which generate sufficient dust to create a static charge and can also occur within the ash clouds from volcanic eruptions.

Though lightning and thunderstorms are vital to our life as they make nitrogen and also oxygen and free radicals available to the plants and other terrestrial organisms, these are capable of causing wild land fires, human and animal death through electrocution and if in close proximity, temporary deafness and rupturing of the ear's tympanic membrane. The action of lightning's electrical and magnetic fields and the lightning current on industrial premises, power transmission lines, underground communications, aircraft and their electrical circuits and induction of dangerous over-voltage are well known. Lightning is known to have caused extensive exterior and interior damage to structures, particularly churches, since ancient period. Mixail Lomonosov in 1753 and also Benjamin Franklin around the same time proposed the use of lightning rods to provide a safe path of the lightning current to ground, but Maxwell in 1876 suggested that such rod system attracted more lightning strikes than the surrounding area. Therefore a metal enclosure of sufficient thickness, called Faraday Cage, was devised to store gunpowder and inflammable material. Modern lightning protection schemes for structures containing computers and electronics employ a technique known as topological shielding with surge suppression which is the updated version of the Faraday Cage concept.

Lightning is a natural hazard that causes serious economical losses and personal injuries and deaths in many parts of the world. Especially in South and East Asia, Africa and South America the problem is quite acute due to the high occurrence density of lighting, the large population and the rapid and unplanned industrialization. The lack of information in the NAM and other developing countries regarding the lightning related characteristics is one barrier that hinders the development of protection systems. The other barrier is the poor knowledge among the engineering community on lightning and lightning protection and the lack of awareness among the general public in lightning safety. In order to address some of the pertinent issues related to lighting, such as its detection and warning systems, safety and education, protection of structures, power systems, communication and data lines, and the latest status of development in surge protective devices and resolve these concerns through North-South and South-South collaborations, the Centre for Science and Technology of the Non-Aligned and other Developing Countries (NAM S&T Centre) organised an International Roundtable on Lightning Protection during 22-25 May 2007 at Colombo, Sri Lanka jointly with the National Science and Technology Commission (NASTEC) of Sri Lanka.

After inauguration of the Roundtable by Prof. Tissa Vitarana, Minister of Science and Technology of Sri Lanka, seven technical sessions were held to discuss, namely, Lightning and Atmosphere; Detection and Safety; Structural Protection; Protection Standards, Risk Analysis and Other Issues; Overall Protection Measures & Lightning Environment; Protection of LV & Communication Systems; and Protection of HV Systems and Other Concerns. The overall technical programme of the Roundtable was coordinated by Prof. Chandima Gomes, Chairman, Expert Study Group on Lightning Protection Measures of NASTEC and Professor in the Department of Physics, University of Colombo. A field trip and excursion to Kurunegala was arranged on the concluding day of the Roundtable to acquaint the participants with real life lightning situation.

The Roundtable was attended by 52 scientists from 12 countries. The overseas participants were from Bangladesh [Dr. Munir Ahmed, Executive Director, Technological Assistance for Rural Advancement - TARA); Botswana [Mr. Oarabile Nnabu, Electronics Engineer, Botswana Technology Centre]; India [Dr. Ing. Ravindra Arora, Professor, Department of Electrical Engineering, Indian Institute of Technology, Kanpur; Mr. Manish Ranalkar, Meteorologist, India Meteorological Department, Pune; and Dr. C. Lakshmi Narasimhan, Earthquake Engineer, Vellore Institute of Technology

University]; Indonesia [Mr. Hary Soebagyo, Head of Div. of Roadmapping of S&T Program, State Ministry of Science and Technology (RISTEK)]; Malaysia [Mr. Wan Mohd Nazri Wan Daud, Principal Assistant Director, KLIA Meteorological Office, Selangur Darul Ehsan and Mr. Hartino Zainal Abidin, President / R&D Consultant, Lightning Research SDN BHD, Kuala Lumpur]; Mauritius [Mr. Prabhakar Sembhoo, Transmission and Distribution Manager, Central Electricity Board, Curepipe]; Myanmar [Dr. Salai Tluang Za Thang, Lecturer, Power Engineering Department, Mandalay Technological University]; Pakistan [Mr. Mozzam Ali Toor, Chief Executive Officer, Capital Consultants]; Saudi Arabia [Prof. Mohamed Hamid Shwehdi, Electrical Engineering Department, College of Engineering Sciences, Dhahran]; Serbia [Dr. Mladjen Curic, Professor, Institute of Meteorology, University of Belgrade]; and South Africa [Mr. Ngcobo Abednego Maliwa, Senior Technician, Telekom College], who also made their presentation during the event.

The participants from Sri Lanka, who presented their papers during the workshop, were Prof. Chandima Gomes (on 'Fundamental Concepts of Lightning', 'Concepts of Building Protection' and 'Lightning Surge Protection in Power Systems'), Dr. Chandana Jayaratne (on 'Atmospheric Conditions Favouring Thunderstorms'), Dr. Mahendra Fernando (on 'Methods of Lightning Detection & Warning Systems'), Mrs. J. Dewasurendra (on 'Development Concerns of Sri Lanka Standards'), Mr. Kamal Illeperuma (on 'Effects of Lightning on Power Systems in Sri Lanka') and Dr. Mahesh Edirisinghe (on 'Special Concerns of Protecting LV and Communication Equipment').

During the Concluding Session an invited lecture was delivered by Mr. Shailendra Kumar, Senior Regional Sales Manager, Thomas & Betts, Dubai, UAE on the subject 'BSEN 62305:2006 Protection against Lightning: An Overview' and a Panel Discussion was chaired by Prof. C. Gomes, Prof. R. Arora and Prof. M. Curic to discuss and adopt the 'Colombo Declaration on Lightning Protection and Safety'. A copy of the Colombo Declaration follows this Report. The Roundtable ended with the distribution of participation certificates to the participants.

On behalf of the NAM S&T Centre, I express sincere gratitude to Prof. Tissa Vitarana, Honourable Minister of Science & Technology of Sri Lanka for his absolute support and patronage for this Roundtable, and to Prof. Nalini Ratnasiri, Chairperson, NASTEC and Dr. R. D. Guneratne, Director and CEO, NASTEC for hosting and making splendid arrangements for holding the event in Sri Lanka. I have a very special word of appreciation for Prof. Chandima Gomes of NASTEC who along with Dr. Muditha Liyanagedara had been the real force behind the successful management of the event, and also because he toiled hard along with Prof. Ravindra Arora of the Indian Institute of Technology (IIT), Kanpur, India, to whom also I wish to express my deepest gratitude, for jointly editing the present publication. I acknowledge with thanks the kind words from Prof. Vladimir A. Rakov from University of Florida about this publication. My grateful thanks are also due to the National Science and Technology Commission (NASTEC), Sri Lanka for providing generous financial support to bring out this publication. Last, but not the least, I would like to appreciate the valuable services provided by the entire team of the NAM S&T Centre under the guidance of Mr. M. Bandyopadhyay and Dr. V.P. Kharbanda specifically by

Mr. Gaurav Gaur and Mr. Pankaj Buttan, who coordinated the work on the organisation of the Roundtable and subsequent compilation of the material in bringing out this publication.

I trust that the material presented in this volume will be highly useful not only for the scientists and professionals engaged in the field of Lightning Physics, but also for the concerned authorities in the governments of the developing countries in taking appropriate policy measures to create awareness among masses about this natural phenomenon and to provide necessary safeguards to mitigate possible disasters.

Arun P. Kulshreshtha
Director, NAM S&T Centre

Colombo Declaration on Lightning Protection and Safety

We, the participants of the International Roundtable on Lightning Protection held from 22nd to 25th May 2007 at Colombo, Sri Lanka, jointly organized by the National Science & Technology Commission of Sri Lanka (NASTEC) and the Centre for Science and Technology of the Non-Aligned and Other Developing Countries (NAM S&T Centre),

Realizing the gravity of the hazards of lightning that lead to deaths, injuries and economic losses and the need for scientific and technological advancement, proper engineering and technical practices, dissemination of knowledge and public awareness with respect to lightning protection,

Recommend the following to be adopted by the authorities in all concerned countries and practiced with immediate effect.

Recommendations

A. Promotion of Safety Awareness Among the Public

- Deaths and injuries due to lightning shall be minimized and public safety shall be improved by:
  I. Organizing educational and awareness programs for different target groups by the government and non-government organizations.
  II. Including basic concepts of lightning and lightning protection/safety in the school curriculum.
  III. Publishing information on lightning, its hazards and precautions.
  IV. Displaying proper lightning safety instructions at vulnerable locations such as playgrounds, beaches, etc.

B. Enhancing Technical Knowledge and Skills Among Professionals Dealing with Lightning Protection

- Theoretical, technical and practical knowledge as well as skills necessary for implementing lightning protection measures of professionals shall be improved by:
  - I. Organizing technical workshops, seminars, training programs.
  - II. Arranging national/international training events with the support of the government and non-governmental organizations.
  - III. Facilitating professionals to get access to the up-to-date scientific and technical information through electronic media and other means.

C. Protection of Buildings and Structures for the Safety of Occupants and Property

- Buildings shall be protected against lightning through:
  - I. Education and encouragement to the public by adopting scientifically validated lightning protection measures.
  - II. Development of national standards or adoption of international standards for lightning protection.
  - III. Constitution of an authorized body to make recommendations on protection systems and taking necessary steps for minimizing lightning damages.

D. Mitigation of Adverse Effects on Equipment and Systems

- Damage to electrical, electronic & communication equipment, computer networks and other related systems shall be minimized by:
  - I. Establishing awareness programs for administrative and technical personnel in all sectors of the economy about appropriate lightning surge protection solutions.
  - II. Sensitizing manufacturers, importers, designers and installers of protection systems on the need to use the most appropriate lightning surge protection equipment.
  - III. Developing country standards or adopting international standards for lightning surge protection solutions for different sectors (viz. power, communication, computer and data networks, PABX systems, electronic process control systems etc.).
  - IV. Monitoring and certifying the quality of protection devices manufactured in the country and/or imported, as well as certifying the installation of these devices by the authorized body.

E. Protection of Towers and Safety Concerns in Adjacent Areas

- Protection of tower related equipment and safety of the adjacent areas shall be ensured by:

I. Training the professionals to identify protective measures for towers and related equipment to ensure appropriate protection measures.
II. Investigating and taking safety measures for possible increase of lightning hazards in areas adjacent to the tall structures.
III. Making it mandatory to have effective earthing systems for towers.
IV. Making it mandatory for the tower owners to take appropriate measures to protect the adjacent areas.

F. Protection of Power Systems and Communication Networks

- Damage to power systems shall be minimized by:
  I. Investigating the conditions of the existing lightning protection scheme in the power systems.
  II. Including appropriate earthing practices and accepted standards in the curricula of engineering institutions.
  III. Mandating engineers to maintain regular inspection records.
- Damage to communication networks shall be minimized by:
  I. Ensuring compliance with ITU Standards.
  II. Encouraging research in the quality of high frequency earthing systems and communication equipment protection technologies in order to make recommendations to the concerned institutions/service providers to rectify shortcomings.

G. Protection of High Risk Installations

- Damage to storage of hazardous materials such as inflammable chemicals, explosives, petroleum and ammunition dumps and other high risk installations shall be minimized by:
  I. Organizing awareness programs about lightning threats to storage facilities and institutions that transport or use hazardous materials.
  II. Making highest level of structural protection mandatory in such cases.
  III. Inspecting the lightning protection systems in such cases on regular basis.
  IV. Incorporating lightning protection of high-risk installations in national standards.

H. Development of National Standards on Lighting Protection and Safety

- Adherence to proper lightning safety and protection practices in the country shall be promoted by:
  I. Developing, improving and upgrading national standards/codes for lightning protection systems for buildings/equipment and their installations.

II. Conducting awareness programs to popularize the standards/codes among the professionals and public.

III. Making standards mandatory to concerned parties.

I. Testing and Research Facilities and Data Collection

- Services provided to manufacturers and importers of lightning protection equipment to test their products against national standards shall be enhanced by:

  I. Establishing new laboratories and supporting research institutes to upgrade the existing ones.

  II. Providing training in modern techniques and methodologies to test facility providers.

  III. Providing required facilities to researchers on lightning and lightning protection to commence/continue research on lightning.

  IV. Networking the country with a lightning detection system so as to enable lightning forecast and data collection.

  V. Establishing research groups and institutions to develop databases on lightning accidents and other lightning related occurrences.

J. Local Manufacture of Protective Devices

- Local entrepreneurs, inventors and researchers shall be encouraged to produce lightning protection equipment and technologies suitable to local conditions and national standards through:

  I. Financial grants, working facilities, market information, foreign training, etc.

  II. Collaborative programs and forums for exchange of information and sharing their views and work experience.

K. Protection of National Heritage Sites

- Lightning damage free environment shall be ensured for national heritage sites by:

  I. Investigating the present status of archeologically important sites.

  II. Designing and implementing effective and durable protection systems.

  III. Regular inspection of the protection systems.

WE FURTHER RECOMMEND the establishment of an International Institute for Lightning Protection and Safety in Sri Lanka in a phased manner, subject to the availability of donor funds, to address various issues with respect to lightning safety and protection, especially to create awareness among the public about the lightning hazards and mitigation measures, and to promote collaboration between the lightning institutions in the world.

Signed this day, 24th of May 2007 at Colombo, Sri Lanka.

Mr. Hartono Zainal Abidin Malaysia	**Dr. Munir Ahmed** TARA-Bangladesh	**Mr. M. A. Ahmed** Capital Consultants -Pakistan
Dr.-Ing. Ravindra Arora Indian Institute of Technology-India	**Prof. Madjen Curic** University of Belgrade-Serbia	**Mr. W. M. Nazri Wan Daud** KLIA Meteorological Office Malaysia
Prof. A. P. Kulshreshtha (NAM S&T Centre)-India	**Mr. A. M. Ngcobo** Telkom College-South Africa	**Dr C.Lakshmi Narasimhan** Vellore Institute of Technology University, India
Mr. Oarabile Nnabu Botswana Technology Centre Botswana	**Mr. Manish Ranalkar** India Meteorological Department India	**Prof. M. H. Shwehdi** King Fahd University of Petroleum & Minerals, Saudi Arabia
Mr.PrabhakarSembhoo Central Electricity Board Mauritius	**Mr. Hary Soebagyo** Ministry of State of Science and Technology, Indonesia	**Dr. Seiai Tiaung Za Thang** Mandalay Technological University Myanmar
Mr. K. R. Abeysinghe Dept. of Meteorology Sri Lanka	**LCDR C. A. P. Anthony** Sri Lanka Navy Sri Lanka	**Mr. L. Athukorala** Sri Lanka Telecom Sri Lanka
Mr. P. Athukorala Ceylon Petroleum Storage Terminals Sri Lanka	**Wg. Cdr. J. P. Balasooriya** Sri Lanka Air Force	**Mr. L. R. J. De Silva** Sri Lanka Air Force
Mr. S. M. I. B. Dedunupitiya Provincial Environmental Authority (NWP), Sri Lanka	**Ms. P. C. Devasurendra** Sri Lanka Rupavahini Corporation	**Mr. Prasanna Dharmapriya** Richardson Projects (Pvt) Ltd Sri Lanka

Mr. W. A. Dilhara Heyleys Dipped Products Ltd Sri Lanka	**Mr. Thusitha Dissanayake** Dialog Telecom Ltd Sri Lanka	**Dr. Mahesh Edirisinghe** University of Colombo Sri Lanka
Ms. T. G. A. Eronie Sri Lanka Telecom	**Mr. K. S. K. Ettipola** Ceylon Petroleum Corporation Sri Lanka	**Dr. Mahendra Fernando** University of Colombo Sri Lanka
Dr. Chandima Gomes University of Colombo Sri Lanka	**Mr. Keerthi Goonathilake** University of Colombo Sri Lanka	**Mr. J. A. S. Gunanandana** TRC Sri Lanka
Mrs. P. N. Gunawardena Sri Lanka Railways	**Fl. Officer A.N. Hathurusinghe** Sri Lanka Air Force	**Mr. Prasad Indrasiri** Dialog Telecom Ltd Sri Lanka
Mr. Kamal Illeperuma Ceylon Electricity Board Sri Lanka	**Mr. G. M. L. P. Jeyathilake** Chemical Industries (Col.) Ltd Sri Lanka	**Mr. V. Jeyanthiran** University of Colombo Sri Lanka
Mr. J. I. D. Jayasundara Sri Lanka Railways	**Mr. A. M. Jayathilaka** Richardson Projects (Pvt) Sri Lanka	**Mr. B. C. Jayawardena** Ceylon Petroleum Corporation Sri Lanka
Wg. cdr. R. A. P. U. Jayawickrama Sri Lanka Air Force	**Mr. S. K. Lenaduwa** Provincial Environmental Authority(NWP) Sri Lanka	**Mr. Malinda K.Liyanage** Dialog Telecom Ltd Sri Lanka
Mr. Nazri Nizar Richardson Projects (Pvt) Sri Lanka	**Mr. Susantha Paranagama** Richardson Projects (Pvt) Sri Lanka	**Mr. Nimalasiri Pemmawadu** Bata Shoe Co. of Ceylon Ltd Sri Lanka

Contents

Part I
Lightning Activity Mapping

Chapter 1

Study of Lightning Activity Over Indian Sub-continent

Manish Ranalkar[*1], *Amit Kesarkar*[**2], *Rudra Pratap*[*3] *and R.D. Vashistha*[*4]
**India Meteorological Department, Pune, India*
***Centre for Development of Advance Computing, Pune, India*
E-mail: mranalkar@yahoo.com[1], *manish_ranalkar@hotmail.com*[1], *akesarkar@cdac.in*[2], *rpmishra_2006@yahoo.co.in*[3], *ramdhanv@hotmail.com*[4]

ABSTRACT

Distribution of lightning flash activity over the Indian sub-continent (EQ-35°N and 60°E-100°E) is studied using the quality checked monthly lightning flash data obtained from Lightning Imaging Sensor (LIS) on board the Tropical Rainfall Measuring Mission (TRMM) satellite. The LIS data for the period of 1998 to 2005 are in the grid to 0.2° Latitude X 0.2° Longitude. The diurnal, seasonal, annual and latitudinal variation of the lightning activity has been studied over this region and results are presented in this paper. The diurnal variation of lightning flash count shows tendency of maximum convection during afternoon hours with the peak maximum flash rate at 11 UTC (1630 IST) and minimum at 05 UTC (1030 IST). The spatial distribution of time of maximum flash rate over oceanic regions indicated that the peak thunderstorm activity occurs during local late night and early morning hours. However, over land regions the thunderstorm activity peaks during local late afternoon/evening hours. This signifies the role of temperature as a key parameter to govern convective activity over this region.

The study of seasonal total lightning flashes indicated that the lightning flash density values are in qualitative agreement with the convective activity observed over this region. It is observed that, the maxima in seasonal total flash counts occur during the monsoon season. It is in conformity with the propagation of Inter-tropical Conversion Zone (ITCZ) over this region. The mean monthly flash counts show maxima in the month of May, which is the month following period of maximum temperatures over this region. This accounts the hysteresis effect of heating of the atmosphere and conditioning of the atmosphere with suitably available potential energy required for convection. During pre-monsoon season, the flash density maxima of 40.2 fl km^{-2} $season^{-1}$ is observed at 25.2°N/91.6°E and the annual maximum flash density of 28.2 fl km^{-2} yr^{-1} is observed at 33.2°N/ 74.6°E. The latitudinal variation of lightning flash density shows that, the northern latitudes have comparatively more lightning activity than that in the southern latitudes during entire year. The study of inter-annual variability of flash counts shows the bimodal nature with the principle maxima observed during April/ May and secondary maxima observed in the months of August/September.

Keywords: LIS, TRMM, Thunderstorms, Lightning flash density.

Introduction

In principle, lightning may occur from any type of cloud but most of the lightning owes its existence to the cumulonimbus clouds (Uman and Krider, 1989) and hence the lightning is a very good tracer of convective activity over the region. Although, the tropical areas are known for vigorous convective activities manifested in the form of thunderstorms, dust storms etc., the ground based lightning detection networks are very rare in this region. The surface synoptic observations of conventional observatories report the occurrence of lightning/thunderstorm activity in preceding and past hours. These observations are based on the visual observations by weather observer. However, these observations may have personal biases because of limit posed by the laws of Physics to detect the occurrence of lightning from about more than 30-40 km. Therefore, many thunderstorms and lightning activities may go undetected. However, these observations have climatological value because it is useful for characterization of a particular day as thundery and non-thundery. However, weather forecasters want to reveal more information such as whether thunder is due to individual cell of a storm or separate storm in a line or cluster (Asnani, 1993), microphysical characteristics of storm, nature of organizations of precipitating cells. Such information has forecasting value and can enable weather forecaster to understand the evolution of the convective systems. This highlights the lack of observational network for meso-scale severe weather generating systems. In recent years, lightning data has proved to be a powerful tool to get an insight into the storm related parameters such as convection strength and estimation of convective rainfall (Peterson *et al.*, 1998, Tapia *et al.*, 1998). Information about lightning parameters such as multiplicity, polarity of charges being lowered to the earth and the peak current during a flash find applications in tracking the storm (nowcasting), fault analysis on transmission lines (Cummins *et al.*, 1993, Cummins *et al.*, 1998) identifying lightning induced forest fires (Krider *et al.*, 1980, Graham *et al.*, 1997). In spite of such requirements there is a lack of in-situ observational dataset of lightning activity over Indian sub-continent which results into limited knowledge of lightning activity over this region.

The recent developments in space technologies enabled detection and spatial location of the lightning from the space using optical sensors. Despite large background optical signals from clouds and ground surface, lightning signals can be detected using telescopic techniques. NASA's Marshall Space Flight Centre (MSFC) in Huntsville, Alabama had developed an optical lightning detection sensor. A prototype (OTD, Optical Transient Detector) was launched in 1995 (Boccippio *et al.*, 2000) and its improved version LIS (Lightning Imaging Sensor) was launched on board the Tropical Rainfall Measuring Mission (TRMM) in 1997 (Christain *et al.*, 1999). LIS instrument is revolving around the earth at an altitude of 350 km with an orbit inclination of 35°. Therefore it has short sampling time and which in turn results in snapshots of few minutes of the lightning activity within a given area of interest. Data obtained from this system is freely available for scientific studies and is useful for lightning analysis especially for the tropical region. The availability of lightning data and its utilization in the operational weather forecasting has seen phenomenal increase over the last decade. In the recent study made by Kandalgaonkar *et al.* (2005), the LIS data have been utilized for the study of lightning activity over India. They have divided the Indian sub-continent into 5° X 5° latitude X longitude grids. However, since lightning is associated mostly with the meso-scale convective systems, it has very high temporal and spatial variability. According to authors' opinion, it would be appropriate to study such activity with higher spatial resolution. In this study we have used the LIS flash data to study the spatial and temporal distribution of lightning activity over the Indian sub-continent with the grid resolution of 0.2° X 0.2°.

This paper is organized as follows. The section 2 discusses about data and methodology. The results and discussions are described in section 3. The conclusions drawn from the study are given in section 4.

Data and Methodology

LIS observes lightning activity over the tropical region bounded by 35°N-35°S. This instrument detects total lightning which include cloud-to-ground, intra-cloud and cloud-to-cloud discharges. The LIS is useful for identifying spatial location of lightning, time of lightning events, and radiant energy from lightning activity. It samples lightning at the rate of approximately 500 frames/second and can view a 600 km X 600 km area of the earth with spatial resolution between 3 to 6 km (3 km at nadir and 6 km at limb). The low orbit of this satellite allows the snapshot for about 90 seconds of individual storm to be monitored by LIS as it passes over (Christain *et al.*, 1999). The quality checked monthly LIS data obtained from Marshall Space Flight Centre for the period of 1998-2005 is used in this study (http://thunder.nsstc.nasa.gov/lightning-cgi-bin/lis/LISSearch.pl). Figure 1.1 shows the extent of the Indian sub-continent selected for this study.

For this study, the region is divided into a grid for the monthly total lightning flash counts with spatial resolution of 0.2° X 0.2°. It is assumed that 0.2 degree is enough distance to separate two simultaneous events of thunderstorms and this will give more representative values of localized lightning flash densities. It is also believed that, there is no need to mask ocean in coastal regions as high grid resolution will lead to very low error in the prepared datasets. The detection efficiency of LIS varies with local time therefore its corrections are applied to this dataset. The detection efficiency is approximately 90 per cent for most of the regions.

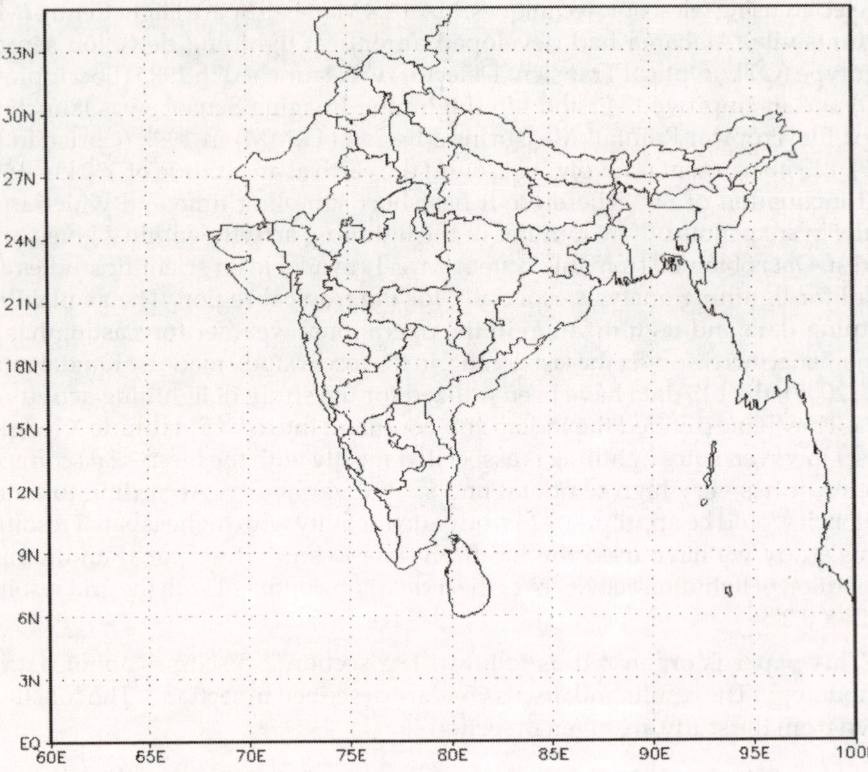

Figure 1.1: Map Showing Region of Indian Sub-continent Considered in this Study

It is known from the results of Manohar and Kesarkar (2003, 2004) that this region shows east-west contrast in thunderstorm activity. It is strongly governed by maximum temperature prevailing over this region in preceding months (Manohar and Kesarkar, 2005) and convectively available potential energy over this region (Manohar and Kesarkar, 2003, 2004, 2005). To take this behaviour into account the entire sub-continent is divided across the longitude of 80°E. The west region is represented by 60°E-80°E and east region is represented by 80°E-100°E. To study the seasonal latitudinal variation of lightning activity the zonal averages computed for these two regions for different season *viz.* Winter (Jan-Feb), Pre-monsoon (Mar-May), Southwest Monsoon (Jun-Sep) and Post-monsoon (Oct- Dec). These are represented in Figures 1.2(a-d) and 1.3(a-d). To study the seasonal spatial distribution of lightning activity the computed flash densities are presented in the Figure 1.4(a-d). In the computation of flash densities a grid area of 484 km^2 was approximated. Figure 1.5 shows variation of seasonal total lightning flash counts.

Figure 1.6 shows the spatial distribution of annual lightning flash density. Variation of mean monthly flash counts is presented in Figure 1.7. The interannual variations of lightning flash counts are shown in Figure 1.8. The diurnal variation of maximum lightning flash rate is presented in Figure 1.9 and the seasonal diurnal variation of maximum flash rate is plotted in Figures 1.10 (a-d).

Figure 1.2: Latitudinal Variation of Lightning Flash Density Over West Indian Sub-continent (0º to 35º N and 60ºE–80 ºE) for the Period of 1998–2005 during the (a) Winter season (Jan-Feb) (b) Pre-monsoon season (Mar-May) (c) Southwest monsoon season (Jun-Sep) (d) Post-monsoon season (Oct-Dec)

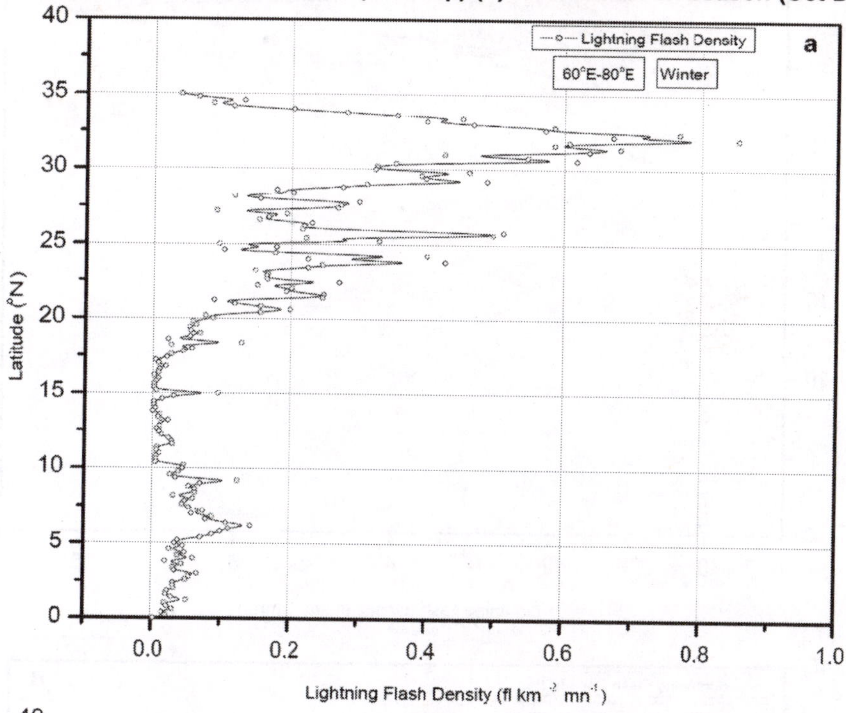

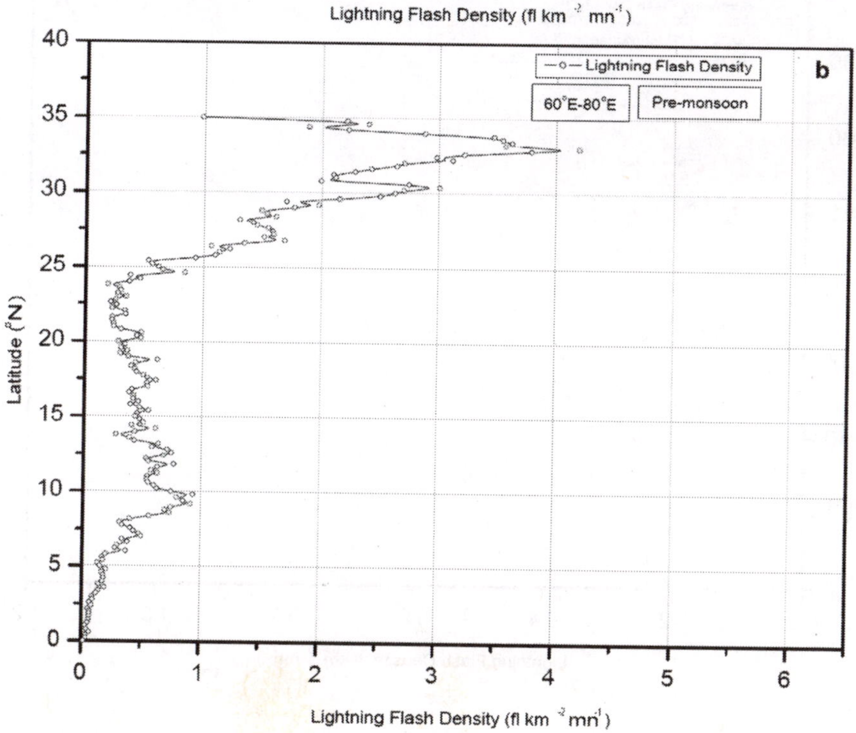

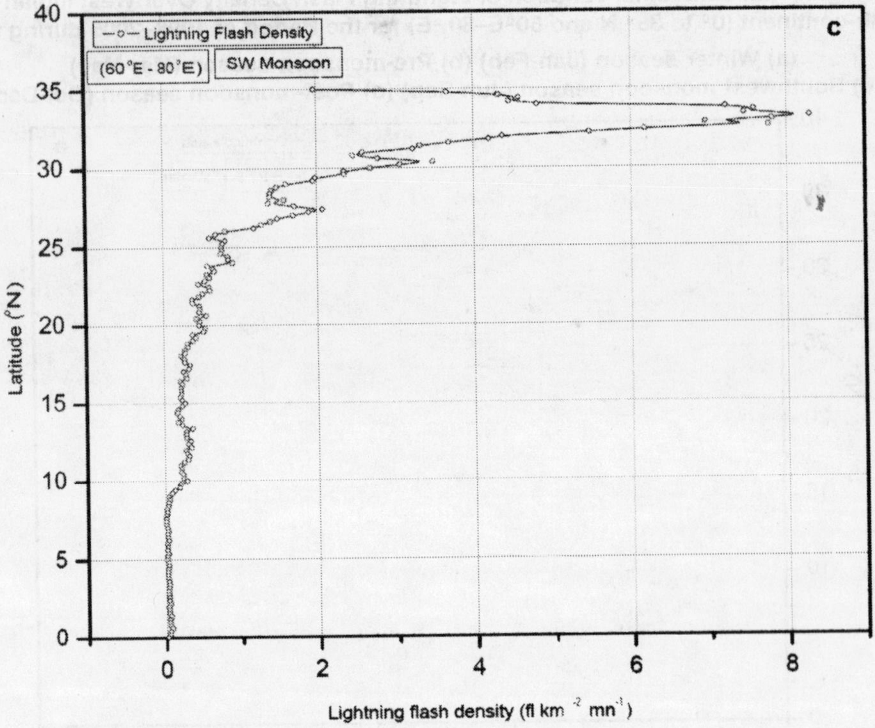
Lightning Flash Density
c
(60°E - 80°E)
SW Monsoon
Latitude (°N)
40
35
30
25
20
15
10
5
0
0
2
4
6
8
Lightning flash density (fl km⁻² mn⁻¹)

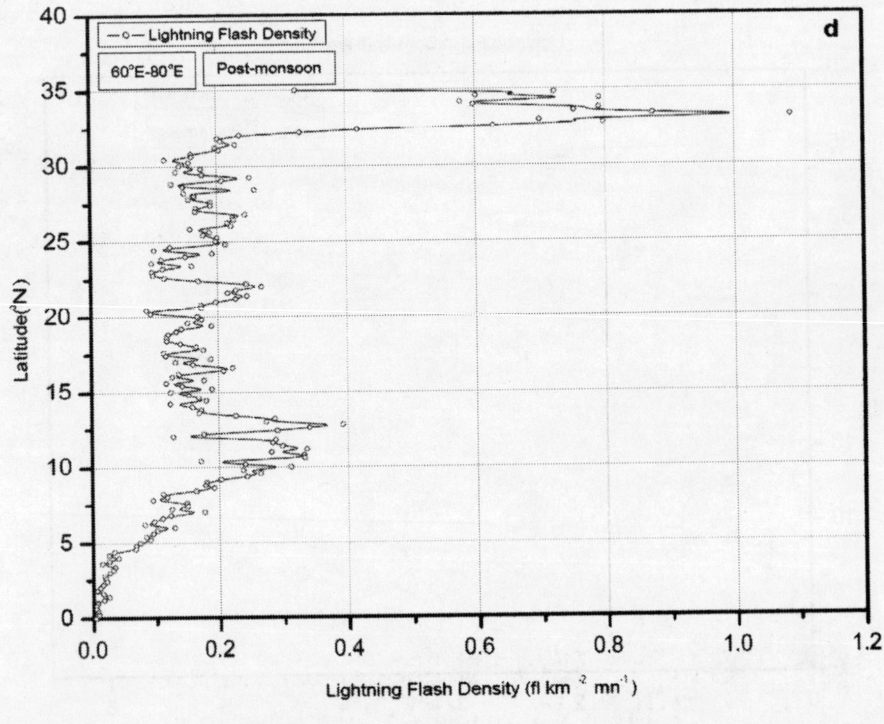
Lightning Flash Density
d
60°E-80°E
Post-monsoon
Latitude(°N)
40
35
30
25
20
15
10
5
0
0.0
0.2
0.4
0.6
0.8
1.0
1.2
Lightning Flash Density (fl km⁻² mn⁻¹)

Figure 1.3: Latitudinal Variation of Lightning Flash Density Over West Indian Sub-continent (0º to 35º N and 60ºE–100 ºE) for the Period of 1998–2005 during the (a) Winter season (Jan-Feb) (b) Pre-monsoon season (Mar-May) (c) Southwest monsoon season (Jun-Sep) (d) Post-monsoon season (Oct-Dec)

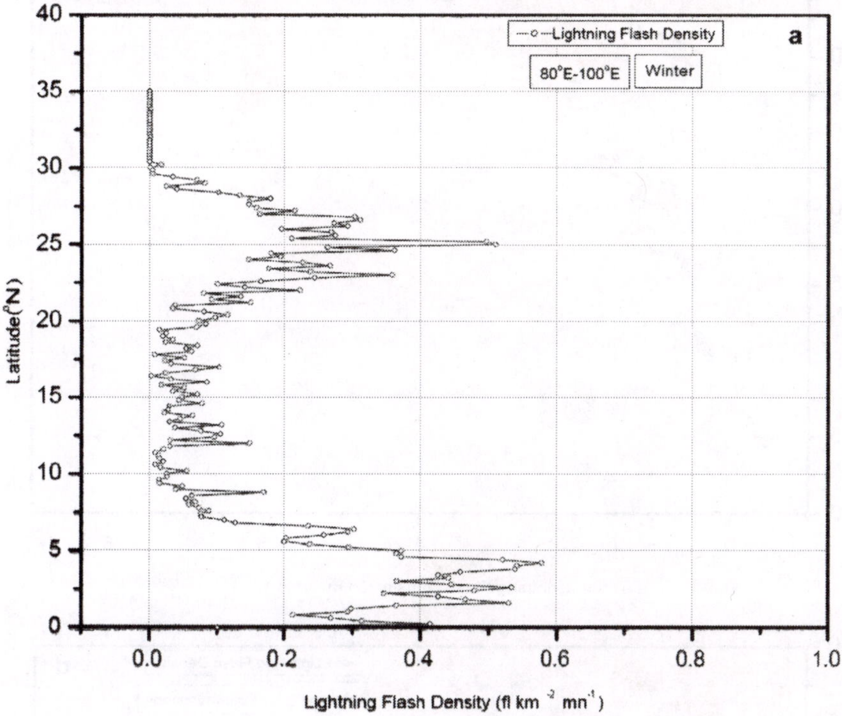

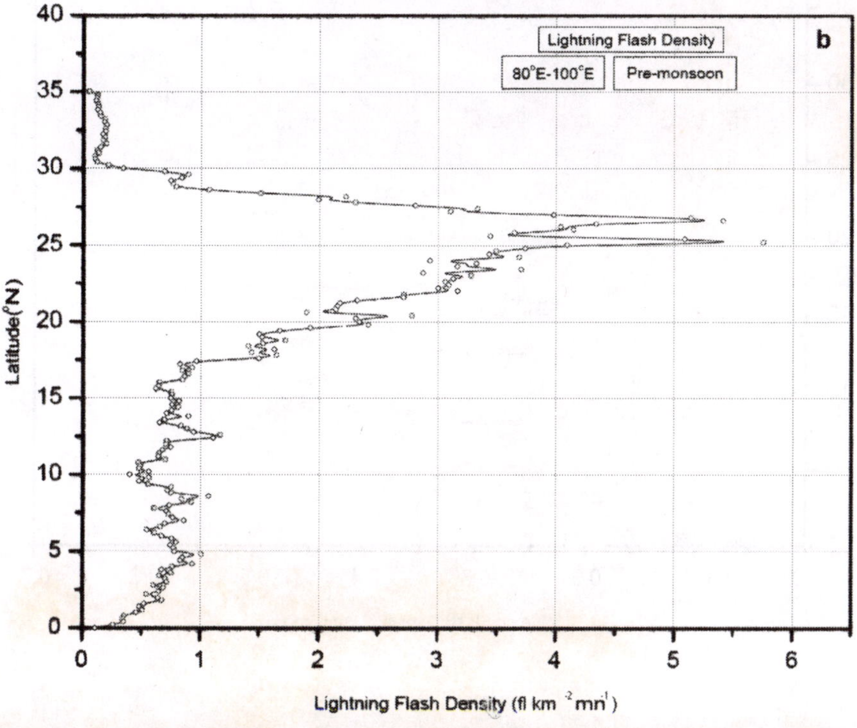

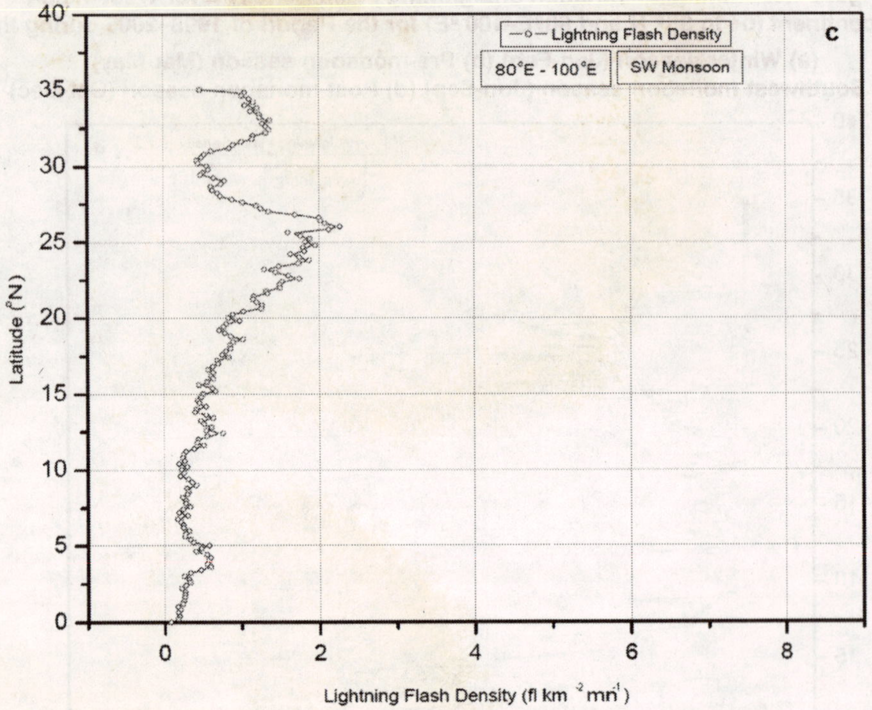
Lightning Flash Density
c
80°E - 100°E
SW Monsoon
Latitude (°N)
Lightning Flash Density (fl km⁻² mn⁻¹)

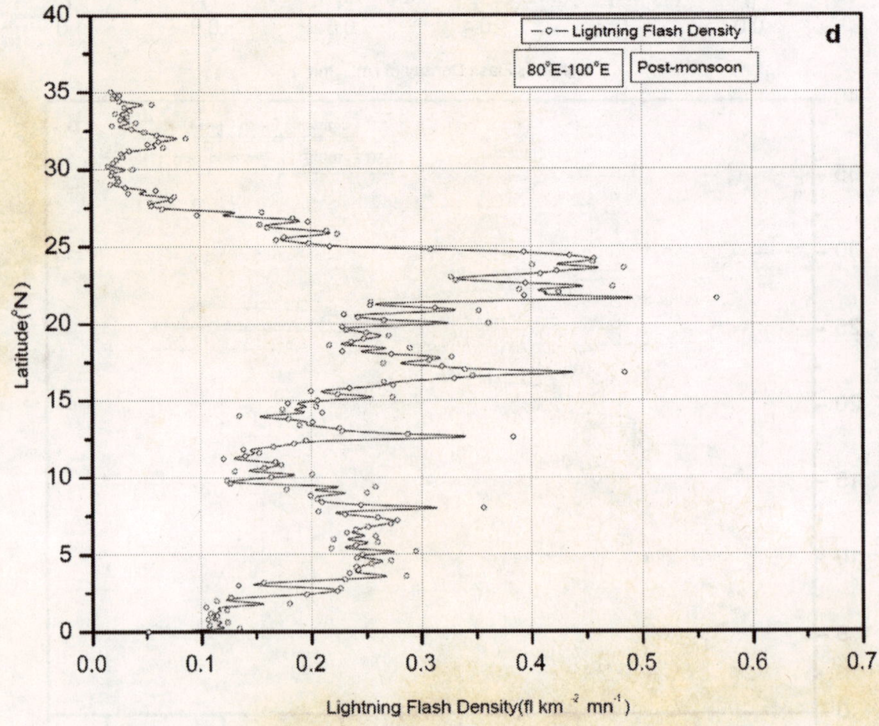
Lightning Flash Density
d
80°E-100°E
Post-monsoon
Latitude(°N)
Lightning Flash Density(fl km⁻² mn⁻¹)

Figure 1.4: Spatial Distribution of Lightning Flash Density (fl km^{-2} season^{-1}) Over Indian Sub-continent (0º to 35º N and 60º–100 º E) for the Period of 1998–2005 during the

(a) Winter season (Jan-Feb) (b) Pre-monsoon season (Mar-May) (c) Southwest monsoon season (Jun-Sep) (d) Post-monsoon season (Oct-Dec)

a)

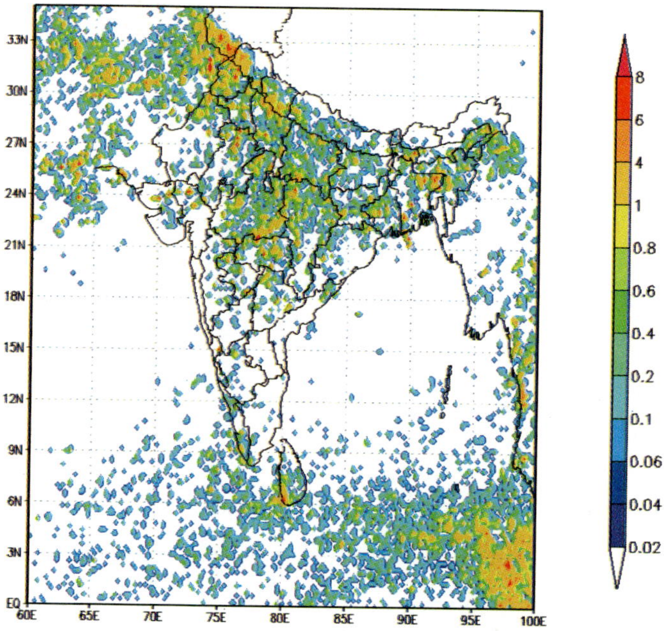

b)

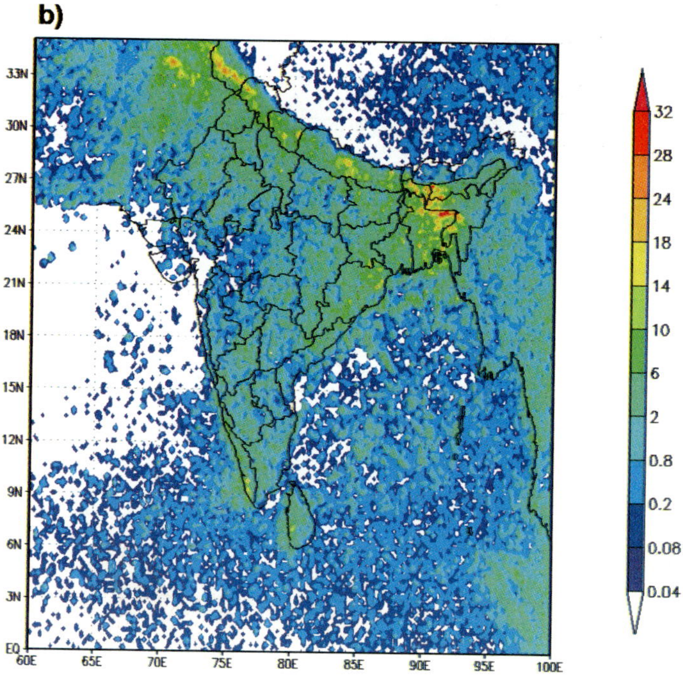

c)

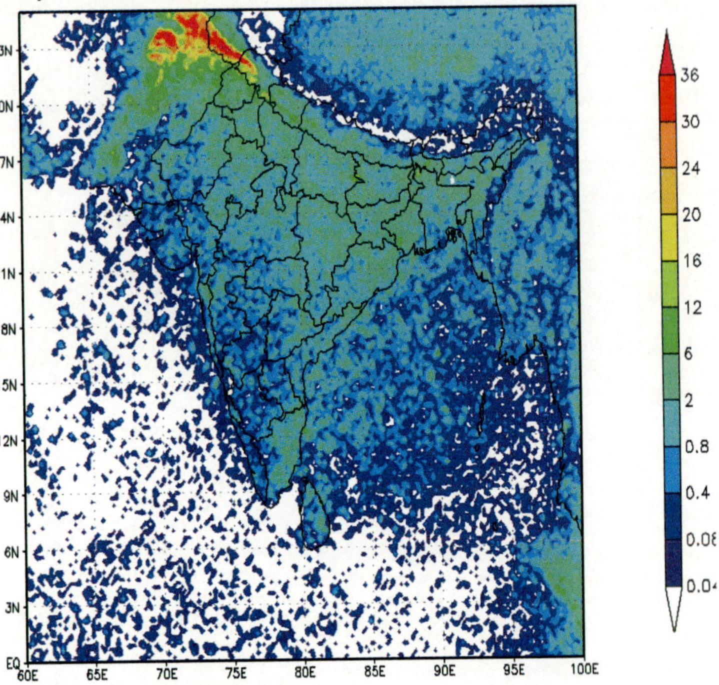
33N
30N
27N
24N
21N
18N
15N
12N
9N
6N
3N
EQ
60E
65E
70E
75E
80E
85E
90E
95E
100E
36
30
24
20
16
12
6
2
0.8
0.4

d)

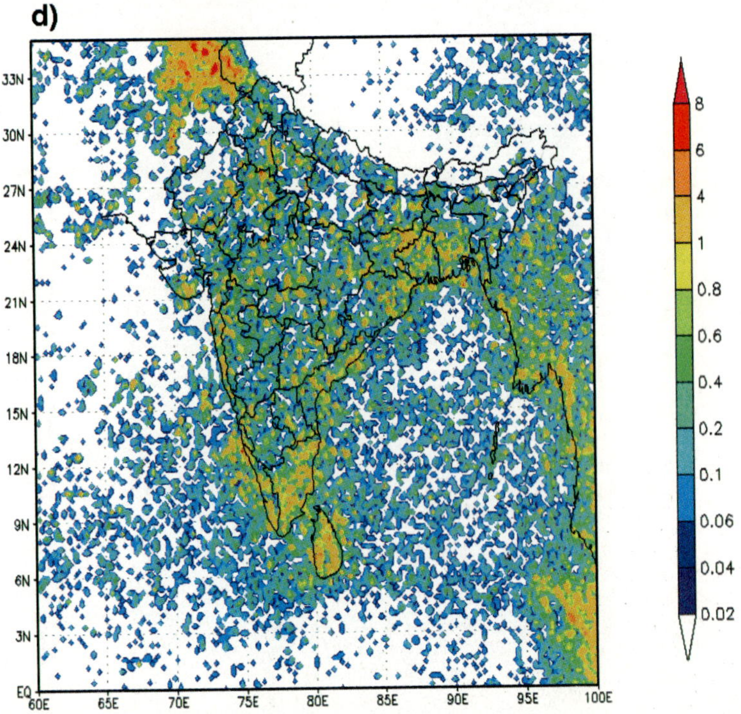
33N
30N
27N
24N
21N
18N
15N
12N
9N
6N
3N
EQ
60E
65E
70E
75E
80E
85E
90E
95E
100E
8
6
4
1
0.8
0.6
0.4
0.2
0.1
0.06
0.04
0.02

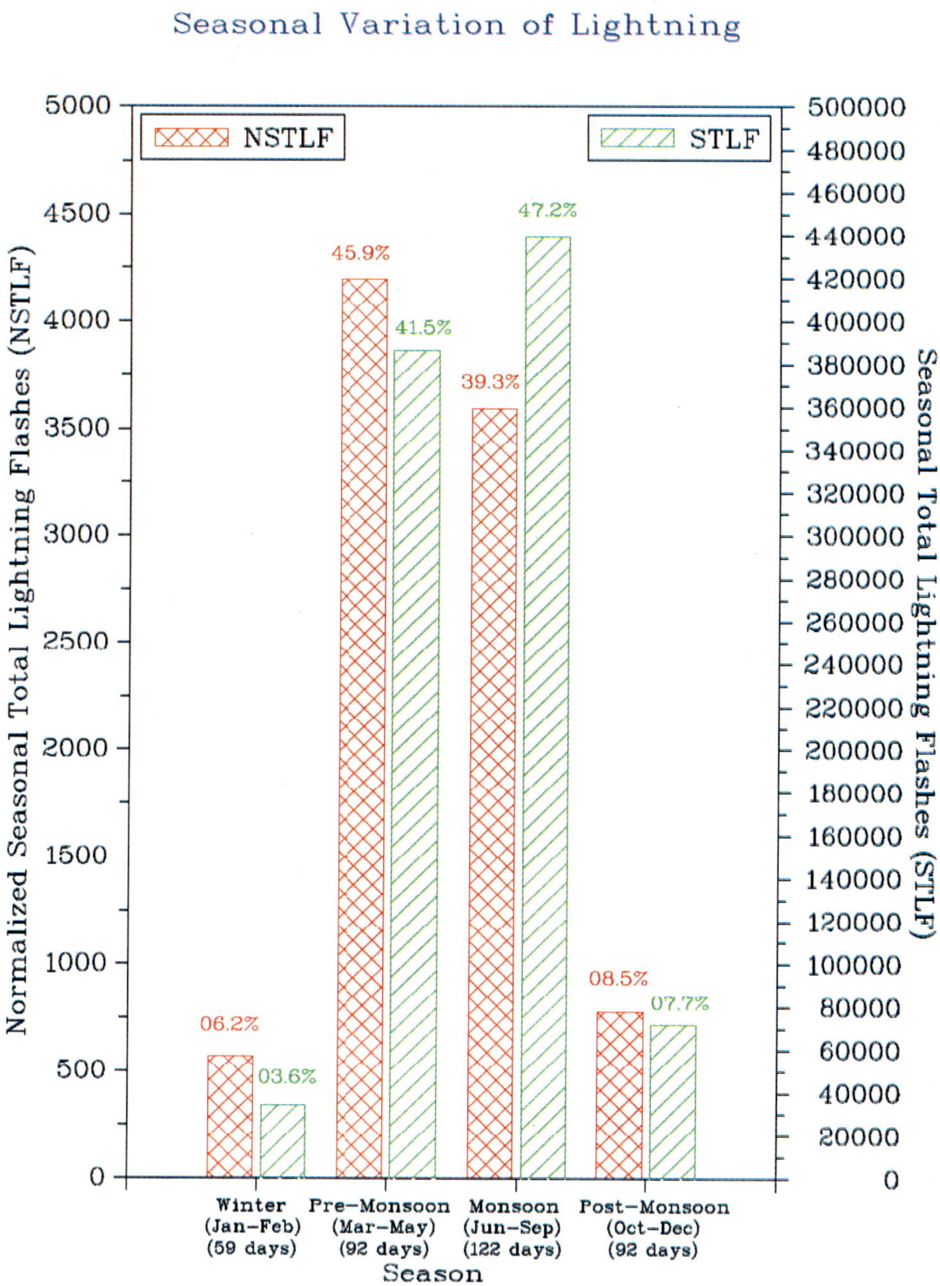

Figure 1.5: Seasonal Variation of Lightning Flash Counts and Normalized Lightning Flash Counts

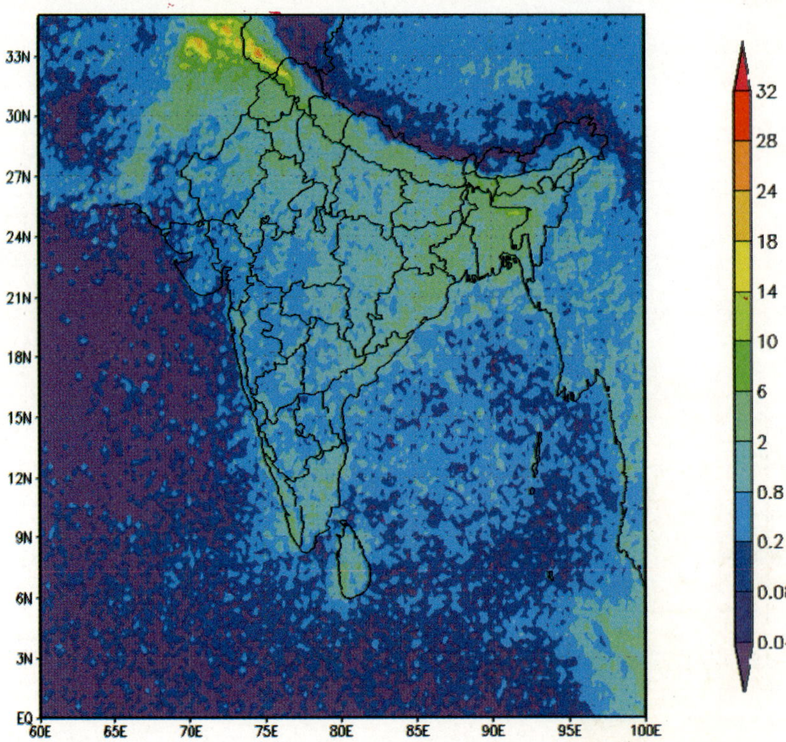

Figure 1.6: Annual Distribution of Lightning Activity over Indian Sub-continent (0º–35º N and 60º–100 º E) for the Period of 1998–2005

Results and Discussion

Latitudinal Variation of Lightning Activity

It would be appropriate at this point to note the conditions that favours genesis of convective activity. The first requirement is clear skies so that the insulation can come uninterruptedly. The insulation heats up the surface and convective current builds up. High instability, low level convergence due to any system (so that the air can rise and vertical development of clouds can take place) and adequate supply of moisture are also favourable for generation of thunderstorms.

Winter Season

The lightning activity is observed to increase with latitude. It can be seen from Figure 1.2(a) that the lightning flash density during winter is more over the northern parts of India with a maximum of 0.85 fl km^{-2} mn^{-1} over a latitudinal belt 31.8 °N–32.0 °N. This may be attributed to lower tropospheric low pressure system called western disturbances that pass through the northern latitudes of India during winter. It may also be seen from Figure 1.2(a) that north of 20 °N lightning flash density gradually increases and it is maximum at 32 °N. This may be due to induced low

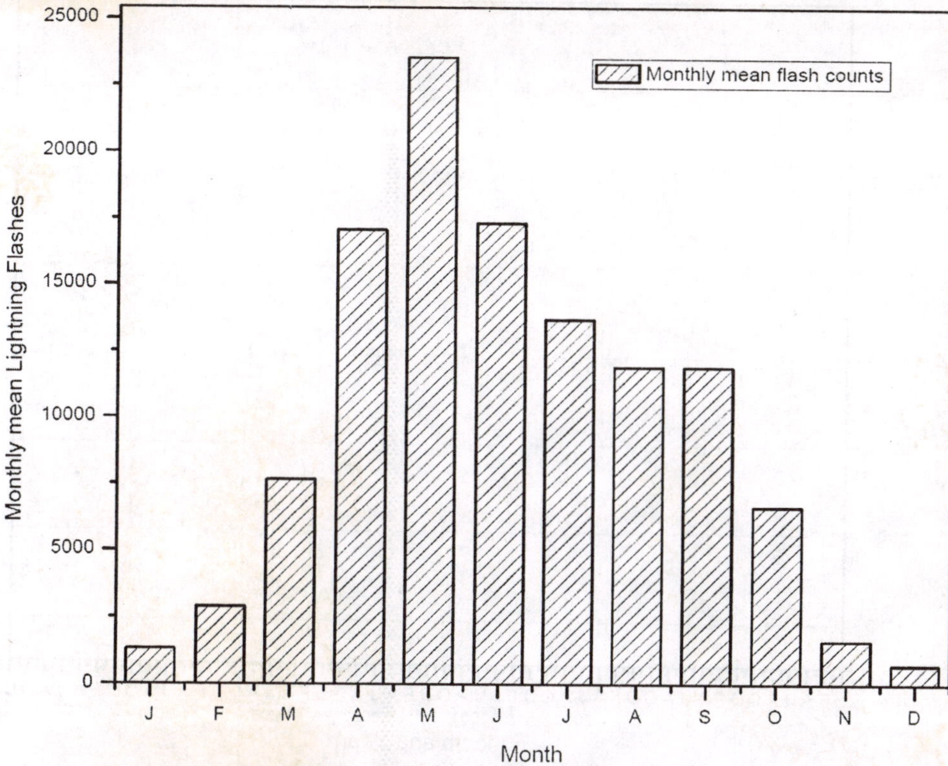

Figure 1.7: The Mean Monthly Flash Counts Over Indian Sub-continent (0° to 35° N and 60°–100 ° E) for the Period of 1998–2005

pressure systems formed in the lower latitudes at the surface under the influence of western disturbances.

Figure 1.3(a) shows that the latitudinal variation of lightning activity over the longitudinal belt 80 °E-100 °E is high in the equatorial region of EQ-5 °N with a peak value of 0.58 fl km^{-2} mn^{-1} at 4.0 °N–4.2 °N. It then gradually decreases northward. North of 20 °N it again increases and attains maximum of 0.5 fl km^{-2} mn^{-1} at about 25°N. Figure 1.4(a) displays the spatial distribution of lightning flash density over the Indian region during winter season. The maximum lightning flash density of 12.66 fl km^{-2} season^{-1} is observed at a 32 °N/74 °E.

Generally in winter season the flow over Indian lower troposphere is dominated by the location of an anticyclone over north Maharashtra and adjoining areas. Sometimes the induced systems of the western disturbance push the anticyclone eastward to the northern parts of the Bay and a trough from western disturbance and its induced systems extends into the north Arabian Sea in this situation the WD gets fresh moisture supply from both the Arabian Sea and Bay of Bengal. This convection along with supply of moisture is favourable for genesis of thunderstorms and may be

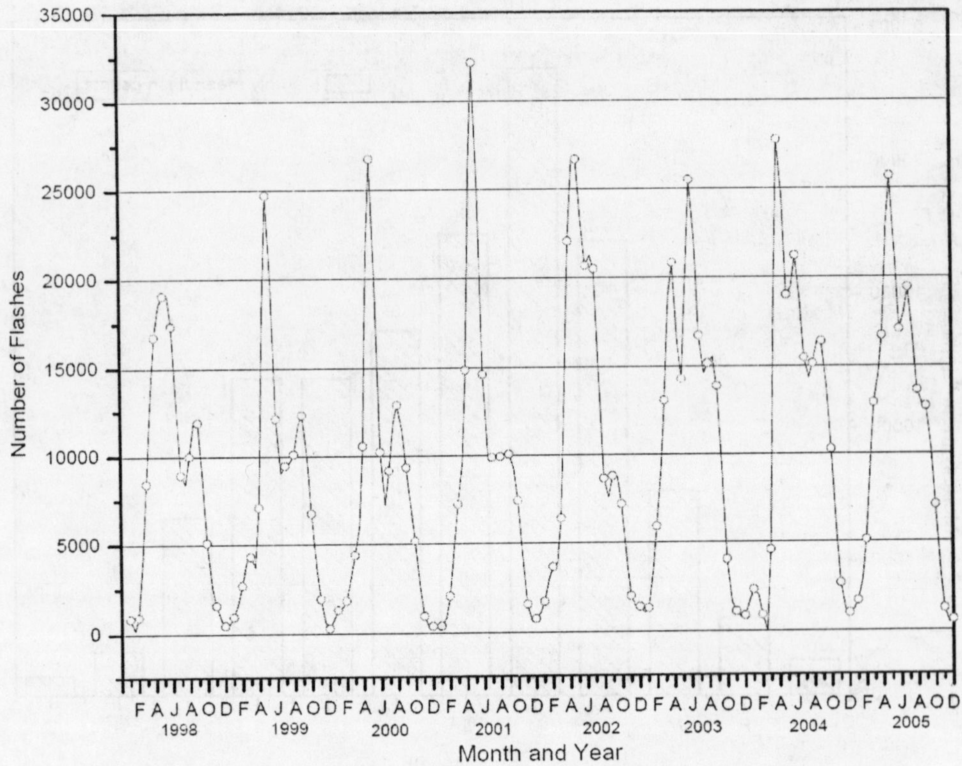

Figure 1.8: Interannual Variability of Lightning Flash Counts Over Indian Sub-continent (0° to 35° N and 60°–100° E) for the Period of 1998–2005

the reason for increased lightning activity over the northern India during winter and post winter season.

Pre-monsoon Season

From Figure 1.2(b) it can be seen that the lightning flash density in the region 60°E–80°E shows a secondary maxima of 0.93 fl km^{-2} mn^{-1} at 9.8°N. The flash density has a decreasing trend up to 24°N thereafter it increases and principle maxima of 4.2 fl km^{-2} mn^{-1} occurs at 33°N. Figure 1.4(b) reveals that lightning flash density is high over southern peninsular India especially over Kerala and western coast of Sri Lanka. This may be attributed to the westward movement of the synoptic scale systems such as cyclonic circulations or trough of low from SW parts of the Bay of Bengal to the Arabian sea during later part of the pre-monsoon season. These synoptic scale systems give rise to necessary convergence for development of thunderstorms. During second half of May when ITCZ is located close to Sri Lanka and southern tip of India convective activity increases over the areas north of ITCZ especially over Kerala where intense thunderstorm activity takes place.

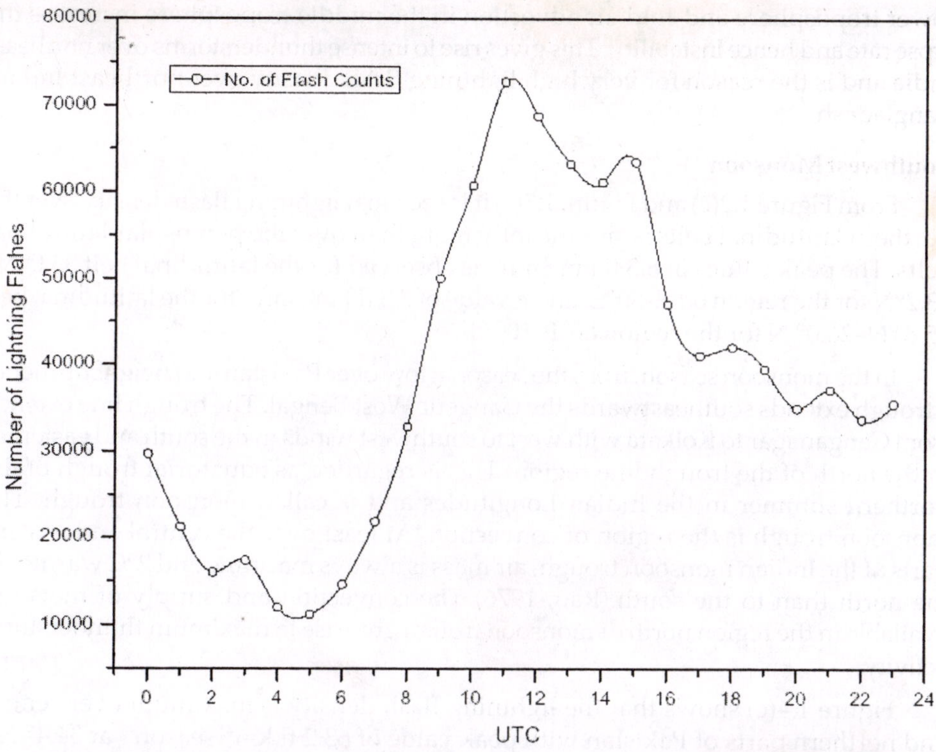

Figure 1.9: Diurnal Variation of Mean Total Number of Lightning Flashes Over Indian Sub-continent (0° to 35° N and 60°–100° E) for the Period of 1998–2005

From Figure 1.3(b) it is seen that in the region of 80°E-100°E, north of 15°N lightning activity increases steadily and peaks in the latitudinal belt 25.2 °N–26.6 °N with mean flash density values of 4.56 fl km^{-2} mn^{-1}. North of 28 °N the flash density decreases steeply. From Figure 1.4(b) it is seen that the lightning flash density maxima of 40.19 fl km^{-2} season^{-1} occur at 25.2 °N/91.6°E. Flash density is observed to be high over the northeast India/Bangladesh. One of the synoptic conditions that lead to maximum number of thunderstorms and hence lightning over northeast India is the presence of an anticyclone over north and adjoining central parts of Bay of Bengal on lower tropospheric levels and high pressure area on the surface. Intensity and location of this anticyclone contributes significantly to the incursion of moisture in different parts of northeast India. Sometimes during pre-monsoon season a wind discontinuity or trough extends from central India to south peninsula as a result the flow over northeast India is southerly to southwesterly. If within this wind flow there exist areas where wind speed decreases, down stream velocity convergence occurs which leads to intense convective activity and hence thunderstorms/lightning. The thermal structure of the troposphere during the season also favours strong convection. There is a warm air advection over northeast India during the season due to southerly or southwesterly wind flow. In the middle troposphere there is a cold air advection as the winds are from northwesterly direction. The increased warm air advection in lower troposphere and cold air advection in the middle troposphere increases the lapse rate and hence instability. This gives rise to intense thunderstorms over northeast India and is the reason for very high lightning flash density over northeast India / Bangladesh.

Southwest Monsoon

From Figure 1.2(c) and Figure 1.3(c) it is seen that lightning flash density over the northern latitudinal belts is significantly more than over the peninsular latitudinal belts. The peak values of 8.3 fl $km^{-2} mn^{-1}$ is observed for the latitudinal belt 33.0°N–33.2°N for the region 60°E-80°E. and a value of 2.3 fl $km^{-2} mn^{-1}$ for the latitudinal belt 25.8 °N–26.0° N for the region 80°E-100 °E.

In the monsoon season, from the seasonal low over Pakistan and neighbourhood, a trough extends southeastwards the Gangetic West Bengal. The trough line extends from Ganganagar to Kolkata with west to southwest winds in the south and easterlies in the north of the trough line region. This is regarded as equatorial trough of the northern summer in the Indian Longitudes and is called monsoon trough. The monsoon trough is the region of convection. At least over the central and eastern parts of the Indian monsoon trough, air mass is always maritime and 2°C warmer in the north than to the south.(Rao, 1976) The convection and supply of moisture available in the region north of monsoon trough give rise to maximum thunderstorm activity.

Figure 1.4(c) shows that the lightning flash density is maximum over central and northern parts of Pakistan with peak value of 63.2 fl $km^{-2} season^{-1}$ at 34.4° N/ 74.4° E. During SW monsoon season a heat low appears over this region which is a semi-permanent system. There is a frictional convergence in the heat low and weak ascent in it. It is believed that the configuration of the mountain ranges in the northwest corner of the sub-continent and adjustment of wind field give rise to low pressure over central and northern Pakistan. The Himalayas provide orographic flow barrier for development of thunderstorms. A careful examination of Figure 1.4(c) also reveals that the lightning flash density in the region of monsoon trough is comparatively more than over other areas.

Post-monsoon Season

From Figure 1.2(d) it is seen that the lightning flash density is maximum in the northern latitudinal belts with a peak of 1.1 fl $km^{-2} mn^{-1}$ at 33.2° N. It may be attributed to passing western disturbances over the northern India. The flash density then decreases southward and again increases over the latitudinal belt of 20° N-22° N *i.e.* central parts of India with peak value of 0.3 fl $km^{-2} mn^{-1}$ at about 22° N. Figure 1.3(d) also shows maximum flash density in this region. Kandalgaonkar *et al.* (2005) have attributed this to the retreating ITCZ and convection associated with large scale convection.

Figure 1.4(d) shows the spatial distribution of lightning flash density over the region. In the post monsoon season the seasonal synoptic patterns and disturbances which are associated with the occurrences of thunderstorms are western disturbances and cyclonic circulation formed over the Arabian Sea and Bay of Bengal. From Figure

Figure 1.10: Time of Maximum Flash Rate Over Indian Sub-continent (0º–35º N and 60º–100 º E) for the Period of 1998–2005 during the (a) Winter season (Jan-Feb) (b) Pre-monsoon season (Mar-May) (c) Southwest monsoon season (Jun-Sep) (d) Post-monsoon season (Oct-Dec)

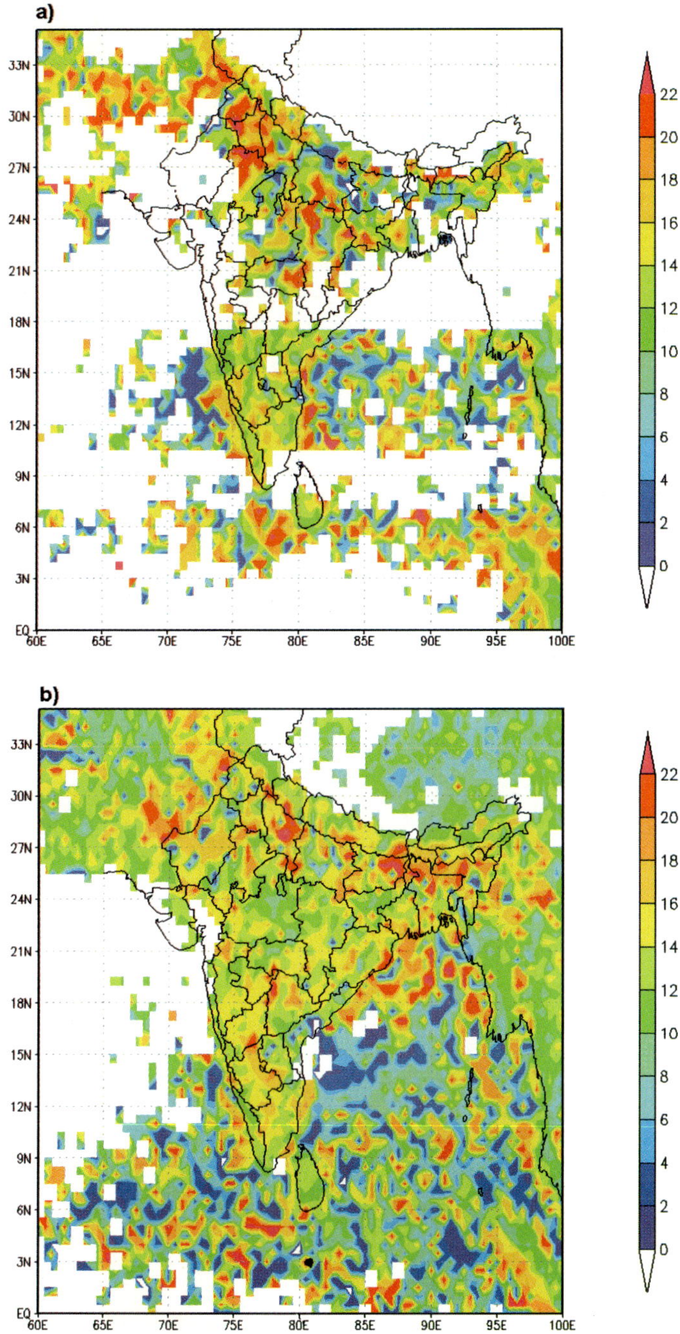

c)

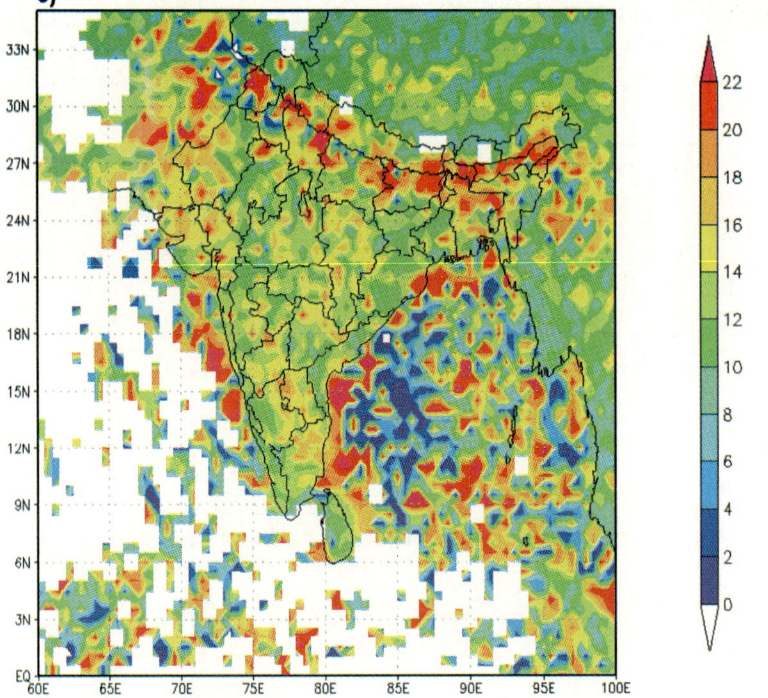
33N
30N
27N
24N
21N
18N
15N
12N
9N
6N
3N
EQ
60E
65E
70E
75E
80E
85E
90E
95E
100E
22
20
18
16
14
12
10
8
6
4
2
0

d)

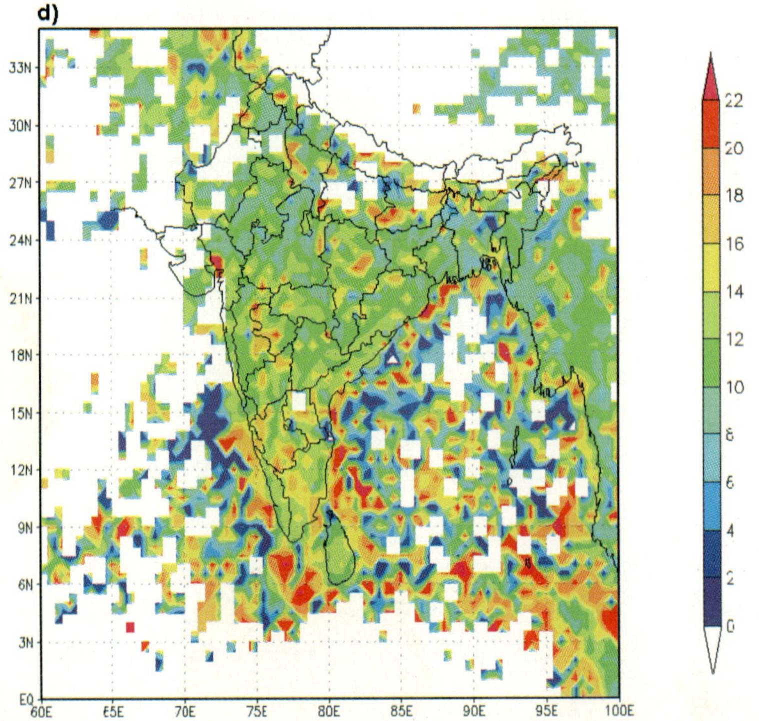
33N
30N
27N
24N
21N
18N
15N
12N
9N
6N
3N
EQ
60E
65E
70E
75E
80E
85E
90E
95E
100E
22
20
18
16
14
12
10
8
6
4
2
0

1.2(d) and Figure 1.4(d) it is seen that the flash density is more over the peninsular India. This may be attributed to the waves/troughs in the equatorial easterly winds which are observed over Indian seas during November to March. There is low level convergence and upper level divergence on the east side (rear) of the wave. The convective shower activity is therefore more in the rear of the wave.

The seasonal variation of lightning flash counts is shown in Figure 1.5. It is observed that the maxima in the seasonal total lightning flash count occur in the monsoon season (47.2 per cent). This result is in agreement with Manohar and Kesarkar (2005) who have studied the climatology of thunderstorm activity over Indian region and observed that the maximum numbers of annual total thunderstorms occur in the monsoon season. Figure 1.5 also depicts the seasonal total lightning flash counts normalized using number of days of the season. It is seen from this Figure 1.5 that the maxima in the normalized seasonal total flash count occurs in pre-monsoon season with 45.9 per cent of total flashes as compared to 39.3 per cent of total flashes in the monsoon season. It may therefore be inferred that the thunderstorms in pre-monsoon season are more intense than in monsoon season.

Annual and Inter-annual Variation of Lightning Activity

Figure 1.6 shows the annual variation of lightning density over the sub-continent in units of fl km^{-2} yr^{-1}. The flash density distribution is in qualitative agreement with the climatology of thunderstorm days (WMO 1953). The peak lightning flash density of 28.2 fl km^{-2} yr^{-1} is observed at 33.2°N/74.6°E. Earlier studies have reported annual flash density maximum over the Indian sub-continent to be 33.3 fl km^{-2} yr^{-1} at 33.75°N/73.25°E (Christian *et al.*, 2003). The high flash density over northern Pakistan is attributed the Himalayan orographic barrier. It may also be seen from Figure 1.6 that there is a sharp decrease in the lightning flash density to the north of the Himalayan ranges.

The dynamics of convective systems over ocean is not as well studied as overland. The meteorological features that delineate convective activity over ocean and land are described in the following: There is no orographic lifting mechanism over oceanic areas. The Sea Surface Temperature (SST) is fairly homogeneous hence pressure gradient is uniform over large oceanic areas in the absence of any synoptic situation. Convective Available Potential Energy (CAPE) over the ocean is relatively weak for severe thunderstorm to occur because convection over ocean is very weak due to low external trigger energy to overcome Convective Inhibition Energy (CINE). Specific heat capacity of the ocean is very high. Insulation of short wave energy is mostly reflected back from calm seas whereas from rough seas the incident energy is reflected at various angles. Some of the incoming energy is absorbed up to the mixed layer depth.

These features lead to significantly low lightning flash density over Arabian Sea and Bay of Bengal compared to adjoining land areas (Figure 1.6). Most of the lightning activity over the ocean areas is associated with cyclonic circulations.

The annual variation of lightning is further split into monthly mean lightning flash counts and is presented in Figure 1.7. It is seen that most of the lightning flashes occur during April to June with peak in May.

Figure 1.8 shows the interannual variation of lightning flash count over the Indian sub-continent. It can be observed that the flash counts in general show primary maxima in the month of April/May and secondary maxima in the month of August/ September. Kandalgaonkar *et al.* (2005) have shown that the lightning activity is strongly dependent upon the surface air temperature which also shows bimodal variation.

Diurnal Variation of Lightning Activity

Based on the time of occurrence of lightning flash counts the diurnal variation of lightning activity over the Indian region is presented in Figure 1.9. It can be seen that maximum lightning flash counts occur at 11 UTC (1630 IST). The maximum flashes occur during late afternoon and evening hours. This result is in agreement with the diurnal variation thunderstorms over Indian region. The lightning flash counts during morning hours are observed to be low with minima at 04 UTC (1030 IST). The maximum flash counts during late afternoon and evening hours are the result of solar forcing. The Sun heats up the surface during the day. Solar radiations are absorbed within few millimeters of the surface during the day. At night this radiation is easily radiated back to space from the land surfaces as they cool. Thus the diurnal temperature range is much more over the land surfaces which affect the diurnal variation of thunderstorms and hence lightning.

The time of maximum flash rate was calculated with respect to UTC (IST-0530) for each season and results are plotted in Figure 1.10(a-d) with a resolution of 2 hours. Note that for all seasons, maximum flash rate over land surfaces occur during late afternoon to evening hours. There are regions where flash rate maxima occur during late night hours. Over the Arabian Sea and Bay of Bengal the lightning flash rate maxima has propensity to peak at early morning hours or late night hours. This result is in agreement with Orville and Huffines (2001). From Figure 1.10(b) it may perhaps inferred that during pre-monsoon season there is a west to northeastward drift of thunderstorms.

Conclusion

Seasonal latitudinal variation of lightning flash density during winter season has maxima in the northernmost latitudes of Indian region. During pre-monsoon season the lightning flash density in the region 60°E–80°E increases northward from the equator and peaks up at 9.8°N. It then decreases northward up to 24°N. North of 24°N it increases steeply and peaks at 33°N. In the region 80°E-100°E the flash density peaks in the belt 25.2°N-26.6°N which is the region of intense convective activity over northeast India. In the monsoon season the flash density in the southern parts of India is much low but to the north of 25°N the flash density increases gradually and peaks at 33°N. During monsoon season in the region 80°E–100°E the flash density gradually increase from 20°N to 25°N. Thus along the monsoon trough flash density is more. During the post-monsoon season in the region 60°E–80°E the lightning flash density in the northern latitudes and peaks at 33.2°N. Then it decreases southward. The flash density is more again in the belt 20°N-22°N. The flash density over the peninsular latitudinal belt from 10°N-13°N is also high during post-monsoon season. It has been seen that, the seasonal total flash counts are maximum during the monsoon season. It is in agreement with the propagation of Inter-tropical Conversion Zone (ITCZ) over this region.

The mean monthly flash counts show maxima in the month of May, which is the last month of season maximum temperatures over this region. This accounts the hysteresis effect of heating of the atmosphere and conditioning of the atmosphere with suitably available potential energy required for convection. During pre-monsoon season, the flash density maxima of 40.2 fl km^{-2} $season^{-1}$ is observed at 25.2 °N/ 91.6° E. The annual maximum flash density of 28.2 fl km^{-2} yr^{-1} is observed at 33.2°N/ 74.6°E which is the region of seasonal low during pre-monsoon and monsoon seasons. The flash densities over the Arabian Sea and Bay of Bengal are significantly low as compared to that over land. Seasonal total flash counts during monsoon season are comparable to pre-monsoon season. However, the normalized seasonal total flash counts are observed to be more during pre-monsoon season. Thus the thunderstorms during pre-monsoon season are more intense. The interannual variation of flash counts shows principle maxima during April/May and secondary maxima during August/September.

The diurnal variation of maximum flash rate is observed to peak at 11 UTC and minimum at 04 UTC. Thus it clearly shows that maximum thunderstorm activity occurs during late afternoon to evening hours. However, it is observed that over the oceanic areas maximum flash rate generally occur during late night and early morning hours.

Acknowledgement

The authors are thankful to the Director General of Meteorology, India Meteorological Department, New Delhi, Director, C-DAC, Pune and Group Coordinator, Computational Atmospheric Science Team, C-DAC, Pune for continuous encouragement for research. The authors are also thankful to Global Hydrology Resource Centre (GHRC), Marshall Space Flight Centre (MSFC), Huntsville, USA for providing the LIS Science data on CDs and also on the website.

References

1. Asnani, G.C., 1993, Tropical Meteorology. G.C. Asnani, Pune, pp. 179-190.
2. Boccippio, D.J., 2000, The optical transient detector (OTD): Instruments characteristics and cross sensor validation, J. Atmos. Oceanic Technol., 17, pp. 441-458.
3. Christain, H.J., 1999, The Lightning Imaging Sensor, 11th International Conference on Atmospheric Electricity, Natl. Aeronaut. and Space Admin., Guntersville, AL, USA.
4. Christain, H.J., *et al.*, 2003, Global frequency and distribution of lightning as observed from space by the Optical Transient Detector, J. Geophys. Res., 108(D1), 4005, doi:10.1029/2002JD002347.
5. Cummins, K.L., Burnett, R.O., Hiscox, W.L., and Pifer, A.E., 1993, Line reliability and fault analysis using the National Lightning Detection Network, Precise

Measurements in Power Conference, National Science Foundation and Centre for Power Engineering at Virginia Tech., VA, USA.

6. Cummins, K.L., Krider, E.P., and Malone, M.D., 1998, The U.S. National Lightning Detection Network™ and applications of Cloud-to-Ground Lightning Data by Electric Power Utilities, IEEE Transactions on Electromagnetic Compatibility, 40, pp. 465-480.
7. Graham, B.L., Holle, R.L., and López, R.E., 1997, Lightning detection and data use in the United States, Fire Management notes Published by the U.S. Department of Agriculture (Forest Service), 57, No.2.
8. Kandalgaonkar *et al.*, 2005, Spatio Temporal variability of lightning activity over Indian region, J. Geophys. Res., 110:10.1029/2004JD005631.
9. Krider, E.P., Noggle R.C., and Uman M.A., 1976, A gated wide-band magnetic direction finder for lightning return strokes, J. Appl. Meteorol., 15, pp. 301-306.
10. Krider, E.P., Noggle, R.C., Pifer, A.E., and Vance, D.L., 1980, Lightning Direction-Finding Systems for Forest Fire Detection, Bull. Amer. Met. Soc., 61, pp. 980-986.
11. Manohar, G.K. and Kesarkar, A.P., 2003, Climatology of thunderstorm activity over Indian region: I. A study of east-west contrast, Mausam, 54, 4, pp. 819-829.
12. Manohar, G.K. and Kesarkar, A.P., 2004, Climatology of thunderstorm activity over Indian region: II. Spatial Distribution, Mausam, 55, 1, pp. 31-40.
13. Manohar, G.K. and Kesarkar, A.P., 2005, Climatology of thunderstorm activity over Indian region: III. Latitudinal and Seasonal Variation, Mausam, 56,3, pp. 581-592.
14. Peterson, W.A., and Rutledge, S.A., 1998, On the relationship between cloud-to-ground lightning and convective rainfall, J. Geophys. Res., 103, pp. 14025-14040.
15. Rao, Y.P., 1976, Meteorological Monograph on Southwest Monsoon, Synoptic Meteorology No. 1/1976, India Meteorological Department.
16. Tapia, A., and Smith, J.A., 1998, Estimation of Convective Rainfall from Lightning Observations, J. Appl. Meteorol., 37, pp. 1497-1509.
17. Uman, M.A. and Krider, E.P., 1989, Natural and Artificially Initiated Lightning, Science, 246, pp. 457-464.

Chapter 2

Seasonal and Annual Lightning Thunderstorms Day Maps for Saudi Arabia

M.H. Shwehdi
Electrical Engineering Department,
King Fahd University of Petroleum and Minerals,
Dhahran, 31261, Saudi Arabia
E-mail: mshwehdi@kfupm.edu.sa

ABSTRACT

The objective of this work is to establish and develop the actual Isokeraunic level (IKL) maps, which is the number of annual thunderstorm days (Thunders days (Td/yr)); both annual and seasonal maps are developed for the country.

On the basis of these maps, distribution of thunderstorms over the country is analyzed in terms of its development factors. It is an important information required for determining lightning performance of the transmission lines and power systems. From the contours of the thunderstorm days (Td/yr) in different areas of Saudi Arabia illustrated in the maps, engineers and meteorology personnel can easily find where lightning strikes are more likely to occur. The work in this paper is based on database and records available on lightning incidence in Saudi Arabia at the Presidency of Meteorology and Environment (PME).

The new maps will be of great help in assisting electrical engineers in Saudi Arabia. Such an information is very valuable for designing quality lightning protection systems for the power transmission in the country.

Thunderstorms are most frequent over the southwest of the country. Their frequency generally decreases towards the west direction. Thunderstorm activity does not, in general, appear to vary in any consistent way with temperature. There appears to be no evidence of any widespread temporal trend in thunderstorm frequency.

Keywords: *Lightning research, Saudi Arabia, Isokeraunic level, Thunderstorm days, Spatial and temporal mapping, Annual, Seasonal thunder day map and Contours.*

Definitions

Flash: The total lightning discharge.

Flashover (General): A disruptive discharge through air around or over the surface of solid or liquid insulation, between parts of different potential or polarity, produced by the application of voltage wherein the breakdown path becomes sufficiently ionized to maintain an electrical arc.

Ground flash density (Ng): The average annual ground flash density is the number of lightning flashes per square kilometre per year.

Isokeraunic (Or Isokeraunic): Value (number) of thunderstorms measured daily (Td/yr.) *i.e.* Kampala, Uganda 185 Td/yr.; Florida 110 Td/yr.

Lightning flash: The complete lightning discharge, most often composed of leaders from a cloud followed by one or more return strokes.

Lightning outage: A power outage following a lightning flashover that results in system fault current, thereby necessitating the operation of a switching device to clear the fault.

Overview

Some of the major incidences of lightning which were reported in Saudi Arabia took place in the Southern area city of Abha. Large number of distribution transformer failures occurred. The report of transformer failure rate in the Southern Electric Company (SCECO) prepared by Power Technology Inc. (PTI) based on the possibilities of the cause of transformer failure. The fact of using a lower Isokeraunic level Td/yr for shield wire design and other lightning protection design seem to be low and not reflecting the real amount of lightning incidences. The PTI report speculates that Td/yr was obtained from the old map, Figure 2.1.

A comprehensive study was conducted. It recommended that SCECO-South should keep track of lightning data records and consider installing lightning detection network. Many utilities in world have justified the cost of lightning detection network system compared to equipment loss, operation and maintenance, crew scheduling cost etc. Such data, obtained by acquisition detection network, are valuable for designing transmission line shield wires and lightning protection systems that correlate Td/yr data with transmission and distribution equipment failures and outage rate.

There are no archives on losses caused by lightning in Saudi Arabia. Reports from some farmers and public individuals, who frequently reported the loss of human lives as well as camels, and palm tree burning in different areas of Western Province (TAIF), are known.

In the Central Province (Al-Qaseem) lightning strike rendered many livestock dead, and burned crops. In the north Saudi Electric Company (SEC) experienced many incidences in which transmission lines lightning arrestors, and stage arrestors at 132/33 kV substations did not operate during lightning and caused burning of Coupling Capacitive Voltage Transformers (CCVT), and other valuable distribution equipments. Lightning had caused damages in different industrial locations. The

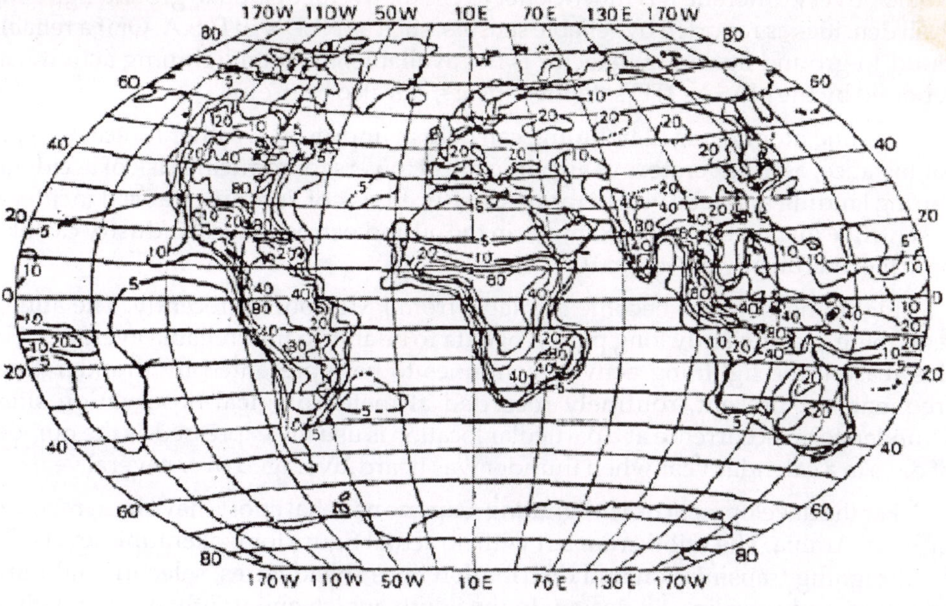

Figure 2.1: World Isokeraunic Map (1956)

large amount of surface losses has initiated the idea of this lightning research project, and lightning mapping. Based on many facts mentioned above, one can say that the exact Td/yr activities are not truly found. This research is seeking to obtain a current TD mapping for the whole country since Td/yr is one of the essential factors which will help calculate ground flash densities which are used to calculate the outage rate and failures due to lightning. The lightning protection systems in transmission and distribution systems were not properly designed and well coordinated with other insulation system in the SEC power system.

Thunderstorms are spectacular but hazardous weather phenomena. Together with high temperature, winds and safety now tops the list of concerns in the Presidency of Meteorology and Environment of Saudi Arabia (PME) as well as SEC. Thunderstorms are most frequent over the southwest of the country, and generally decrease towards the west direction. North and central parts have also experienced recently more frequent thunderstorms.

PME does not use any detection and monitoring network at present. It still uses human observation at its sites scattered all over the country. This method of observation may have some unrealistic records. Thunderstorm-days is a poor metric for lightning activity, specifically when observers often have had other duties than just reporting the weather. They may not hear somewhat distant thunder while indoors, or may not be cautious in reporting a perceived unimportant change in the observation like thunder. One lightning flash that generates thunder-sound is one thunderstorm-day. On the other hand ten thousand lightning flashes that generate thunder also counts as one thunderstorm-day, even though the description of lightning on those would be very different. It is much better to use the average cloud to ground lightning flash densities as reported by reliable sensors, such as NLDN in U.S.A. Or if a reliable cloud-to-ground lightning detector is not available, the total lightning activity, as reported by the NASA OTD satellite sensors, can also be useful.

On-line monitoring of lightning can help in improved weather forecast. It can, for instance, assist operators of airport control towers for reducing risk of accidents during landing and take off operations. Reduced risk of lightning-caused incidents at sensitive installations, for example, in the oil and petrochemical industry can also be achieved (Burrows *et al.*, 2001).

Lightning data has become available from PME sources recently. The author feels there is sufficiently long period of data to be able to find reliable averages. For this reason, the lightning activity continues to be represented by thunderstorm frequency at present, routinely recorded at meteorological observation sites. Thunderstorm occurrence at a particular location is usually expressed as the number of days in a calendar year when thunder was heard, averaged over several years.

For the development of TD lightning maps no national efforts have been reported in Saudi Arabia. The utilities are left with no actual figure for Isokeraunic level (TD) for designing transmission and distribution lines shield wires, selecting lightning arrestors, and coordinated design. In the South, which apparently has the highest lightning frequency, there seems to be very little information found on lightning activity. The world Isokeraunic map shown in Figure 2.1 established in 1956 indicates that the Isokeraunic level in the southern Saudi Arabia is between 5 and 15 thunderstorms days per year (www.pme.gov.sa).

Thunderstorm frequency does not, in general, appear to vary in any consistent way with rainfall (The IEEE Working Group, 2001). There appears to be no evidence of any widespread temporal trend in thunderstorm frequency (The IEEE Working Group, 2001). PME has been gathering lightning data at 28 observation locations around the country since 1951, whereas SEC has installed recently outages recording and monitoring for some of its power system regions.

Lightning research in Saudi Arabia is continued. The search and collection of all existing and available data on lightning occurrences recorded by utilities, industries, and those kept at PME, going on.

Saudi Arabia Meterological Information

Introduction

Lightning accounts for most of the power supply interruptions in power lines. It is one of the leading causes of disturbance in transmission and distribution systems. In U.S.A. alone, an estimated 30 per cent of all electric power outages are related to lightning every year. The estimated total costs approaching one billion dollars. This includes equipment damage, loss of lives etc. during thunderstorms (Rosa *et al.*, 1994; Boccippio *et al.*; Rosa *et al.*, 1995; Rosa *et al.*, 1998).

The Isokeraunic level (Td/yr) is an indication of regional lightning activity based on average quantities derived from historically available ground-level observations. A more detailed depiction of lightning activity may be obtained from lightning ground flash density (GFD) maps, which are created from information obtained with the help of lightning detection networks, or by historical lightning incidence records that include, current, time, frequency, date, intensity, etc, from online lightning detection stations (Rosa *et al.*, 1995).

Presidency of Meteorology and Environment (PME)

As a result of the comprehensive national economic growth occurring in Saudi Arabia, and especially with the introduction of air transport in line with global activity, the need arose for an efficient meteorological service. Accordingly in 1951, the Department of Meteorology was established within the Civil Aviation Directorate. During the last two decades Saudi Arabia witnessed very rapid development in economic and industrials sectors, and the necessity to take care of environment affairs emerged. In all the aspects of land, water and air activity to avoid duplication and dissipation of efforts between different government departments involved in these matters, the General Directorate of Meteorology was designated as central agency to be responsible for environmental protection. The title of the organization is recently changed into Presidency of Meteorology and Environment (PME) (www.pme.gov.sa).

Saudi Arabia Geographical Facts

Saudi Arabia is located in Middle East, bordering the Persian Gulf and the Red Sea, north of Yemen. Its geographic coordinates: 25 00 N, 45 00 E, with a total land area of 1,960,582 sq km, with a coastline of 2,640 km, and it is slightly more than one-fifth the size of the US.

Climate is harsh, dry desert with great extremes of temperature. Extreme heat and aridity are characteristic of most of Saudi Arabia. The Arabian Peninsula is one of the few places in the world where summer temperatures above 48° C (120° F) are common. In winter frost or snow can occur in the interior and the higher mountains.

Precipitation is scarce throughout the country. Annual rainfall in Riyadh averages 100 mm (4 in). It rains almost exclusively between January and May. The average in Jeddah is 61 mm (2.4 in) and occurs between November and January. Saudi Arabia has no permanent rivers or lakes. Terrain is mostly not inhabited, sandy desert. Elevation extremes are lowest point: Persian Gulf 0 m, highest point: Jabal Sawda' (south) 3,133 m (www.pme.gov.sa).

Lightning Frequency in Saudi Arabia

Weather and Thunderstorms in Saudi Arabia

The location of the Saudi Arabia is in the orbital overheated region that has low clouds which cause thunderstorm. The clouds are present on the land of the Kingdom usually in the winter and spring seasons. Clouds are there rarely in the summer season except in the southern region because of the southern west winds carrying the clouds.

Winter thunderstorms in Saudi Arabia develop with cold and very unstable air over relatively warm sea. High Cb-clouds develop and occasionally thunderstorms follow. Thunderstorms during the summer time are on the other hand mainly formed due to climatic condition inland. As the sun warms the land, the air above it also becomes warmer, thus the air may become so unstable that thunderstorm may develop. The frequency of thunderstorms in Saudi Arabia is lower during spring (April-May) and fall (September–November), May being the quietest month (www.pme.gov.sa).

Thunderstorms can therefore occur in two very different environments. First, the tropical air mass type thunderstorms resulting from the diurnal heating of the surface of the Earth. These late afternoon thunderstorms occur mainly in the tropics but can also occur during summer months in mid-latitudes where instabilities can develop in the afternoons on hot summer days. Second, the frontal thunderstorms which occur primarily in mid-to-high latitudes where different types of air masses interact and result in instabilities (baroclinic instabilities) along cold and warm fronts. Frontal thunderstorms can occur at any hour of the day, and over continent and ocean, during summer and winter. What is needed for these thunderstorms to develop is a stronger density gradient between adjacent air masses. These density gradients can be caused either by different temperatures, different humidity, or a combination of both, which is the case in Saudi Arabia during six months of the year. This supports the increased activity of thunderstorms in the Saudi Arabia over those activities reported in Figure 2.1.

Thunder and lightning observations are more during winter season on many PME locations such as in Riyadh and vicinities AL-Qaseem, Dhahran and vicinities, Abha, Taif, Al-Baha and surrounding.

The average of the annual thunderstorms doesn't exceed thirty two. Thunderstorm on the major part of the land of the country, except in the Southern west regions, is about 97 in an year. On the other hand only about 10 thunderstorms on the shores of the Red Sea are present. While in the winter, the average of the thunderstorm on the shores of the Arabian Gulf (other side of the country) is approximately 5, it is two 2 on the shores of the Red Sea.

The weather of Saudi Arabia is characterized in summer season by a clear visibility and no thunderstorm except the Southern West region. In Saudi Arabia the seasons are defined as follows:

1. Winter Season months are (December, January, February).
2. Spring Season months are (March, April, May).
3. Summer Season months are (June, July, August).
4. Autumn Season months are (September, October, November).

Lightning Thunderstorm Data Resources in Saudi Arabia

PME data observed manually at different stations spread over the country on day to day basis is sent to PME central office in JEDDAH where it is collected and stored in computer database. The need for validation is required for more accurate mapping.

The PME records show that thunderstorms are most frequent over southern, eastern, and central regions especially during the winter months (December-February). It extends to the northern region, and north-western parts also. In the central inland and eastern parts thunderstorms occur during the summer months (June–August).

The number of thunderstorms in different areas are; about 3-8 days in the west and in the northern part are 3-10. In the east 5-10 days whereas in the north-east 1-5 days and north-west part about 2-6 days, in the south-west about 3-10 days, and in the south 5-15 days and south-eastern part about 8-15. It is interesting to note that thunderstorm activity seem to concentrate around the southern mountain region.

The data has been collected from 29 PME stations during the past 19 years at some stations, 24 years from other stations and many years from the other. The average data collection from all the stations is 19 years. Table 2.1 shows a sample for the month January, 2003 for all the 29 stations.

Table 2.1: Sample of Data from PME During One Month for 29 Stations

Station Number	*Year*	*Month*	*TS*	*Station Area*
41112	2003	1	0	Abha
41055	2003	1	0	Al Baha
40420	2003	1	2	Alahsa
40361	2003	1	0	Al-Jouf
40357	2003	1	0	Arar
41084	2003	1	0	Bisha
40416	2003	1	4	Dhahran
40405	2003	1	2	Gassim
40360	2003	1	0	Guraiat
40377	2003	1	5	Hafr Albatin
40394	2003	1	2	Hail
41140	2003	1	0	Jizan
41024	2003	1	0	Kaia Jeddah
40417	2003	1	5	Kfia
41114	2003	1	0	Khamis Mushait
40437	2003	1	1	Kkia Riyadh
40430	2003	1	0	Madinah
41030	2003	1	0	Makkah
41128	2003	1	0	Najran
40373	2003	1	1	Qaisumah
40362	2003	1	2	Rafha
40438	2003	1	3	Riyadh Old
41136	2003	1	0	Sharorah
40375	2003	1	0	Tabuk
41036	2003	1	0	Taif
40356	2003	1	0	Turaif
41061	2003	1	0	Wadialdawaser
40400	2003	1	0	Wejh
40439	2003	1	0	Yanbu

Source: SEC data.

The need to collect as many records of outages of the SEC transmission line systems and their details may assist in the validation of PME lightning records. At some of the SEC regions the outages records are usually detected on a real time and direct protection devices, which give such data from more reliable automatic detection system over that by human observation.

The outages data is usually classified in a table which contains information such as; the type of fault, equipment type, date of fault and restart of line, fault area, number of circuit in which fault occurred, cause of fault and category, duration of fault and other description of the cause.

This method followed was to collect from different SEC regions all available outages records representing the whole country, and then classify all lightning caused outages with time, date in each of the regions. Once these are classified according to lightning or weather related outage, the PME weather records are made available to check on the status of the weather on each of the SEC lightning recorded data. If the weather was thunderstorm and heavy clouds then that record will be considered as a lightning caused outages. It will be then entered as a lightning event with the day, month, and year information. All the SEC lightning classified records were compared and validated and then if valid, considered as SEC Lightning Record.

Summarizing the criterion used in this research project for sorting and collecting lightning caused outages from the utilities, outages records from each utility is classified as follows:

- If the fault is clearly listed fault due to lightning this will be taken as a first lightning incidence, a check with PME weather is verified.
- If it is classified as transient over voltage cause, this will also be taken as lightning caused fault for PME weather reference.
- The third categorization of lightning caused outages is those of the weather related faults which are rarely added to lightning, and after PME weather reference.

The SEC regions are classified as follows:

- Central region from SEC which include Riyadh, AL-Qassim, Hail, Dawadmi, around Riyadh, and AL-Kharj.
- West and South region from SEC. which includes Makkah, Jeddah, Madïna, Taif, Abha, Al-Baha, Khamis Mushait, Bisha; Najran, Jizan, and Shrowra
- East and North region from SEC outages for the eastern area which includes Al-Hasa, Dammam, and north area, and Tabouk and Hail in the north

SEC obtained recorded causes category of the faults is classified as the following:

a) Equipment's Problem, b) Relay Problem, c) Human Error, d) Contact, e) Weather, and f) Unknown.

From SEC lightning records only the faults occurring due to the lightning were recorded in this project and the rest outages are not of interest for this research and are neglected.

Records and Outcome

Mapping of the Thunderstorm Days

Data was received from PME for 29 locations all over the Kingdom and during different periods ranging between 24 years and 19 years. Only the 19 year data were used here which is believed to be complete and reasonable. From the rest of the data, some were omitted due to incomplete records in many months and some were available from few stations only. The author believes this data base is complete; seems consistent, and sufficient for the lightning records.

Excel, Access, Arc-View software and statistical methods were utilized to evaluate how such data could be analyzed and mapped. Tabularization and plotting using the Excel program was useful to determine the approach of analysis. Moreover, research experience that made possible USA and other countries to make Td/yr maps were also helpful to look into the seasonal categorization as a method for analysis and finding the highest lightning density (Rosa *et al.*, 1994; Janischewskyj *et al.*, 1998; Boccippio *et al.*; Rosa *et al.*, 1995; Rosa *et al.*, 1998; Torres, *et al.*, 1996).

The total annual average thunderstorm days along with the total seasonal average lightning flashover were determined in table and plot forms for further use by the Simulation GIS Arc-View software.

Figure 2.2 shows the bar chart of the incidence of PME TD data for Al-Hasa observation location as an example. The data is sorted out for all the four seasons as well as the annual. Similar bar charts for all stations were performed for the analysis. Table 2.2 illustrates the seasonal and the annual average data obtained from all PME locations as classified.

Lightning frequency varies throughout the country. It also varies from month to month and from year to year. For a long time now, PME has collected the information which is used to develop formal thunderstorm day's map using Arc-view GIS. Figures 2.3 and 2.4 show the total number of thunderstorms days expected annually, averaged over a number of years using colour and number contours respectively.

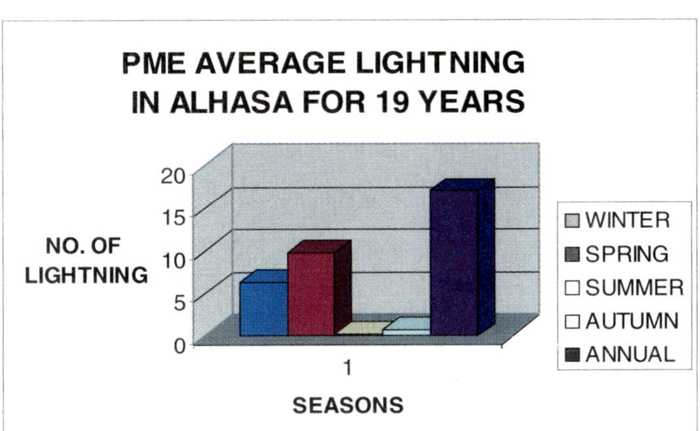

Figure 2.2: ALHASA Average Lightning for 19 years from PME data

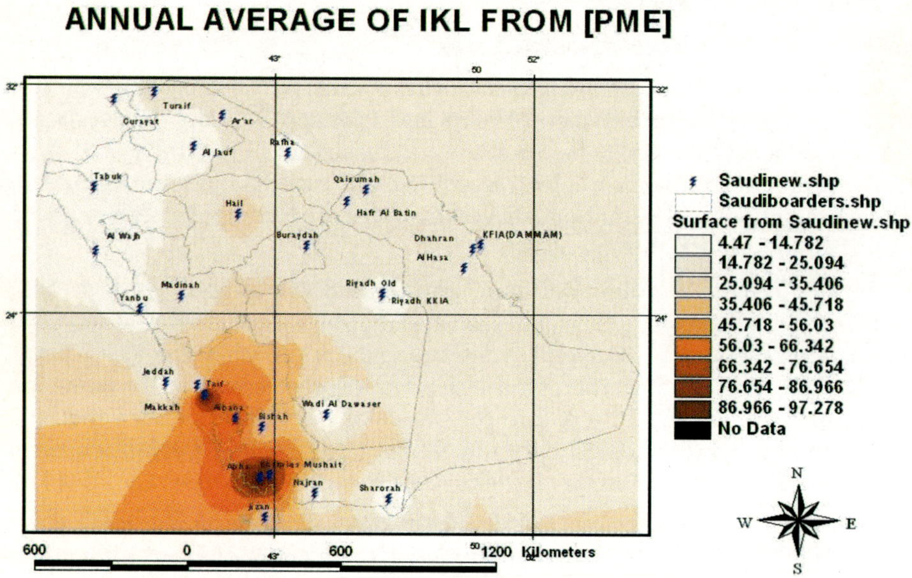

Figure 2.3: The Mean Annual Td/yr for Saudi Arabia (Colour contour)

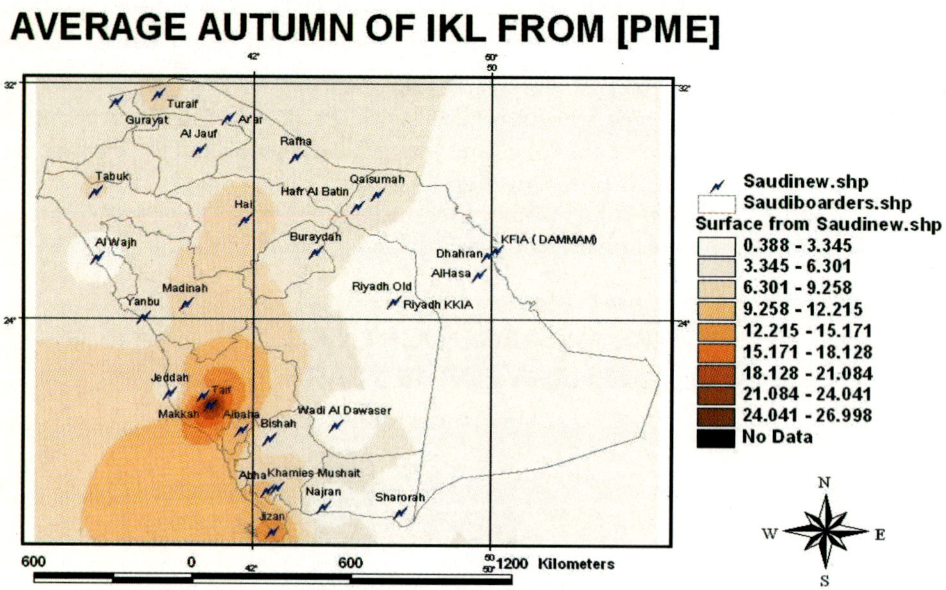

Figure 2.4: The Mean Annual Td/yr for Saudi Arabia (Line contour)

Figures 2.5–2.8 were drawn to show the seasonal lightning activity in the various regions of the country.

ANNUAL AVERAGE OF IKL FROM [PME]

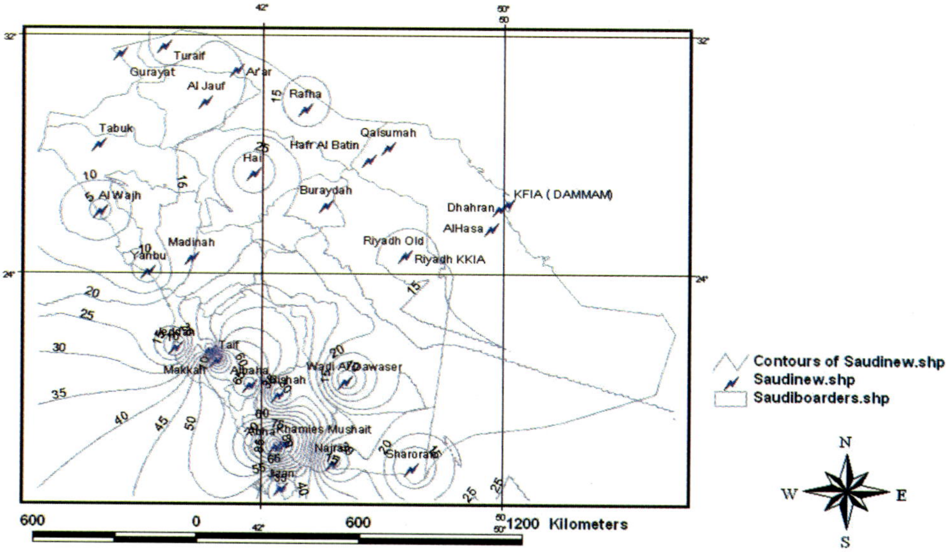

Figure 2.5: The Mean Annual Td/yr for the Autumn Season

AVERAGE SPRING OF IKL FROM [PME]

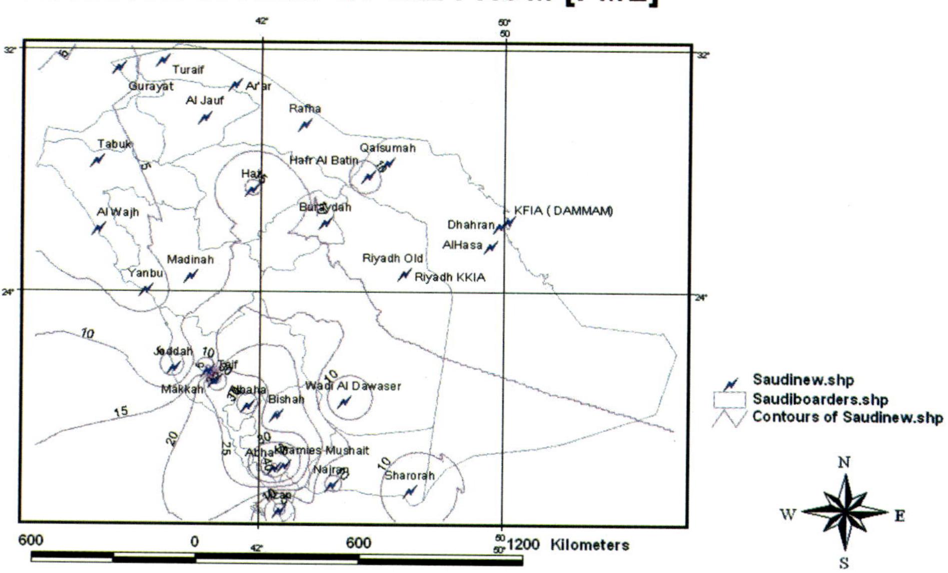

Figure 2.6: The Mean Annual Td/yr for the Spring Season

It is obvious that, the highest concentration of Isokeraunic level (IKL) during the whole year is located in the southern and mountain regions such as Taif, and Abha, while it is very low on the beach sides of the Red Sea such as Jeddah. Moreover, the

AVERAGE SUMMER OF IKL FROM [PME]

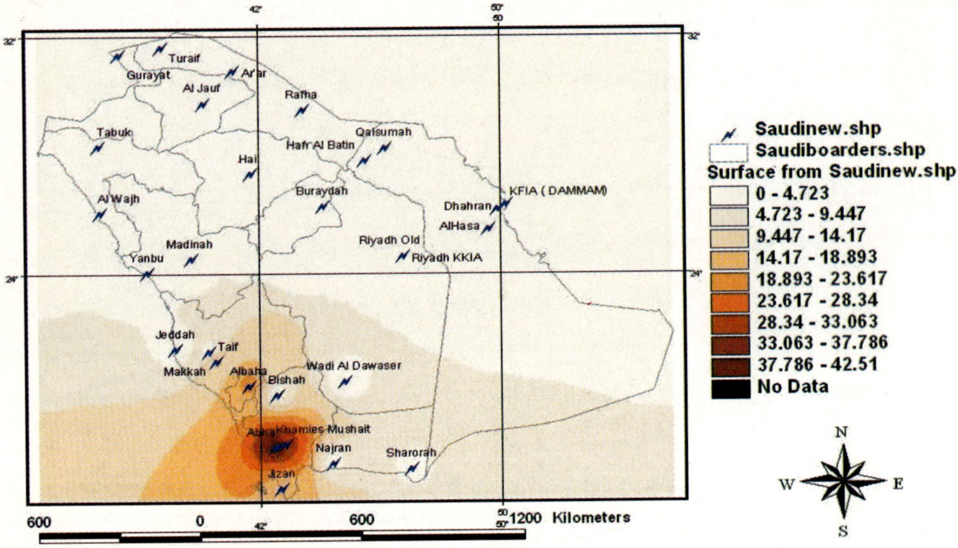

Figure 2.7: The Mean Annual Td/yr for the Summer Season

AVERAGE WINTER OF IKL FROM [PME]

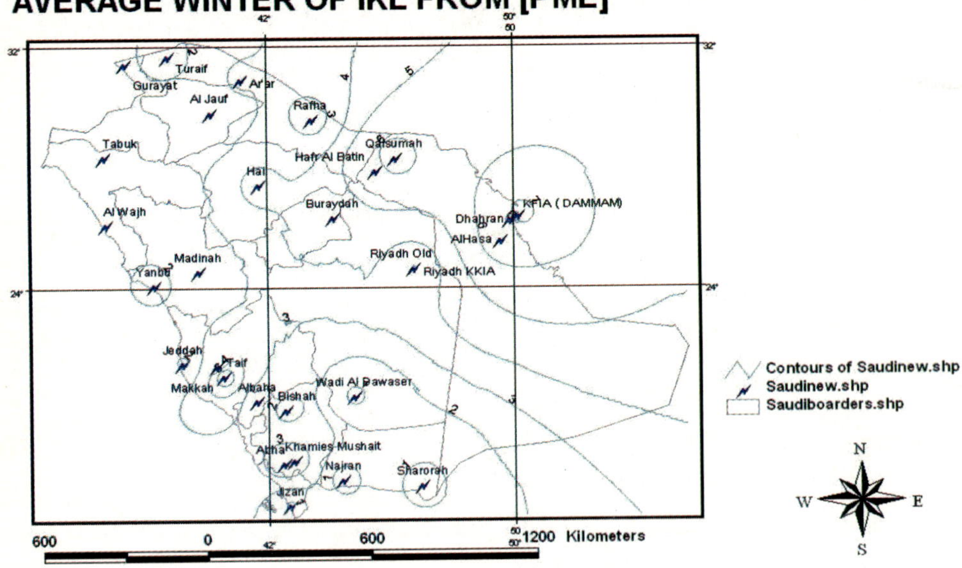

Figure 2.8: The Mean Annual Td/yr for the Winter Season

seasonal average within the same period was published in the map form using GIS as shown. Such a map is called an Isokeraunic level (IKL) chart. This chart does not give information on the severity of lightning, but it supplies valuable data on the relative probability of lightning in different regions of Saudi Arabia. Table 2.2

illustrates that the highest average of IKL happened in spring season, while the lowest average happened in summer season.

Table 2.2: The Total Annual and Seasonal Average Td/yr for the 19 Years

City	*Total Average*				
	Summer	*Autumn*	*Winter*	*Spring*	*Annual*
Abha	42.54	10.25	3.541	41	97.33
Alabha	21.05	11.16	2.63	32.58	67.42
Alahsa	0.26	0.79	6.26	9.74	17.1
Al Jouf	0.16	4.25	2.04	5.54	11.96
Arar	0.29	5.54	3.13	6.17	15.13
Bisha	3.89	4.05	2.11	25.16	35.21
Dhahran	0.042	1.67	5.88	8.58	16.17
Qassiem	0.21	5.53	5.47	12.63	23.84
Gurayat	0.05	5.58	2	3.89	11.53
Hafr	0.23	3.31	5.92	10.54	20
Hail	0.58	8.92	4.25	15.46	29.21
Jizan	17.14	16.38	1.1	4.14	38.76
Jeddah	1.17	4.08	1.92	1.83	9
Kfia	0	2	7.75	5	14.75
Khamis	29.83	7.33	3.42	35.52	76.13
Kkia	0.13	0.83	2.67	8.33	11.96
Madinah	2.83	7	2.67	7.71	20.21
Makkah	2.89	9.95	2.95	3.68	19.47
Najran	3.74	0.47	0.79	11.11	12.75
Qaisuma	0.37	5.4	8.12	11.58	25.5
Rafha	0.13	4.54	2.67	5.96	13.29
Riyadh Old	0.25	1	4.46	10.04	15.75
Sharorah	3.37	0.89	0.74	5.05	10.1
Tabuk	0.79	6.54	2.63	4.54	14.5
Taif	16.86	29.59	6.55	43	96
TURIEF	0.32	6.95	1.68	6.95	15.89
Wadi Dwaser	0.78	0.5	0.89	5	7.17
WAJH	0.042	1.38	2.1	0.96	4.46
YANBU	0.47	3.82	1.77	1.14	7.14

Conclusion and Recommendations

- Developed Annual and Seasonal maps of the IKL (Td/yr) are the first to be published in the history of Saudi Arabia. These maps are useful for PME, SEC transmission and distribution engineers.

- The annual mean lightning thunderstorm days were represented. The four seasonal records of all stations were available.
- There is a need to make the PME data of the average lightning activity for nineteen years (19) years more validated with some other Saudi Arabian lightning data records.
- It is observed that, the highest concentration of Isokeraunic level (IKL) during the whole year is located in the southern and mountain regions such as Taif, Abha, and Al Baha while it is very low on the shore of the Red Sea such as Jeddah.
- The average of the annual thunderstorms doesn't exceed thirty (30) on the flat land of the Kingdom of Saudi Arabia except in the Southern and West regions. However, it reaches in some mountain regions to about ninety seven (97) thunderstorms per year. It is very low, around nine (9) thunderstorms, on the coast of the Red Sea.
- Table 2.2 illustrates that the highest average of Isokeraunic level (IKL) happened in spring season. While, the lowest average happened in winter season.
- The areas in which maximum flash density was measured were Abha, Taif, Khamis and Al-Baha based on PME lightning records which give actual lightning days. In Abha, the maximum flash density exceeded 12 flashes per square kilometer per year.
- Some improvement in various aspects of the estimation process should be studied further.

Acknowledgements

The author appreciates the full financial support by the City of King Abdul Aziz of Science and Technology (KACST), also continued support of KFUPM. Without such support this work on Lightning research and new mapping of IKL and GFD could not have evolved.

References

1. Anderson, R.B. and Eriksson, A.J., 1980. Lightning parameters for engineering application, *Electra*, 69, 65-102.
2. Anderson, R.B., Eriksson, A.J., Kroninger, H., Meal, D.V. and Smith, M.A., 1984. Lightning and thunderstorm parameters, IEEE Int Conf Lightning and Power Systems, London, UK.
3. Burrows, W. R., King, P., Lewis, P.J., Kochtubajda, B., Snyder, B., Turcotte, V., 2001. "Lightning Occurrence Patterns over Canada and Adjacent United States from Lightning Detection Network Observations", *Atmosphere-Ocean*, 13 Aug.
4. Boccippio, D.J., Cummins, K.L., Christian H.J. and Goodman, S.J. "Combined Satellite- and Surface-Based Estimation of the Intra-cloud-Cloud to Ground Lightning Ratio over the Continental United States", Monthly Weather Review Vol.129, pp 108-122.

5. CIGRE Lightning flash counter. Part 1 Specification. Part 2 Guide for estimating ground flash density CIGRE lightning flash counter. Electra, 22, 149-171.

6. De la Rosa *et al.*, 1995. "Lightning Characteristics Relevant for Electrical Engineering: Assessment of Sensing, Recording and Mapping Requirements in the Light of Present Technological Advancements", CIGRE TF-33.01.02, Report No. 94, July.

7. De La Rosa, F., Chisholm, W., Galván, A., Heidler, F., Rakov, V., 1994. "Lightning Characteristics Relevant for Electrical Engineering: Assessment of Sensing, Recording and Mapping Requirements in the Light of Present Technological Advancements", CIGRE Task Force 33.01.02 Brochure 94.

8. De la Rosa, F., Nucci, C.A., Rakov, V., 1998. "Lightning and its Impact on Power Systems", CIGRE SC33 International Conference, Zagreb, Croatia.

9. De la Rosa *et al.*, 2000. "Characterization of lightning for application to electric power systems", CIGRE TF Report, Electra, December.

10. http://www.pme.gov.sa/, Presidency of Meterological & Environment (PME).

11. IEEE STD. 1243-1997, IEEE Design Guide for Improving the Lightning Performance of Transmission Lines.

12. Janischewskyj, W., Beattie J. and Chisholm, W. A., 1998. Lightning Ground Flash Density Measurements in Canada: 1990-1996. Final Report for Canadian Electrical Association Contract 179T382A, Sept.

13. Torres, H. *et al.*, 1996. "Experiences and first results of Colombian lightning location network" Proceedings 23rd International Conference on Lightning Protection, pp. 186-190, Firenze.

14. The IEEE Working Group, 2001. "Guide for Improving Lightning Performance of Electric Power Overhead Distribution Lines," Approved as IEEE Standard P1410.

Part II

Awareness and Damage Caused by Lightning

Chapter 3

Lightning Safety Awareness Programme Especially in South Asia to Minimize Loss of Human Lives and Properties

Munir Ahmed and Chandima Gomes***

**Lightning Awareness Centre and Technological Assistance for Rural Advancement (TARA), Dhaka, Bangladesh*

E-mail: tara@citechco.net, munir_tara@yahoo.com, tara@ranksitt.com

***Department of Physics, Colombo University, Sri Lanka*

E-mail: chandima.gomes@gmail.com

ABSTRACT

Lightning is a natural phenomenon that has been striking the earth from very long past all over the world. It has caused and is causing big losses to mankind. The losses include casualty of human and animal lives, buildings, communication, power system and other infrastructures. People have been helpless in overcoming the problem and remain affected. The issue has received attention of scientists since ages and work is going on for the mitigation. Many studies have been conducted but the science behind the lightning is not completely understood yet. Some technology has been developed in protecting the infrastructure (mainly buildings) but it has limitations.

It has been revealed that the preventive safety measures are still the main issue in fighting the problems with lightning. Awareness among general people has been identified as one of the important factor. Programmes have been taken in this regard and people are working continuously. Lightning Awareness Cell (LAC), Lightning Research Centre (LRC) have been opened in many countries and working on research and awareness building. It is quite prominent in South

Asian countries and Sri Lanka, India, Bangladesh, Nepal and Bhutan have LAC. These countries have strong coordination with each other and achieved good success in increasing the awareness. LAC-Bangladesh has been able to reach at community level with the awareness. The safety awareness encompasses the mass awareness to people by different means, technical education, demonstrations and training. Individual lightning safety awareness programme might have limitation in running along. As it is a part of natural disaster, there is a strong need for the incorporation of lightning as a natural disaster in National Disaster Management Programmes of each country. It should get equal importance like other disasters and proper strategy and action plan should be adopted and implemented for sustainable management.

Keywords: *Lightning, Safety, Awareness, Mitigation, Bangladesh, South Asia.*

Introduction

Lightning is a natural phenomenon which originates from the clouds. It is produced by high voltage electricity and strike down on the earth causing damage to life and property. Lightning is usually accompanied by thunder. The lightning strikes have been continuing since the origin of the earth. It occurs throughout the world though the severity is observed to vary over the regions.

The damage from the lightning is quite significant. Many people die due to lightning every year. According to an estimation, more than 500 people die every year in South East Asia alone. However based on data of Bangladesh it appears that about 1000 people die in SAARC countries. In Sri Lanka more than 50 people die every year. In Nepal 15 people died in August 2006 only. For an example, on the 5th April 2002–five women working in a farm in Moneragala were killed on the spot, as the tree they were underneath for shelter from a thin drizzle, was struck by lightning. The lives of these people could have been saved if they were given proper education in lightning protection. Not only human lives but there are losses in livestock, buildings, infrastructure, communication, power plant, tree etc. from the lightning. On the Sinhala-Tamil New year day of 2001, a thirty-year-old elephant, Seetha Menike, belong to the Dalada Maligawa was killed by lightning. The annual damage of assets and properties is very significant although there is no specific information. However, according to an information source, in Sri Lanka every year lightning causes property damage estimated at over US$ 3.0 million (SARI 2006).

Lightning Protection is a specialized topic. The field of Lightning Protection is being updated frequently at international level. New concepts, techniques and products are constantly introduced into the market and most importantly, based on the scientific discoveries, some products, techniques and even entire concepts are rejected from the standards and engineering practice. Our engineers are at a distinct drawback for not getting opportunity to access such knowledge. Unfortunately in Sri Lanka, Bangladesh and many other countries in South Asia do not have proper guidelines for protection. In the absence of such guidelines the engineers are advised to follow other recognized standards such as International Standards (IEC) British Standards (BS) Australian National Standards, American Standards (ANSI) etc.

However, only the standards will not improve the situation unless a proper programme is launched aiming at educating the masses and the people concerned with Lightning Protection. Although a notable effort is made by the scientific community during the last several years to educate the public in the prevention of lightning hazards, still the number of deaths, injuries and property damages due to lightning is unacceptably high. At present protection devices are imported. These are trusted upon by the test certificates issued at foreign laboratories. The local distributor has no way of verifying the claimed properties of the products due to the lack of test facilities. Practically all the products related to lightning protection, now available in South Asia have been produced to with stand the characteristics of lightning currents and lightning generated fields measured in temperate regions and sub-tropical regions. A considerable number of scientists believe that characteristics of tropical and oceanic regions may be different to what is observed in the above-mentioned regions. Thus there has been a need to acquire more knowledge on tropical lightning. Regarding the products, there should be an independent body to check and approve lightning protection installations and import of products.

In almost all developed countries and in many newly industrialized and developing countries, the lightning localizing system has become an important part of the day-to-day operations of the civil administration and the defence. In addition, the need for a lightning protection system is badly felt in meteorology, power sector, communication sector, industrial sector, defence, hydrology, ports and fisheries and hence the research related to lightning.

Although the lightning has been a problem and cause of loss ever since, not much attention was paid until the last few decades. Recently it has got good attention and people across the world are working on this issue. Scientists from different parts of the world are getting together. Activities are being taken up for creating awareness among the common people and mitigation measures are applied although it is in an early stage. Forums and workshops are organised with continued efforts. The Lightning Awareness Centre (LAC) has been established in the countries like India, Nepal, Sri Lanka and Bangladesh with the objective of building awareness among people. Bangladesh has a Lightning Research Centre at Jahangirnagar University, which works closely with LAC for mitigation measures. Several Regional Workshops were held in India and Sri Lanka with the initiative from UNESCO where participants from several countries attended. There has been a plan for Lightning Safety Awareness up to 2010. Some programmes like South Asia Initiative for Energy (SARI) have shown interest and support to lightning programmes.

Many states in India and other neighbouring countries such as Sri Lanka, Bangladesh, Bhutan and Nepal are prone to lightning hazards. Proper dissemination of knowledge of lightning protection and safety measures is expected to minimize the death toll and other hazards to the human beings and live stock as well as to properties, industries and services such as power and communication. In Sri Lanka the properties damaged in the power, communication and industrial sectors and at domestic level, during the two lightning seasons of the year. This amount does not take into account the billions of indirect losses due to the loss of manhours caused by the damaged and malfunctioning equipment and loss of data in the microprocessors. The equipment damage is on the increasing trend for the last few decades due to the wide spread use of electronics, extension of the national power grid into rural areas and mushrooming communication towers all over the country. Many archaeological structures, which have irreplaceable high value, are either totally unprotected or not-properly protected at present. Thus, these structures are highly vulnerable to damage due to lightning.

Although a notable effort is made by the scientific community during the last several years to educate the public in the prevention of lightning hazards, still the number of deaths, injuries and property damages due to lightning is unacceptably high in India especially in Eastern India. According to the National Crime Record Bureau, India, 1507 persons died in India during 2001 because of lightning, which is about 1 per cent of the natural and unnatural accidental deaths in the country. In Orissa (a state in Eastern India) alone, about 300 people were struck by lightning and subsequently died in 2004. Further, the equipment damage is also increasing due to the wide spread use of electronics, extension of the national power grid into rural areas and the mushrooming communication towers all over the country (Gomes 2006, personal communication).

In Bangladesh, more than 100 people die and another 100 get injured every year from lightning. In 2006, in Bangladesh 127 people died and 78 got injured. A power plant of 33 kV was destroyed and few livestock died (TARA, 2006). There are death and property losses in other south Asian countries also.

Though various lightning protection and safety measures are available internationally, but it is very limited to South Asian countries. Some engineers and scientists are involved with lightning protection but still knowledge is limited in this field. Lightning Protection is a field that requires high specialization for an electrical engineer to become an expert. New concepts, techniques and products are constantly introduced into the market and most importantly, based on the scientific discoveries, some products, techniques and even entire concepts are rejected from the standards and engineering practice.

Having limitations on safety measures equipment, there has been an emerging need for proper dissemination of lightning protection and safety measures to minimize the death toll and other hazards to the human beings and live stock as well as to minimize the lightning damages to properties, industries and services such as power and communication in South Asian countries. Although a notable effort has been made by the scientists community during the last several years to educate the public in the prevention of lightning hazards, still the number of deaths, injuries and property damages due to lightning is unacceptably high in those countries. This paper deals with the issues, achievements and requirements of lightning safety awareness programme especially in South Asia.

Basics of Lightning/Fundamentals

Lightning is a natural atmospheric phenomenon, which is caused by the instability of charge distribution within a cloud. It also occurs due to the charge separation in the mass of ash and dust ejected due to volcanic eruptions and nuclear explosions. Lightning physics is the study of the various aspects of lightning such as background conditions for formation, corresponding activities, variation, distribution based on the geographical location and effects on human beings and structures.

A lightning flash originates inside a cloud, several kilometres above the ground level. Except for ball lightning, which is a very rare phenomenon, lightning is simply an electric spark between a cloud and ground, between two clouds or between two parts of a cloud. The spark that jumps between the ends of two wires, which are connected to the terminals of a car battery, is a very basic form of lightning.

In the first stage of the lightning strike, a channel of charge flows towards ground from the cloud. When this channel is about 50-100 meters above, earthbound objects in the vicinity (eg. trees, buildings, human beings, animals etc.) start sending upward channels of opposite charge to meet the downward channel from the cloud. One of these upward channels succeeds in meeting the downward channel first. Subsequently a large current will flow through the object, which sent that upward channel. Then we say that the object is lightning struck. If a given building is a tall protrusion in a certain landscape it may be the unfortunate object that sends the first upward channel that meets the downward stream of charge from the cloud.

Thus, most of the casualty takes places in the open field. The property damages occur mainly in high-rise buildings and electric networks such as electricity plants, telephone lines etc. The passing of electricity through living bodies, especially mammals, makes huge electric shock and heat that burns and kills the animal. Lightning causes fracture to complete damage to buildings, bursting of electric transformers and equipments. In a study, Gomes *et al.* (2006), has shown that the casualties are more (70 per cent) from indirect effect than direct strike (30 per cent) by the lightning in Sri Lanka and Bangladesh. The indirect casualties occur by the side flashing when people run indiscriminately for shelter. It usually occurs during the dry and hot period of the year. In South Asia the period of lightning is from March to June as peak time and September-October as second peak time in many places. Figure 3.1 shows the process of lightning.

One of the remarkable drawback of lightning mitigation is the prejudice and misconception among general people. Most of the people are ignorant about the cause of lightning. This is very high among the people of South Asian countries. People tend to believe that lightning comes from the God. It is a punishment for vigorous misconduct and can't be avoided. People tend to behave badly to affected person or family instead of cooperation, sympathy, assistance and support. Some people rely on spiritual measures as a remedy.

Lightning Safety and Mitigation Strategy

The lightning safety and mitigation are of mainly two types 1) Protection through technical way and 2) prevention through taking safety/precautionary measures through building safety awareness.

Protection Through Technical Ways

There has been technological advancement on the protection of lightning. The main effort is on the protection of valuable infrastructure. The available techniques are;

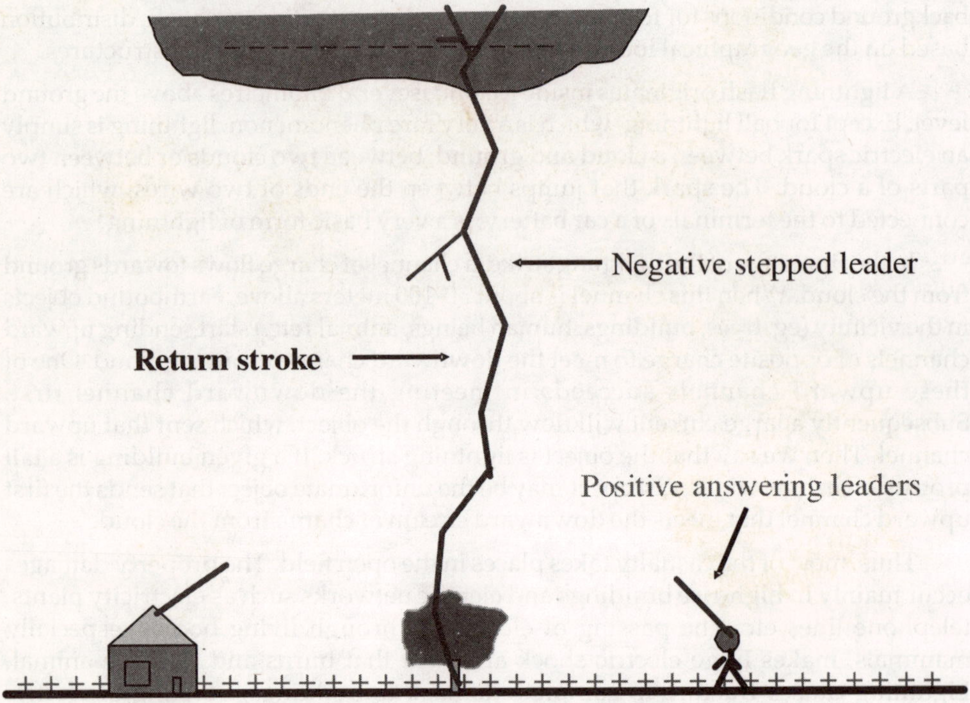

Figure 3.1: Shows the Meeting of Negative and Positive Step Leader that Leads to Lightning Strike (Courtesy: Chandima Gomes)

Building Protection Against Lightning

Lightning may cause damages to buildings and equipment in three ways. When a building attracts a downward lightning leader (direct strike) or attract a part of a lightning flash that hit another structure in the near proximity (side flash) it will get the maximum damage. The lightning current reaches a maximum value of about 30,000 Amperes on average but currents in the range of 300,000 Amperes are also reported. The lightning current heats its path to a temperature of about 40,000 Celsius. The enormous current involved with the lightning flash may destroy the entire power and communication networks in a building including all the equipment connected to the networks. The high temperature resulted by both the current that flows in the lines and the sparks that jump in between different parts of the building may trigger fires that will completely burn out the installation. Direct lightning (or side flashes) cause damages at a very rapid rate so that once the building is lightning struck it is very unlikely that one can prevent any of the damages to the equipment and human injuries (still one can prevent the spreading of the fire by acting quickly).

The second way lightning currents enter into installations is through the service lines such as power, communication and cable TV. Once lightning strikes a service line, part of the lightning current enter all the nearby buildings which may destroy all the equipments that are plugged into the system. The lightning current may also injure the users of equipments connected to service lines. This mode of intrusion of the lightning current cause less damages than a direct strike, yet service lines are subjected to lightning strikes much more frequently than buildings themselves.

The lightning current discharge from cloud-to ground is a good emitter of electromagnetic radiations. Thus, once a lightning hits a nearby object (say at 500m) even the building is exposed to a strong dose of electromagnetic radiation. When this radiation passes through electronic equipments such as computers, medical equipments, military equipments etc. the sophisticated parts of them can be destroyed. This may happen even when the equipments are unplugged from service lines. However, the chances of ordinary electrical equipments getting damaged due to such radiation is very slim.

In the commercial language a building protection system is referred to as a network that is meant to protect a building from direct lightning strikes and side flashes. An ordinary building protection system consists of one or several sharp pointed rods (or a mesh of metal strips/wires) installed at the roof of the building, several metal stripes or metal wires from roof to base and one or several conducting rods buried in the ground. When a downward channel comes from a cloud, the air termination sends an upward channel much faster than the other parts of the building thus the lightning is attracted to one of the rods (or to the metallic mesh). Then the lightning current is safely passed into earth through the rest of the system. Thus, instead of repelling, a lightning protection system attracts a lightning channel. And as the lightning current is safely driven into earth the building is saved from damage. The system is called the "Franklin Rod System", named after Benjamin Franklin who first proposed lightning rods in 1749.

Surge Protection

With the system described above a building is protected only from direct strikes and probably from side flashes. Still buildings can be penetrated by lightning currents that propagate along service lines (power, telecommunication etc.). These lines are more probable to be exposed to lightning electrical environment than individual buildings as they stretch a long distance over the land. There are special devices (surge diverters or surge suppressors), which prevent these current impulses from entering the building. A surge diverter is connected at the entrance of the service line to the installation. At high level of protection they are connected at the power socket of each electrical or electronic equipment as well. Under normal operation the surge diverter does not interfere with the line signals. In the case of a lightning strike it provides a convenient path for the lightning current to divert into the earth without permitting it entering into the building or the equipment. Surge suppressors, which have to be connected to protect power lines, communication lines and data lines, are different from one another.

Electromagnetic Compatibility (EMC)

The sophisticated electronics in a building can also be damaged by radiation, which will be emitted from the lightning flash. Electromagnetic radiation propagates in free space. This radiation can be prevented from entering the building by taking suitable protection measures. The typical method of radiation prevention is to screen the building with a conductive material so that the building becomes a "Faraday Cage". As it is very costly and unnecessary to screen the whole building it is recommended to take safety measures only to compartments of the building where sophisticated electronics are installed (such as computer rooms, medical theatres and scanning rooms, control chambers of power plants, airports, military bases, and communication bases etc.). Design and implementation of protection systems that prevent the intrusion of undesired electromagnetic impulses through both radiation and conduction is termed Electro Magnetic Compatibility (EMC).

Lighting Prevention Through Safety/Precaution Measures (Mitigation Approach)

The main destruction of lightning is the loss of human lives and other living beings and nonliving assets. The Safety Mitigation Measures are:

Local Safety Measures for Individuals

In the context of Bangladesh and other countries in the region having similar physical environment farmers and fishermen work in the open fields and open waters respectively during lightning prone season. The farmers work to harvest and transplant paddy during March to July during high lightning strike period. During the same time fishing is also important as fish migrate with the onset of pre-monsoon rain. Another peak time is September-October when fishermen are busy in fishing soon after flood recession and farmers work on paddy fields. These two periods are prime period in Bangladesh and some other South Asian countries. Many human lives are lost along with other livestock in this period. It makes an irreparable loss to poor families due to loss of the earning member or their main assets. Hence the individual safety measures are very important and can play significant role for reducing the losses due to lightning. No safety measures for the individuals have been proposed so far.

Building Safety

The technical safety for building has been mentioned before. Other important infrastructures like fly over, bridges, airports, archaeological sites etc. are also sometimes affected by lightning and require protection and more safety measures to be adopted.

Telecommunication Network Safety

The telecommunication, including mobile phone service providers systems are prone to lightning. Preventive measures are required to be developed and enforced.

Electricity and Power Safety

It is another area of huge asset damage. No technical and preventive measure is in place. Action is required to save this sector as this support most of the economic activity like garments, manufacturers etc. Interruption in electricity due to lightning may not only damage equipment of that industry/office but may contribute in failure of shipment within deadline and thus consequently business loss of million dollars.

Target Achievement

Awareness to Common People

The common people who are affected by the lightning need to be made aware and educated with all the safety issues and precautions.

Awareness to Technical People

Technical people should also be made aware about the types of losses and damage through lightning so that they can take steps for technology development for further improvement.

Research and Studies

It should be continued in order to find the mechanism of lightning causes and its mitigation.

Way of Achievement

The awareness can be achieved by organizing workshops, seminars, posters, advertisement etc. It can be done by more conventional way of dissemination *i.e.* workshop cum training. For the participants the following issues would be useful;

- Fundamentals of lightning mechanism
- Personal lightning safety
- Common lightning accidents
- Lightning safety of household equipment and of outdoor workers
- Alternative lightning protection systems

Lightning Safety Programmes in South Asia

Initial Educative Programmes

Several Regional Workshops have been held in India and Sri Lanka with the initiative from UNESCO Delhi where participants from several countries attended. Teachers from Colleges and Universities from Bangladesh also attended these workshops. In all the workshops second author of this paper attended and worked as resource person.

One of the major recommendation of these workshops was to carryout more awareness programmes on lightning Physics in South East Asia. Later UNESCO nominated second author (Dr. Chandima Gomes) as one of the leader in awareness education programme for this region.

Under this context and UNESCO recommendations to promote awareness among the people, scientists and academicians Dr. Gomes launched a project where he conducts workshop/lectures in Sri Lanka, Bangladesh and Bhutan. This project was supported partially by UNDP/UNESCO and SARI Energy.

Development of Lightning Awareness Research Centres and Programmes

To carry out programmes on lightning safety, awareness and mitigation work, workshops alone are not sufficient. There is a need for continuous support from institutions. As the existing 'disaster management organizations' do not consider this issue as a severe one, need was felt for the development of 'Lightning Awareness and Research Centres' in this region. Several LAC and LRCs have been established in Bangladesh, Bhutan, India and Nepal.

Sri Lanka

The National Institution for Lightning Protection (NILP) in Sri Lanka is recently formed. The executive members have done a remarkable service to the nation in the last few decades with regard to lightning protection. So far they have been involved as a coordinator, moderator and active resource person for over 100 workshops, conferences and training programs at international, regional and national levels. These programs have been funded/sponsored by various institutions such as UNESCO, SARI/Energy (USAID), IEE Sri Lanka Branch, Sri Lanka Institute for Development of Administration, Sri Lanka Association for Advancement of Science, University of Colombo, University of Moratuwa, Sri Lanka Telephone Regulatory Commission, Institute of Fundamental Studies etc. The executive members have pioneered in establishing Lightning related projects in Sri Lanka, Columbia, Nepal, Bangladesh and Bhutan. They are also engaged with the first lightning physics research group in South Asia which has a history of over 40 years. The coordinator of the executive member panel is the group leader of South Asian Lightning Awareness Program.

India

Kerala

The Lightning Awareness Cell, Kerala was formed in June 2005 following a dialogue initiated with the SALAP team at SARI/Energy Regional meeting held in Colombo in May 2005. The institution was formed under the umbrella of Regional Energy centre Kerala, which is a not for profit organisation registered under the Travancore Cochin Literary, Scientific and Charitable Societies Act–XII of 1955. The LAC Kerala is now strengthened with the active contribution of a number of senior academics and professionals in the region. First committee meeting to discuss the structure and work plan of LAC, Kerala was held on the *12th July 2005*. The LAC of Kerala conducted a Lightning workshop at Mysore on 07-08-06. They also organized another programme in Cochin in March 2006.

Bangalore

Department of High Voltage Engineering under Indian Institute of Science, Bangalore has been very active in lightning related research and has designed and built the lightning protection system for the satellite launch pad at Sriharikota, India, lightning test facility for aircrafts at Bangalore, lightning protection system for HANSA aircraft etc. In addition, several students have worked on lightning related area for their Ph.D. as well as masters degrees at the dept. In addition, the author has delivered several talks on lightning at different meetings in the country.

Guwahati

The Lightning Awareness Cell, Guwahati was initiated in August 2005. The cell has been formed under the umbrella of 'The Energy and Resources Institute' (TERI), which is a not for profit autonomous organization registered under the Society Registration Act 1856 and headquartered in New Delhi. The LAC Guwahati is now strengthened with the active participation of a number of senior academics and professionals in the region. The cell has also initiated contacts with various national and international institutes working on lightning protection and safety. LAC has organized a two day workshop on Lightning in Guwahati on 26-27 April 2006. Planned programmes are:

- Workshop on lightning protection and safety for school and college teachers in various regions of the Guwahati
- Awareness programmes on lightning safety for panchayat members and villagers
- Awareness programme for media professionals in different regions of the country.
- Entrepreneurship Development Programmes involving participants from different states
- Mapping on Lightning Affected areas of India by detailed Survey

Bangladesh

The Lightning Awareness Centre (LAC), Bangladesh was first proposed and formed during the workshop on 15 December 2004 held at CEGIS by Technological Assistance for Rural Advancement (TARA), Dhaka. Later during the workshop at Jahangirnagar University (JU) on 17 December 2004 this was further strengthened and decided to function closely with Bangladesh Lightning Research Centre (BLRC) at JU and South Asian Lightning Awareness Centre (SALAC) in Sri Lanka and National Lightning Safety Institution (NLSI), USA and other organizations. The first two workshops were conducted under South Asia Lightning Awareness Programme (SALAP) Phase-1, supported by SARI/Energy.

In recent past LAC/TARA alone and jointly with BLRC, JU and local NGOs conducted several awareness programmes/activities like workshop at CEGIS jointly with JU, workshop jointly conducted at JU, Seminar in Chandranath College, Netrokona, Bangladesh, Awareness programme with school children in Sreemangal, Bangladesh SPOSP and SERRE, Awareness programme with fishermen and farmer community, workshop with NGO workers and its beneficiaries at Bhurungamari, Kurigram (Hashem and Chowdhury 2005, TARA 2005a, 2005b, 2005c, 2005d, JU 2005. LAC TARA also started maintaining a lightning database. In addition to work in Bangladesh LAC/TARA has also been associated with lightning safety related programs abroad. LAC representative attended SARI Energy Regional meetings in Delhi, Colombo, Dhaka and Kathmandu. It also took part in Lightning programmes in Sri Lanka, Bhutan and USA. LAC TARA also produced number of reports of its events.

Under the LAC TARAs future plan following approach and strategy has been identified:

- Workshop/Programmes considering most Lightning affected areas
- Formal Presentation/workshop at Divisional, District and Upazila Level Programme
- Rural Level Programmes in village, bazar/hats/growth centres/schools with Jarigan/Folksongs for the profession wise such as: Farmers, Fishermen, Boatmen, Housewives, Students, Teachers
- Mobile Units with a vehicle with necessary presentation equipment
- Awareness materials to develop are Posters, Brochure, Flyer, Calendar, Booklet, Bill Board, Newspaper Ad, Communicating with Principals of Colleges and other institutes to organize small presentations, communicating with Editors of local newspapers/media person to publish articles
- To organize a Regional Workshop
- Mapping on Lightning Affected areas by detailed Survey
- New website on Lightning awareness
- Making new Documentary/DVD in the Bangladesh context on lightning awareness and safety
- Creating a database on Lightning

Bhutan

BLARC (Bhutan Lightning Awareness and Research Centre) was formed during a two days workshop held at RBIT (Royal Bhutan Institute of Technology) in Phentsholling in December 2004 with the initiation of SALAC.

Nepal

Nepal Lightning Awareness Centre (NLAC) was formed on 28th August, 2006 and a workshop has already been conducted in Kathmandu.

Pakistan

Number of workshops and seminars conducted in Pakistan with the initiative of SALAC, Sri Lanka.

Maldives and Myanmar

It has been planned to organize lightning safety programme and to initiate LACs in these two countries.

Later Stage/Present Status

Lightning Safety Awareness has been planned up to 2010. Under this plan number of awareness workshop and training are planned in Bangladesh, Bhutan,

Nepal, India, Sri Lanka. It is planned to have more linkages with Kenya (country experiences more than 215 Thunder day / Year in some areas, Prof. Robert Jallan'go Akello has been a lightning safety advocate since the early 1980's). It is also planned to have more interaction with Lightning Data Centre, St. Anthony Hospital, Colorado, USA, Lightning Research Team of Uppsala University, Sweden and with National Lightning Safety Institution (NLSI).

Conclusion

Though lightning is an age old phenomenon, it is not yet fully understood. This paper does not advocate prevention from lightning but to promote take up lightning safety measures. Many damages may be avoided if proper lightning safety measures are taken. Lightning safety measures can be achieved mainly by mass awareness, technical education, demonstrations and development of lightning and surge protection devices through research and development. It is needed to consider lightning as one of the 'natural disasters' and incorporate it in National Disaster Management Programmes with priority.

Acknowledgements

We acknowledge the information, which is used mainly from the programme/ activities of LAC-TARA, Prof. Dr. Parashuram Sharma, Bhutan, Dr. Mannan Chowdhury, Jahangirnagar University, Dhaka, Mr. Richard Kithil, CEO, National Lightning Safety Institution (NLSI), USA, Mr. Kamal Raj, Nepal, Mr. Debajit Palit and Mr. Hari Kumar of India and Mr. Akello, Kenya.

References

1. Hashem, A. and Z H Chowdhury 2005. Report on Sreemangal Programmes 06-07 May 2005; TARA Report Date 11th May 2005, 25 pages, Dhaka
2. JU 2005. Report on Lightning Workshop of 17th December 2004. Dept. of Physics, Jahangirnagar University, Dhaka
3. SARI 2006. A Compendium of activities 2003-2006. SARI Energy, Small Grants Program, USAID.
4. TARA 2005a. Report on Lightning Workshop of 17th December 2004. Dept. of Physics, Jahangirnagar University, Dhaka
5. TARA 2005b. Report on Lightning Awareness workshop held at CEGIS on 15 December 2005. TARA, 17 pages Dhaka
6. TARA 2005c. Report on Nertrokona Programme of 24th March 2005; Report date 25th March 2005, 13 pages , Dhaka
7. TARA 2005d. Draft Report on Participation to Lightning Programmes in USA of 11-13 August 2005; Report Date 20th September 2005, Dhaka
8. TARA 2006. Lightning Database. LAC-TARA, Dhaka

Abbreviations

BLARC: Bhutan Lightning Awareness and Research Centre

BLRC: Bangladesh Lightning Research Centre

LAC: Lightning Awareness Centre

NLAC: Nepal Lightning Awareness Centre

NLSI: National Lightning Safety Institution

SALAC: South Asia Lightning Awareness Centre

SALAP: South Asia Lightning Awareness Programme

Chapter 4

Lightning Situation in Botswana

Oarabile Nnabu
Botswana Technology Centre,
Gaborone, Botswana
E-mail: onnabu@mega.bw

ABSTRACT

There is a high incidence of lightning in Botswana. A typical lightning season is from September to May, with a peak between November and January. A study on lightning was performed in Gaborone in the 1990s over a period of five years (Jayaratne and Ramachandran, 1997). During this study, an average of 54 thunderstorm days a year was found. Lightning incidence is high in other parts of the country as well.

Despite the high incidence of lightning in Botswana, lightning is not generally taken very seriously. There is no lightning protection standard in Botswana. However, there is a lot of construction and other developments going on in the country at the moment. Without a proper and enforced standard, it means that the quality of the lightning protection equipment installed, if any, or the way it has been installed, cannot always be guaranteed.

Incidents of deaths and serious destruction by lightning are relatively low compared to those from other mishaps. Most of the damage by lightning is preventable. Loss of life, no matter how relatively few, can never be acceptable, especially when that loss could have been easily prevented. Public awareness is one of the key ways that should be used to correct this situation. Botswana Bureau of Standards (BOBS) should be encouraged to come up with a lightning protection standard as soon as possible. There is also a need to begin research on lightning in the country.

Introduction

Lightning can be described as either a gigantic electric spark between two charged regions in a cloud (Jayaratne and Ramachandran, 1993), or as a tremendous electric current (or electric spark) resulting from a discharge between clouds, within a cloud or between a cloud and the earth (Davidson *et al.*, 1985). The destructive effects to people and property are caused by the cloud to earth discharges. Wikipedia (http://en.wikipedia.org/wiki/Lightning, accessed 19 March 2007) on the other hand describes lightning as 'an atmospheric discharge of electricity, which usually, but not always, occurs during rain storms, and frequently during volcanic eruptions or dust storms.'

Botswana (between 18°*S* and 27°*C* latitudes; between 20°*E* and 29°*E* longitudes) is a landlocked country about 675 km and 1025 km from the Indian and Atlantic oceans respectively. The average altitude is 1000 m, with Kanye Hill being the highest at 1491 m. It is a dry country with a mean annual rainfall varying from a maximum of 650 mm in Kasane, to a minimum of less than 250 mm in Kgalagadi (Tsabong). The dry season is from May to August; pre-rainy season from September to October, rainy season from November to March and the post-rainy season is in April (http://www.weather.info.bw/resources/entry_content.html, accessed 18 April 2007).

There is a high incidence of lightning in Botswana. The estimated number of thunderstorm days per annum show that the incidence of lightning strikes on the ground varies. Despite the high incidence of lightning in Botswana, lightning is not generally taken very seriously. It is one of those things that one only remembers when they occur and completely forgets about them once they end. A number of people still hold some of the superstitious beliefs outlined in (Yeboah-Amankwah and Devan, 1980) about lightning, *i.e.* that lightning is a bird and people with supernatural powers (traditional doctors) can control it to harm those they don't like, etc.

This article appreciates that the amount of destruction by lightning is no longer as much as it used to be. In fact, compared with road accidents, as an example, deaths from lightning appear insignificant. However, it is highlighted that although there may be relatively few lightning related accidents, when they do happen, they can be quite grim and costly. These deaths (no matter how few) and the damage are found unacceptable as most of them can be easily prevented. It is found that there is a general lack of public understanding of lightning and how to protect one against it. The paper therefore, advocates for public education (which should be sustained), a formulation of a national lightning protection standard as soon as possible and a revival of research on lightning.

Incidence of Lightning in Botswana

A study on lightning in Gaborone done in the 1990s over a five-year period (Jayaratne and Ramachandran, 1998) has shown that a typical lightning season is from September to May, with a peak between November and January. The study also found virtually no lightning activity during the dry winter months of June, July and August. During this study, a mean of 54 thunderstorm days a year was found. The Department of Meteorological Services (DMS), on the other hand, puts the figure for annual thunderstorm days for Gaborone much higher at 75 (http://www.weather.info.bw/resources/entry_content.html, accessed 18 April 2007).

According to a map given from Oklahoma Climatological Survey (http://www.physicalgeography.net/fundamentals/7t.html, accessed 12 April 2007) most of the United States experience less than 50 thunderstorm days a year. Thunderstorm days per year in Australia vary from 88 near Darwin to less than 10 over parts of the southern regions (Australia Bureau of Statistics, 2002). High incidence (40 to 60 days per year) occurs over the eastern upland areas. A comparison of annual thunderstorm days of Gaborone with those of the United States and Australia clearly show that there is a high incidence of lightning in Gaborone.

Gaborone is, by far, not an area with the most incidents of lightning in the country. A study carried out in the early 1990s (Jayaratne and Ramachandran, 1994), which came up with what the authors considered to be 'the very first isokeraunic map of Botswana', found that the lightning incidence in Botswana is maximum in the northern most region where ground flash density is over 8 $km^{-2}yr^{-1}$. A secondary maximum region was found in the southeast with 5 $km^{-2}yr^{-1}$. The study identified a ridge of high activity that extends from the northwest corner, southwards towards Gantsi. Many other areas also recorded higher thunderstorm days than Gaborone. For instance, Beetsha recorded 83 thunderstorm days per year. A comparison of lightning activity in Gaborone and Molepolole (Jayratne and Ramachandran, 1997) also found lightning incidence to be far much more in Molepolole than Gaborone. The lightning flash density for Molepolole was found to be 34 per cent higher than that for Gaborone.

From the information above, it can be safely concluded that there is indeed a high incidence of lightning in Botswana. The high incidence is in many other parts of the country and not just in Gaborone, which has a high incidence in its own right.

Local Beliefs

Yeboah-Amankwah and Devan Devan (Yeboah-Amankwah and Devan, 1980) carried out some studies on local beliefs on lightning in the late seventies. One hundred people were interviewed throughout the country. The most common conceptions they found (about lightning) were:

- A ball of fire like a bird (some said peacock) with the colours of the rainbow.
- A bird with long claws which on the occasion of a flash swoops down to either lay an egg or catch a particular reptile or lizard.
- Two birds, one up and the other below. The higher one 'strikes' and the lower one goes to 'pick up' and they both then 'fly away.'
- A ball of fire from the urine of a 'cloud bird.'
- A bullet from the clouds.

Most of the people interviewed (76 per cent of those interviewed) believed that lightning is supernatural and is controlled by human beings with supernatural powers (traditional doctors). A jealous traditional doctor, with a strong desire to destroy a challenger, a competitor or an enemy, could use lightning. It could also be used for revenge, as a display of personal power and a show of anger.

A range of materials and situations were also suggested to have protective properties against lightning. The most common methods of protection suggested by those interviewed were:

- Traditional doctors, who have supernatural ability to arrange protection by the use of herbs or medicines.
- Prayer to God.
- Sacrifice of animals to dead ancestors.
- Light in house, *e.g.* lamps.
- Avoidance of running during rain.
- Bottles containing sand and seawater.
- Burying certain lizards around the house.
- Facing the edge of an axe to the lightning stroke.

Those interviewed also gave a list of materials believed to be capable of attracting lightning. Some of the materials mentioned were:

- Red clothes or colour.
- Certain animals such as 'blue headed lizards' or dog or ostrich eggs.
- Certain trees such as 'Mogotho', 'Mosheshe', 'Mokoba' and 'Mogonono'.
- Seawater.
- White objects.
- Electronic instruments: radio, television, and telephone.
- An axe.
- Grass thatch buildings.
- Certain material such as glass, mirror and silvery objects.

Certain situations were also mentioned as attracting lightning. For instance, using needles, milking cows when it is raining, sweat between saddle and horse, and sweat over the body of a running person.

Given the fact that the above study was undertaken many years ago (about thirty years ago), one would have expected most of the superstitious beliefs to have changed. However, many people still (to some extent) believe in one or more of these even today. Mathe (2006) clearly shows this. In this article, written in 2006, one of the people interviewed mentions the fact that people believe that putting 'dry cow dung in a burning fire would protect them from lightning.' She also explains that people believe that burying the sharp end of an axe in the ground would curb lightning. She is not to take a shower, wash her hands, wash dishes or use water in any other way so she won't be electrocuted. She switches off the television and lights during thunderstorms and uses candles instead. She avoids metal pipes since they are good conductors of lightning. However, she concludes by admitting that she doesn't really have any idea how to protect herself or her house from lightning. Many people (to some extent) share her sentiments. The other person interviewed says that he does not "have any ideas as to what precautions to take against lightning, especially when moving around in rain day." It is thus clear that there is general lack of understanding as regards lightning and lightning protection.

Frequency of Destructive Lightning

Incidents where lightning either kills someone or causes serious damage to property have significantly reduced. As such, people do not normally think about lightning, let alone discuss it. At the time when lightning related deaths were very high, the annual deaths from lightning were estimated to be between 50 and 100 (Jayaratne and Ramachandran, 1994) while an earlier survey (Yeboah-Amankwah and Devan, 1980) put the figure at 90. It is thus safe to assume that, at its peak, lightning killed about a 100 people a year in Botswana. On the other hand, the number of deaths from motor vehicle accidents for 2000 is 529 (with 1858 serious injuries) while for 2001 it is 526 deaths (with 1853 seriously injured) (Botswana Central Statistics Office, 2002). Comparing the two causes of deaths (as an example) could explain why it appears that no one is really that concerned about lightning.

In the 1980s and early 1990s, when lightning damage and deaths were much more common than now, many people, especially in rural areas, lived in huts. These were normally made of mud walls and thatched with grass. The thatch would be gathered together to a metal point at the top of the roof. As observed in (Jayaratne and Ramachandran, 1994), in such a situation, a direct hit to the thatched hut may not only set the hut on fire, but side flashes conduct to the ground through bodies and objects within confines of the hut. The metal point on the roof of the hut exacerbated the situation (during a strike) as it was mostly not earthed at all. However, as the economy grew, many people changed to modern type of housing. This kind of housing normally has walls with steel reinforcement, which safely guides lightning to the ground during a strike. This is probably one of the main reasons why lightning related deaths and damage is now a lot lower than it used to be. Coupled to this is the fact that many people nowadays live in electrified houses. Good earthing practices are strictly followed during electrical installations. Traditional huts are no longer as widely used as they were in the past, although a significant number of people still use them in rural areas.

Destruction by Lightning

'The Dailynews' is a free daily government newspaper, which comes out from Monday to Friday. The newspaper staff works closely with those of the two state national radios, as well as the national television. This means that any major incident that happens anywhere in the country is very likely to appear in one of the Dailynews editions. Incidents like deaths from road accidents, or even just the fact there has been a road accident somewhere in the country, are normally covered. A search through the 2005 editions of the Dailynews revealed only two lightning related incidents. It should be pointed out that 2005 was a particularly dry year. The Department of Meteorological Services recorded 0 mm for both Gaborone and Kasane from May until end of October 2005. This could explain the very low lightning incidents. The first incident happened in February 2005 when an 18-year-old woman was killed by lightning in Mmatshumu. She was with a friend and they had taken shelter under a tree next to an electric pole (Madone, 2005). The second incident was even more tragic. Lightning killed four people in November 2005 at Makgwelekgwele lands, in the Central District. The four, a 45-year-old woman and her three children (two sons and a daughter), were killed when lightning struck the hut they were in (Jabeng, 2005).

A run through the Dailynews for the first quarter of 2006 (January to the end of March), reveals more incidents, with some of the incidents really grim. It must be noted that the country was experiencing above normal rains at this stage, following the very dry 2005. The first incident reported is one that took place on Christmas Day 2005. Lightning struck a flock of 26 sheep, belonging to three farmers at Sesung, Ngwaketsi South (Ntsimane, 2006). The sheep had gone for shelter from the storm under a tree. In a similar incident, a farmer at Temesele cattle-post, east of Artesia, lost ten cattle and six calves to lightning (Galeragwe, 2006). The animals were in a kraal at the time of the strike.

Around the same period, lightning killed a woman and her four children in Radisele. Five other people were killed in Letlhakeng sub-district when a house they were sleeping in was struck by lightning (Mathe, 2006). A Ramotswa family lost its belongings when their house was struck by lightning. (Simon, 2006) reports on two employees of Animal Health who were sent to Letlhakane Clinic to be treated for lightning shock. Lightning hit and cut power supply to the office they were in. One of the two women was on the telephone at the time of the strike. It is also mentioned in the article that telecommunication people advise people not to use telephones during thunderstorms; and that government offices have lightning protection. The other incident in this period is of two brothers, 18 and 14 years old, (and their dog) who were struck by lightning after sheltering under a tree from a storm (Tlale, 2006). Lightning also killed a 22 year-old man when it struck a house he was in (Peloentle, 2006). The person he was with survived. Just recently, March 2007, thousands of hectares of rangeland between Takatokwane, Sekoma, Jwaneng and Dutlwe were burnt by fire, allegedly started by lightning (Mokotedi, 2007).

The above incidents highlight the fact that although incidents of damage may be few and far apart, when lightning does strike, the results can be quite catastrophic. Perhaps with the exception of the last incident, some simple measures could have been taken to prevent these tragic events. The main one is education. Material (*e.g.* Davidson *et al.*, 1985; Jayaratne and Ramachandran, 1993) which was used in the country to educate the public at the time when lightning was perceived to be a problem has to be revised. The loss of life, no matter how relatively few, can never be acceptable, especially when that loss could have been easily prevented.

BOTEC Incident

Botswana Technology Centre (BOTEC), in partnership with the Department of Meteorological Services (DMS), has built a pilot automatic weather station (AWS) at Sir Seretse Khama Airport (SSKA). This station has been built to World Meteorological Organisation standards, *i.e.* all aspects of the station conform to these standards. This includes the sensors, the location of the station, installation of sensors and the way data is collected and processed. The station uses a telephone as a communication medium, and its telephone extension is part of the DMS telephone network at SSKA.

When the station was built in October 2005, lightning and surges were considered. Therefore, a sub-contractor was employed to install an elaborate lightning protection system. The system has been installed primarily to protect the very expensive sensors that are used, and other structures on site. The station electric installations are properly constructed with required earthing. When the electricity enters the cabinet, the central processing part of the system, there are surge arrestors to protect the components inside the cabinet, from power surges or any other surges that may come through the power line. In fact there are two lines of defence from surges that may come through power lines: the protection within the power distribution box and the surge arrestors in the cabinet. There are other protection mechanisms within the cabinet itself, including the use of fuses.

The level of protection used at the AWS appeared to be sufficient. However, there was one possible surge entry point that was not protected: the telephone point. In fact, this entry point had been considered and the purchase of a telephone line surge arrestor was in progress; but no one was overly worried as the chances of there being a lighting strike and a surge entering the cabinet through this point were generally considered almost non-existent. Telephone lines don't normally have any form of surge protection in Botswana, either in the home or in the office.

In January 2006, just under two months after the station had been built, lightning struck. It hit the DMS telephone exchange nearby. The AWS telephone line is part of this telephone network, and surges from this hit travelled through the phone line and damaged our main AWS equipment. The exchange was down for some time. Damage to our equipment completely derailed the project. The project had very little money, and once the damage had been done, it was very difficult to replace the damaged equipment. It took almost a year to get the project back on track.

The above incident goes to show just what lightning can do. It may not strike all the time but when it does, it can be very costly. As is the case with the other incidents, this incident could also have been prevented, *i.e.* the telephone exchange should have had a proper and effective protection, and the AWS should have been protected from all angles. Education and making sure that people never take lightning for granted is what is really needed to avoid such incidents. Contractors, and the general population, should be encouraged to use surge protection products.

Lightning Protection Standard

Botswana Bureau of Standards (BOBS) became a parastatal in 1997, following the adoption of the Standards Act by parliament in 1995. BOBS was formed with the primary objective of formulating Botswana standards and coordinating quality assurance activities in Botswana with a mission to improve the quality of life of Botswana citizens (http://www.bobstandards.bw/web_en/intro/en_bobs.html, accessed 19 April 2007). As of April 2007, there is no lightning protection standard in Botswana. A project to formulate a lightning protection standard was started some time back, but for one reason or the other, was suspended. It is currently in suspension. There is a lot of construction and other developments going on in the country at the moment and without a proper and enforced standard, it means that the lightning protection equipment installed, if any, or the way it has been installed, cannot always be guaranteed to be up to proper levels of quality. The fact that there is currently no lightning protection standard in the country could also be used to explain the general perception on lightning in the country.

Education

There is a need for public education on lightning and lightning protection. As already discussed, many people don't know what lightning is and how they can protect themselves and their property from it. A number of deaths mentioned in this paper resulted from people sheltering in high-risk places during lightning storms, mostly under trees.

Public education should start with the basics about lightning. There is some good educational material that was produced in the past, and there is need to either promote it or come up revised ones. Davidson *et al.* (1985) is such material. It gives the basics of what lightning is and how people can protect themselves. The language used is also simple enough to be understood by many people. It provides some of the information that could have helped prevent the loss of life from some of the lightning incidents described in this paper. Some of the guidelines given are:

- Not to stand alone in a flat field during a storm, as you may become the target of a lightning strike.
- Avoid standing under an isolated tree in a storm. The tree is a likely target and you may suffer an indirect hit.
- Stay in a car and do not get out until the storm is over. You are safe in the car during the storm even if the car is struck. Wait until after the storm before getting out of the car because it is possible to experience a small electric shock from the car body as you climb out if the car was struck by lightning.
- Keep away from wall or metal pipes in a house. If the house is struck, the lightning might follow these paths.
- Do not huddle together even when you are in a hut. This will increase the harm of an indirect hit. This has been the cause of some of the worst hut deaths.
- Stay away from tall masts and lightning conductors. These are likely targets of a lightning strike.

Some simple methods of protecting buildings are also discussed in (Davidson *et al.*, 1985), and these could potentially have prevented some of the damages from lightning, as stated in this article. If a house has a metal or corrugated roof, (Davidson *et al.*, 1985) advises one to connect the roof to the earth conductor with metal down conductors spaced at 30m or less from each other and that all metal parts should be solidly connected together. The use of lightning rods is also advised. It is stressed that the rods do not prevent lightning but do reduce damage to buildings and people in the building. The rod usually has a 'cone of protection' of 45 degrees. The position of the rod depends on the area to be protected but the rod should be at least 1.5m from the outer edge of the building. The electrical down conductor can be of copper, brass, aluminum, galvanised steel, stainless steel or phosphor-bronze. Recommended thicknesses of these are given in this manual. However, it is stated that in cases where a heavy lightning strike hits a thinner conductor, it might burn the conductor but still protect the house, and that the conductor will then have to be replaced.

The manual explains how a tree could be used as the mast of the lightning rod; and other ways of using a lightning rod. Lightning rods are readily available in the country and many people can afford them. The methods described in (Davidson *et al.*, 1985) are very simple and the rewards can be great. What is needed is an education campaign to encourage people to use them. An article that appeared in a science magazine aimed at secondary school students (Jayaratne and Ramachandran, 1993) provides basic concepts on lightning. It also gives out some practical activities to increase the student's understanding of lightning. We need more of such articles and manuals.

Lightning Protection Equipment

Some off-the-shelf surge protection equipment is available locally. Among the brands available are those from Clearline, Digitech, Kolitron, Schneider Electric and ProtectNet. However, for specialised equipment, it is usually necessary to look for the products outside the country. Most of the products are normally bought in South Africa, but it is not unusual to have to order some surge protection equipment from either Europe or America. There is need for the contractors and the general public to be encouraged to use these and the other similar products. Lightning protection manufacturers could also help by actively promoting their products.

Recommendations

Many people don't really understand what lightning is and how they can protect themselves and their property from it. Although deaths and damage from lightning have significantly dropped over the years, lightning still causes a considerable amount of damage when it strikes. This damage is in the form of damage to property, injuries to people and the actual loss of human life. Any preventable loss of life or damage to property can never be acceptable.

A look at lightning incidents given in this article shows that most of them could have been easily avoided. The victims needed to know instinctively what to in the unfortunate situations they were caught up in. They needed to know exactly what they were not supposed to do. This kind of knowledge comes with public education, and the education must be sustained. Educational manuals on lightning should be revised as may be necessary.

It is very unfortunate that there is currently no lightning protection standard in the country. A properly enforced standard could go a long way in promoting best practice; by so doing guarding against avoidable loss to both human life and property. The standard could address the issue of traditional huts and how to best protect them from lightning and lightning related damage. Although it is true that there are not as many traditional huts as they used to be, there is still a significant number being built and used, especially in rural areas. BOBS should be encouraged to come up with a national standard as soon as possible.

Through education, people should be encouraged to take lightning seriously. They should be made to fully appreciate the fact that although lightning strikes don't happen all the time, when they do happen, consequences can be catastrophic. When contractors and designers build their systems, they should be made to always make sure that they lock all avenues through which lightning can get in. They should be made to never take anything for granted. A national standard would go a long way in helping in this regard.

Very little research on lightning (if any) is currently being done in the country. Some substantial research on lightning was done in the 1990s by some University of Botswana academia. Unfortunately, no one carried on with their work when they left. This makes it very difficult to accurately assess the actual state of lightning and its damage. Many incidents probably go unrecorded, and the cost of damage from lightning is probably grossly underestimated. Researchers (both seasoned and upcoming) should be encouraged to take on lightning research. The research doesn't have to cost too much money.

Conclusion

There is a high incidence of lightning in Botswana. Gaborone has over fifty thunderstorm days per year. There is an even higher incidence in other parts of the country, especially in the northern-most region. Despite the high incidence, lightning is not generally taken very seriously in the country. It is one of those things that one completely forgets about once they pass. Compared with some thirty or so years ago, deaths and damage from lightning are no longer that common. This is mostly due to the improved housing that many people now live in. Due to the low incidents of serious damage and deaths as compared to other calamities (*e.g.* road accidents), people tend to completely forget about lightning. Lightning may not strike that often, but when it does, the aftermath can be horrific, both in terms of the loss of human life as well as damage to property. There is evidence of a lack of understanding of lightning and lightning protection among many people. Many still cling to superstitious beliefs of lightning being a bird and traditional doctors being able to control it. The sad truth is that a number of deaths and damage from lightning (in the country) could have been prevented with proper education. Any avoidable loss of either human life or property is not acceptable. Therefore, public education should be restarted and sustained, a national lightning protection standard formulated, and lightning research in the country encouraged.

Acknowledgement

- Department of Meteorological Services for providing all weather data.
- Dr. Rohan Jayaratne, School of Physical and Chemical Sciences, Queensland University of Technology for the information he provided.

References

1. Australia Bureau of Statistics, 1301.0–Year Book Australia, 2002. www.abs.gov.au.
2. Botswana Central Statistics Office (2002). Transport and Communications Statistics: 2001, p 33.

3. Davidson, N., Devan, K.R.S. and Idzenga, S. (1985). Lightning Protection in Botswana. Botswana Technology Centre.
4. http://en.wikipedia.org/wiki/Lightning (accessed 19 March 2007)
5. http://www.bobstandards.bw/web_en/intro/en_bobs.html (accessed 19 April 2007)
6. http://www.physicalgeography.net/fundamentals/7t.html (accessed 12 April 2007)
7. http://www.weather.info.bw/resources/entry_content.html (accessed 18 April 2007)
8. Galeragwe M. (2006). Tladi e bolaile dikgomo. Temesele: Dailynews. January 12, p 12.
9. Jabeng M. (2005). Ba thusa ba ba wetsweng ke seru. Palapye: Dailynews. November 14, p 10.
10. Jayratne E.R. and Ramachandran V. (1997). A comparative study of the lightning incidence in Gaborone and Molepolole. Botswana Notes and Records 29, 45-52.
11. Jayaratne, E.R. and Ramachandran, V. (1998). A Five-year Study of Lightning Activity Using a CGR3 Flash Counter in Gaborone, Botswana. Meteorol. Atmos. Phys. 66, 235-241.
12. Jayaratne, E.R. and Ramachandran, V. (1994). An isokeraunic map of Botswana. Botswana Notes and Records 26, 175-182.
13. Jayaratne, E.R. and Ramachandran, V. (1993). Lightning in Botswana. Botswana Science Association Newsletter 18, 12-15.
14. Madone G. (2005). Mosetsana o rathilwe ke tladi. Letlhakane: Dailynews. February 23, p 10.
15. Mathe T. (2006). Lightning kills 10 people, cattle. Gaborone: Dailynews. January 16, p 4.
16. Mokotedi A. (2007). Fire destroys rangeland. Jwaneng: Dailynews. March 20, p 4.
17. Ntsimane K. (2006). Dinku di rathilwe ke legadima. Sesung: Dailynews. January 5, p 11.
18. Peloentle L. (2006). Legadima le gapile a le mongwe. Letlhakeng: Dailynews. March 30, p 12.
19. Simon K. (2006). Pula e sentse matlo. Letlhakane: Dailynews. February 21, p 12.
20. Tlale B. (2006). Lelwapa le wetswe ke seru. Molepolole: Dailynews. March 1, p 12.
21. Yeboah-Amankwah, D. and Devan, K.R.S. (1980). Studies of Lightning: Its frequency and distribution, damage caused by it and local beliefs associated with it. Progress Report 2B, University of Botswana.

Chapter 5

Technological and Sociological Constraints to Effective Protection from Lightning: The Case of Malawi

Gilbert Reginald Phiri
Centre for Information Research and Development in Southern Africa (CEDRISA), Mzuzu University, Malawi
E-mail: gr_phiri@yahoo.co.uk

ABSTRACT

Malawi is a southeastern country belonging to the Southern African Development Community. It is flanked by the southern section of the Great African Rift Valley. Because of this, the country's physiography is characterized by wide variations in altitude which ranges from a low 66 metres above sea level to a massive 3,000 metres above sea level. Comparatively, plains, which range in altitude between 1,100 metres to 1,500 metres above sea level, are the most extensive and continuous features on which the disjointed plateaus, pointed hills and mountain ranges stand.

Malawi falls within the belt which experiences modified Sudan climate, which is characterized by three distinct seasons, namely, cool, dry season (May to August), hot, dry season (August and September) and hot, wet season (October to April). As expected, lightning is confined to the hot, wet season.

Malawi has a fairly dense network of weather stations. In terms of lightning and thunder, the network is not dense enough since there is a greater concentration of such recording stations in cities, towns and airports. Over and above this problem, Malawi is essentially a rural country with as high as 85 per cent of the population living in the rural areas. The cities, towns and airports are separated by long distances with few or no major settlements. Wide areas between the urban settlements and / or airports are not covered by the weather experts. To this effect, the country's statistics represent a biased picture of the distribution of lightning incidents to say the least, and a gross misrepresentation / underestimation of this weather phenomenon to say the most because the incidents captured in urban centres and at airports are treated as an extrapolation of what should be happening in the areas separating the urban areas.

Malawi's population has a high level illiteracy rate which is standing at high 60%. This means that lightning and other weather phenomena are beyond the comprehension of many Malawians. The most disturbing thing is that the majority of the rural population links lightning as an act of spirits or witchcraft; hence the belief that there is nothing that communities could do to protect themselves. Closely related to this is the fact that all incidents of lightning are not recorded, since doing so would imply ignoring the suffering of the people

Malawi has no policy on protection against lightning. This is exemplified by the sad experiences claimants go through when cases of claims are filed for damage by lightning to the Electricity Supply Commission of Malawi are turned down. The Commission turns such claims down on the grounds that their coverage does not include lightning.

Given the aforesaid it is recommended that any combination of the following strategies should be adopted:

- Increasing the density of recording stations by introducing stations in the areas that are currently not covered. This may call for the installation of equipment exclusively meant to capture data on lightning, analyzing it and making inferences on its occurrence and protecting lives and property from damage.
- Provision of basic/civic education for the rural masses on the basic principles of lightning and its occurrence. This measure would be aimed at dislodging the rural masses from the myths about lightning.
- Formulation of policy or a legislation on mitigation of lightning as a natural disaster.

Keywords: Eye observation, Extrapolation, Institutionalization, Mainstreaming, Mosaic, Myth, Risk mapping, Risk prone areas, Technical flaw.

Introduction

Location

Malawi is a southeastern country belonging to the Southern African Development Community. Malawi stretches from 9.5°S to 17.5°S, and 33°E to 34°E. The country is a narrow country which flanks the southern section of the Great African Rift Valley. The landscape is characterized by what is referred to as accentuated relief. The lowest part of the country which is occupied by Nsanje and Chikwawa districts lie at a low 66 metres above sea level. The upper section of the same rift valley floor rises to 550 metres above sea level. The highest regions in the country having the following plateaus such as Mulanje, Zomba and Nyika; mountain ranges such as Kirk Range. These regions rise to anything from 2,000 to 3,000 metres above sea level. The plains, which are in the most extensive, range lie between 1,000 and 1,500 metres above sea level.

Climate

Because of its location and accentuated relief, Malawi experiences modified Sudanese Climate. This is characterized by three definite seasons, namely; cool dry season (May to August), hot dry season (August and September) and hot wet season (October to April). During this season, an intense migratory low pressure belt called the Intertropical Convergence Zone (ITCZ) hovers over the region of Malawi. The ITCZ draws most air from the Congo Basin on the west of the country, northeasterly monsoon air from the Indian Ocean and southeast Trade winds from the Indian Ocean.

Apart from the ITCZ, the country's climate is also largely influenced by tropical cyclones in the Indian Ocean somewhere in the middle of the wet season. The cyclones draw air from the mainland as long as Hadley Cells are located either in the Atlantic Ocean off the west coast of South Africa. During this time, warm, moist air is drawn from the Congo Basin west of the country. This results in frontal rainfall, which is not associated with lightning. The map below illustrates the position of the three wind systems.

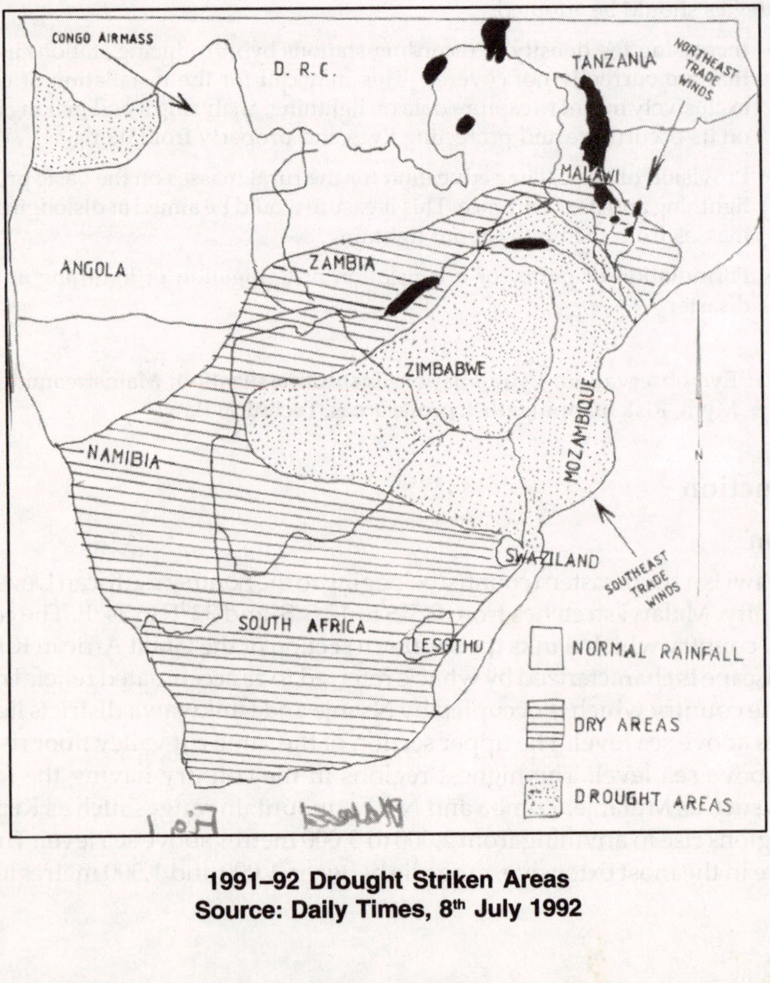

1991–92 Drought Striken Areas
Source: Daily Times, 8th July 1992

Upon entering the Indian Ocean, the Hadley Cells force cyclones into the continent. As this occurs, high rise mountain ranges and pointed hills receive orographic rainfall which is also not in particular associated with lightning activity.

Lightning Risk Mapping

In the beginning of the wet season, and indeed for a good part of the season, Malawi receives convectional rainfall which is associated with lightning and thunder. As expected, the sky is mostly covered with thunderstorm clouds. Since each one of the cells have a potential for lightning, the development of clouds is monitored by the weather stations shown in the map and the statistics is given below in Table 5.1.

Table 5.1: Average Thunder and Lightning Days in Malawi

	May	*Jun*	*Jul*	*Aug*	*Sep*	*Oct*	*Nov*	*Dec*	*Year*
Stn-Name	2	0	0	0	0	8	20	29	150
Bolero	2	3	0	1	2	7	16	21	110
Bvumbwe	1	0	0	0	1	6	14	9	87
Chichiri	1	0	0	0	2	5	11	22	93
Chikweo	1	0	0	0	1	8	17	23	122
Chileka	1	0	0	0	1	5	15	24	112
Chitedze	2	0	0	0	0	5	16	27	133
Chitipa	1	0	0	0	1	6	14	21	102
Dedza	3	0	0	0	0	1	11	22	124
Karonga	0	0	0	0	0	3	15	23	110
Kasungu	2	0	0	0	1	6	16	28	137
Lilongwe (old)	1	0	0	0	0	4	17	28	134
LIA	1	0	0	0	1	5	14	21	92
Makhanga	1	0	0	0	1	7	16	21	106
Makoka	1	0	1	0	2	6	14	23	110
Mangochi	2	3	0	1	3	7	16	22	111
Mimosa	1	0	0	0	0	6	18	25	131
Monkey	1	0	0	0	0	4	13	22	108
Mzimba	2	0	0	0	0	2	12	25	124
Mzuzu	1	0	0	0	1	7	12	23	110
NRC	1	0	0	0	1	5	11	19	91
Ngabu	2	0	0	0	0	2	12	22	123
NkhataBay	2	0	0	0	0	3	13	23	121
Nkhotakota	1	0	0	0	1	5	15	27	131
Salima	1	1	0	0	2	7	17	22	115
Thyolo	1	1	1	0	0	2	17	22	115

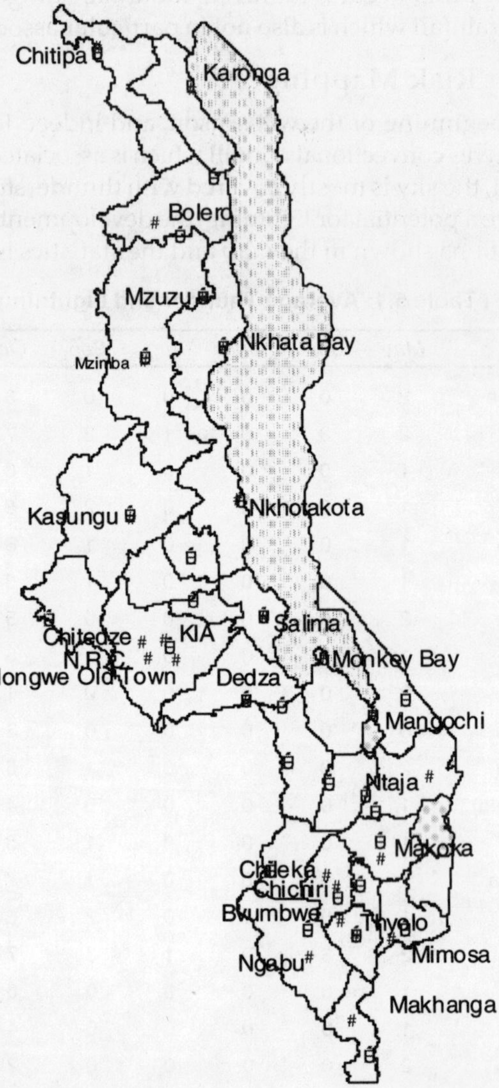

Average Thunder and Lightning Days by Station in Malawi

With such a statistical data collection exercise, there are many flaws. First and foremost, the statistics are presented as monthly and annual averages of frequencies of the development of thunderstorm clouds. This has many technical flaws, one, the potential of each cloud to develop lightning does not always translate into actual lightning.

Secondly, weather stations are very far apart from each another. As such, the averages recorded are a gross representation and/or oversimplification of the reality on the ground. As a matter of fact, the statistics are often muddled up because most weather stations coincide with district headquarters.

Thirdly, most if not all stations, are not adequately equipped with appropriate equipment for detecting the precise location of a lightning event, its magnitude and the frequency of such events at specific points. As a result of the lack of appropriate equipment, more often than not, relief workers are taken up by surprise storms when reports of actual lightning events are transmitted from remote corners of the country.

The fourth technical constraint is that lightning conductors, the copper wires/ conductors, are in extremely short supply in the country partly because they are expensive or, indeed, not available at all. The developers do not consciously include protection against lightning in their development projects, be it the construction of residential units or industrial complexes or indeed office blocks.

Fifthly, the country has no regulation on lightning. This is exemplified by the failure to make claims from the national and or private electricity supply services each time electric surges end up damaging electric apparatus.

Myths about Lightning

A thousand and one times, Malawians wake up to stories of incidents of lightning, which are a reflection of glaring ignorance or deep rooted myths about lightning. To begin with, lightning is regarded as a phenomenon that humans can not do anything about. Secondly, there is the belief that lightning does not strike one object more than once. Obviously, this is in direct contrast with scientific knowledge as exemplified by existing basic literature on the subject (Pole, 1989; Feynman, Leighton and Sands, 2006). What does this mean with regard to protection against lightning? The worst manifestation of such myths is a deafening indifference to realities about live occurrences of lightning. For one thing, each time a structure is struck by lightning, no conscious decision is made to prevent subsequent strike because it is believed that such incidents can never, ever occur again.

The second manifestation of the dire consequences of the same indifference is lack of appropriate action on the rampant lightning strikes which were reported in the year 2005/2006 rainy season. During that season, media newsrooms were flooded with reports of lightning strikes which resulted from transmission of lightning by telephone wires which were hung on big trees on the streets along the major cities and other urban areas. Since lightning is regarded as a mythical phenomenon, street vendors were evacuated from the streets. No efforts has to date been made to provide civic or basic education about the physics behind lightning.

The third manifestation of the myth is the construction of buildings at risk prone areas such as hill tops. One glaring example of such developments is the construction of prayer houses at such locations. Driven by the myth that lightning is a mysterious phenomenon that is beyond human understanding or indeed, a man induced one, such buildings are not protected from lightning. When lightning does strike, no effort is made to turn things as they were even though such buildings are erected by enlightened people in the name of bishops or other religious and other well known leaders.

Finally, because of the deep rooted myths, no effort has to date been made to record the live lightning incidents no matter how disastrous they have been. One major reason for this is the desire to forget these incidents because of the fear among the survivors.

Recommendations

Given the aforesaid, the way ahead should include any combination of the following:

- Increasing the density of recording stations by, among other things, introducing stations in the areas that are currently not covered. This may call for the installation of equipment exclusively meant to capture data on lightning, analyzing it and making inferences on its occurrence. Policies and strategies should be made for protecting lives and property from damage. As for the existing stations, there is a need to introduce appropriate equipment for detecting lightning.
- Providing the rural and urban masses with adequate basic or civil education on effective protection against lightning as well as keeping record of every incident of lightning, including timing, magnitude and frequency of the strikes.
- Formulating policy or even enacting laws on lightning. The said policy or legislation would pave the way for appropriate guidelines to developers regarding effective protection against lightning, mainstreaming/ institutionalizing lightning. Lightning leaves behind a mosaic of damage and loss of life year after year out. Imparting basic information in the school curriculum as extra or co–curricular activities or, indeed, in the form of competitions can help turn things around and make Malawi a safer place to live in as far as lightning is concerned.

References

1. Pole, Stephen 1989. Explaining Physics. Oxford. Oxford University Press, pp 234 – 236.
2. Feynman, R. P., Leighton, R. B. and Sands, M. 2006. The Feynman lectures on Physics – Electricity in the atmosphere. (Definitive edition Volume II) London. Addison – Wesley Publishing Company. Chapter 9.

Chapter 6

Lightning Protection Conducted in Myanmar

Salai Tluang Za Thang

Department of Electrical Power Engineering,
Mandalay Technological University,
Mandalay Division, Myanmar
Email: sanzyu@sailormoon.com, tzthang@gmail.com

ABSTRACT

Lightning is a huge spark caused by the electrical discharge taking place between the clouds, within the same cloud, between the clouds and between the clouds and the earth. Lightning is one of the most serious causes of over-voltages in the power system. If the power equipment, especially outdoor sub-station, is not protected, the over-voltages cause the failure of insulation. The lightning also causes damage to buildings, farms and commercial houses etc. The damage to human life is comparatively less. All the electrical equipments must be protected from the severe damage of lightning strokes. The technique of protection can be studied as protection of transmission lines, power stations and sub-stations from direct strokes and protection of electrical equipment from travelling waves. For lightning protection to be provided in power system such as sub-station, it is necessary to have complete knowledge about impulse voltage withstand characteristics of the substation equipment (outdoor type).The sub-stations have the equipments such as transformers, bus bars, isolation switches, circuits breakers, instrument transformers etc that must be protected from lightning strokes. Especially, transformer is one of the most important and widely used equipment for AC power systems. Therefore, the transformer is the major equipment over which lightning protection must be provided. Furthermore, for lightning protection, the correct selection of lightning arrestor is very important. Lightning strike discharges many thousands of amperes of current in a very short time, in microseconds, it is important to decide the lightning arrestor ratings correctly to be used at sub-stations. To provide protection from lightning to the transmission line from direct strokes, low ground conductor footing impedance and shield or ground wire methods are employed in practice.

Keywords: Buildings, Transmission lines, Transformer, Lightning arrestors, Myanmar, Awareness of lightning safety.

Introduction

The objective of this paper is to present the current practices of lightning protection conducted in Myanmar. Although lightning is hazardous to all the living beings, lightning awareness and education is not conducted in Myanmar because lightning is not considered to be a major threat to the life of the people of Myanmar. However, it is necessary to educate the engineers and technocrats so that they understand the basic concepts of lightning phenomenon, lightning threats in their field of work, safety measures that should be taken to minimize lightning hazards, essentials of lightning protection, selection of protective equipment, and the finer points of implementing, testing and maintaining a proper lightning protection system. In this paper, the methods used for lightning protection for buildings, power systems and the present concern in general about lightning in Myanmar are mainly presented.

Lightning Phenomenon

Lightning can be described as a visible discharge of static electric charges occurring within a cloud, between clouds, or between a cloud and earth. The potential acquired by the clouds depends upon the magnitude of the charge that builds up between the clouds, which are separated by an insulating air gap. When the electrical potential between positive and negative charge build up becomes high enough between the air gap insulation, the charges rush to meet. The action produces in sudden release of energy heating the air to incandescence in the leader core, the intense white spark we call lightning. In general, the negative charges accumulate near the base of thunderclouds with opposite charges developing in the upper portion of the cloud and on the earth's surface with its projecting objects like trees, buildings, chimneys, poles, or wires. Because the potential build up is highest at these projecting objects, lightning opts more often to strike there than on larger and flatter surfaces.

Lightning Protection for Buildings

The fundamental principle of lightning protection is to provide a safe conductor pathway for lightning to follow without destroying a structure or other object. Adequate protection systems for buildings must include; (1) properly sized, placed, and installed air terminals (lightning rods) to receive the lightning strike; (2) conductors designed to carry the discharge from the air terminal to the ground; and (3) ground rods properly sized and installed to carry the charge to the earth. Conductor materials used in protection system must be resistant to corrosion. Copper, copper alloys, copper-clad steel, and aluminium are all approved materials. Copper and aluminium are the most common. Because aluminium conductors corrode when in contact with earth, aluminium should terminate at least one foot above ground level and connected with corrosion-resistant copper conductors and ground rods. A special bi-metal connector is advised too be used to avoid corrosion when bonding aluminium and copper conductors. The installation of lightning protection system is as important as the materials used. A sufficient number of air terminals must be spaced properly. The spacing of air terminals depends upon the roof shape and slope. Generally it is 20-25 feet along the ridge and on any tall projections such as chimneys or vent pipes. Conductors must be properly sized and installed to avoid sharp turns. Metal conduits, gutters, drain pipes, pipe vents, metal water pipe, radio and television antennas, metal roofing, fences and other metallic objects should be bonded properly to main down conductors and ground rods to prevent side flashes. Lightning system ground rods must be driven to a minimum depth of ten feet. Not less than two rods should be used at opposite corners of major buildings. Lightning has a tendency to strike preferably on taller structures and objects. Strikes to ground are, however, quite common where a distance between structures of more than twice their individual heights exist. Current flow in reinforced concrete structures tend to disperse throughout the reinforcement bars with a preference towards those that are towards the external sections of the structure. Thus, a large number of down conductors at the edge of a building greatly reduce magnetic fields inside the building minimizing the risk of transient interference to electronic equipment from the building lightning protection system.

Direct Strikes to High Voltage Power Lines

Lightning strikes on the high voltage overhead power lines are quite common. It is often considered that the high voltage to low voltage transformation action eliminates the resultant transient over-voltages. Although transformers are protected against transient over-voltages between line and earth, line to line transients pass through un-attenuated. When high voltage lines are struck by lightning, they flashover to earth. If a line flashovers before the others, converting a line to earth transient into one between line and line, it easily passes through the transformer. Transformer is one of the most important and widely used equipment for AC power systems. Transformers are the major equipment over which lightning protection must be provided. Since the transformer is very expensive equipment, a lot of care is exercised in selecting its impulse voltage withstand level. The impulse voltage surge penetrates into the winding and thus the core insulation. The impulse voltage level of a transformer is determined by the insulation to earth and the residual voltage of the surge diverter or the lightning arrestors. Modern transformers are designed in such a manner that they pass chopped wave of higher crest voltage than the full wave testing voltage. The chopped wave is created by flashing over of the gaps. The flashover voltage of the bushings must be taken into account while dealing with the problem of insulation co-ordination. The voltage-time characteristics of the bushings differ from those of the internal insulation. The flashover voltage of the bushings is usually higher than that of internal insulation of the transformers.

Direct Strikes to Low Voltage Power Lines

When lightning hits low voltage overhead power or telephone lines, most of the current travels to earth as a result of line flashover to ground. A relatively small portion of the lightning current is transmitted along the line to electronic equipment.

Resistive coupling is the most common cause of transient over-voltages and it will affect both underground and overhead lines. Resistively coupled transients occur when a lightning strike raises the electrical potential of one or more of a group of electrically interconnected building or structures. Common examples of electrical interconnections are power feeders from substation to building, building to building power feeders, power supplies from the building to external lighting, telephone lines from the exchange to the building or between buildings, data communication lines and signal or power lines from a building to external or field based sensors and equipment. Resistively coupled transients can occur when separately earthed structures are only metres apart. Resistive coupling will affect both underground and overhead cables. Inductive coupling is a magnetic field transformation effect between lightning and cables. A lightning discharge causes an enormous current flow and whenever a current flows, a magnetic field is created around it. If power or data cabling passes through this magnetic field, then a voltage will be picked up by, or induced onto it. This frequently happens when lightning discharge takes place close to overhead power or telephone lines. Much the same thing happens when a building's lightning protection scheme is struck. The lightning current flows to earth through the down conductors. The resulting magnetic field may well encroach upon cabling within the building, inducing transient over voltages. Where long lines are well isolated from earth (*e.g.* via transformers or opto-isolators) they can develop high voltages due to capacitance between them and the charged thunderclouds. If the voltage on the lines rises beyond the breakdown strength of the devices at each end (*e.g.* opto-isolators), they will be damaged.

Protection of Transmission Lines Against Lightning Direct Strikes

Effective protection against direct strikes requires a shield to prevent lightning from striking the electrical conductors together with adequate conducting facilities over insulated structures so that the charge could drain to the ground without affecting the conductors. Alternative method of protecting the line is to build it without shielding; but auxiliary discharge paths can be inserted into lines so that any lightning discharge tending to interfere with the normal flow of current is interrupted. The design of a transmission line against lightning for a desired performance is not dependent upon the operating voltage, but the important points for the design of a line for protection against the direct strokes are by using ground wires, clearance of the conductor, and clearance of the ground wires and resistivity of the supports. Ground wires having sufficient mechanical strength must be situated in such a manner so as to shield the line conductors from direct strokes. The ground wires are selected from mechanical strength point of view rather from electrical considerations. Also the ground wires must be non-corrosive. Adequate clearances should be provided between the line conductor and tower and between the line conductor and the earth. These clearances must be maintained according to the flashover strengths of the insulators used. Moreover, sufficient clearances are to be provided between the ground wire and the line conductors. Care should be taken to maintain these clearances at the centre of the span so that there is no flash over. Resistivity of the supports is very important that the tower footings have a low resistance should allow the lightning discharge currents to flow to earth easily.

Awareness of Lightning Safety and Education in Myanmar

In Myanmar, lightning hazard is not considered as a major threat when compared with other natural disasters. Therefore, there is no awareness on lightning safety and education for the people of Myanmar. But it is believed that awareness of lightning safety and education will be taken into consideration in the near future. In Myanmar, most of the buildings in urban areas are well protected with lightning arrestors. Monthly lightning days during Year 2005 in Myanmar are presented in Appendix A. The data expressed in Appendix A can represent the situation of lightning occurrences for the whole Myanmar.

Appendix–A

DEPARTMENT OF METEOROLOGY AND HYDROLOGY

MONTHLY LIGHTNING DAYS

YEAR: 2005

STATIONS	JAN	FEB	MAR	APR	MAY	JUN	JUL	AUG	SEP	OCT	NOV	DEC
Kaba-Aye	0	0	0	0	10	2	4	6	6	11	5	0
Kyaing Tone	0	0	0	0	6	0	8	0	4	0	1	0
Taung Gyi	0	0	2	7	12	6	5	1	6	11	3	0
Lashio	0	0	0	0	1	0	0	0	0	0	0	0
Sittway	0	0	0	2	6	6	2	1	8	6	0	1
Magway	0	0	0	1	2	2	0	1	2	6	0	0
Loikaw	0	0	2	4	3	3	1	0	5	2	1	1
Monywa	0	0	0	0	2	4	5	0	15	0	0	0
Mandalay	0	0	0	3	6	7	14	9	10	7	3	0
Homalin	0	0	2	3	2	7	3	10	8	4	0	1
Dawei	0	0	0	0	2	2	1	0	1	3	2	0
Myintkyina	0	2	2	3	2	1	1	0	4	0	0	3
Hpa-An	0	0	1	3	3	0	0	0	6	5	0	0
Bago	0	0	0	1	4	3	0	3	2	5	1	0
Hakha	0	0	0	0	0	0	0	0	0	0	0	0
Pathein	0	0	0	0	0	0	0	0	0	0	0	0
Malamyine	0	0	0	0	2	4	2	1	5	8	3	1

10.5.07

(Nyein Nyein Naing)
Staff Officer
Record Section
Dept: of Meteorology &
Hydrology

Acknowledgement

The author would like to express his thanks to Daw Nyein Nyein Naing, Staff Officer, Record Section, Department of Meteorology and Hydrology, Myanmar, for her assistance to the improvement of the paper.

Reference

http://www.lightningsafety.com/nlsi.lhm.html (accessed 10 May, 2007).

Part III

Mechanism of Lightning Strikes and Lightning Detection Systems

Chapter 7

A New Approach to the Mechanism of Lightning Strike

Ravindra Arora
Department of Electrical Engineering,
Indian Institute of Technology, Kanpur – 208 016, India
E-mail: rarora@iitk.ac.in

ABSTRACT

Mechanism of breakdown in very long gap distances (upto 25 meters) in atmospheric air has been studied by many authors. In this paper the development of breakdown mechanism between two typical electrodes, a large plane in air and a rod at the ground having a gap distance of five meters, is described. An increasing positive polarity dc voltage is applied to the plane and the rod is grounded. A similar situation is present in the atmosphere when the lightning strikes between the cloud and an object on the ground. The observed audio and visual effects of the stable partial breakdown phenomenon are reported. The development of charge and its movement at the time of lightning is explained.

Keywords: *Breakdown, Long air gap, Lightning, Streamer and leader corona, Movement of charge.*

Introduction

The phenomenon of lightning is as old as this earth. The fury of the lightning strike has always scared the human being. The unpredictable behaviour of lightning and the damage caused by lightning strike continues to terrify the masses and confuse the scientists and researchers in spite of so much of research work all over the world. It is not yet possible to tame the lightning. However, with better understanding of the phenomenon more effective protective measures are being evolved to make the lightning less scary and damaging.

The physics of the phenomenon of lightning is, unfortunately, a matter of controversy among scientists even after the research work over centuries. Inspired by the knowledge of the mechanism of breakdown of atmospheric air in very long gap distances developed in the high voltage laboratories, the phenomenon of lightning strike can be explained suitably. Breakdown of atmospheric air in tens of meters of gap distances has been accomplished by many engineers in the high voltage laboratories spread over many countries of the world (Alexandrov *et al.*, 1969; Pigni *et al.*, 1979; Lemke, 1967). The breakdown characteristics have been measured with different types of voltages, ac, dc and impulse (lightning and switching) of either polarity for different electrode systems up to a gap distance of 25 meters by many researchers. From the knowledge of the development and propagation of the breakdown phenomenon, a good inference can be drawn about the lightning strikes.

Electric Charge Accumulation in the Atmosphere

The earth's atmosphere has many sources through which it acquires electric charge, for example, UV irradiation and cosmic rays from the sun, friction between fast moving air layers and also due to rubbing between two insulating bodies. The charge thus produced rests on the water vapour, clouds and on aerosols available at alarmingly increasing rate in the earth's atmosphere and other ungrounded bodies. Due to the accumulation of charge on a cluster of such particles, the body as a whole acquires static potential. The electric charge has a tendency to orient and segregate itself into the positive and negative charge concentrations. The electric charge rests in dielectrics but it is restless in conductors. The electric charge always tries to adopt least resistance path to flow. Air is the most freely available dielectric which has insulation resistance of the order of tens of thousands of mega ohms. Hence the electric charge in the atmosphere rests in it and remains static and concentrated within a body like clouds. The magnitude of static charge accumulation determines the potential acquired by a cloud. Under unstable thunder conditions, the charge acquired by the clouds increases rapidly. Although static, it gives rise to a rapid increase in the potential developed in the clouds as a body.

The mother earth is God gifted to maintain its ground potential at the zero level. Due to its soil resistivity, the ground may acquire a potential on its surface temporarily by induction or by injection of large quantity of charge. However, as soon as this charge finds passage to go inside the ground, the potential is maintained back to zero level. The extent of rise in ground potential depends upon the magnitude of charge and the soil resistivity. The soil resistivity varies from place to place and it depends highly upon the moisture content of the soil.

The Earth: A Capacitor

A capacitor is formed by a dielectric in between two electrodes. Connected in parallel in an electric circuit, one of the electrodes of the capacitor is applied potential and the other grounded. Our earth can be described to be a large capacitor. The clouds, having static charge, form the electrode with potential and the other electrode, the earth itself, is at ground potential. In between the two, the air as a dielectric, forms the capacitance, Figure 7.1. If the potential acquired by the electrode at high voltage is

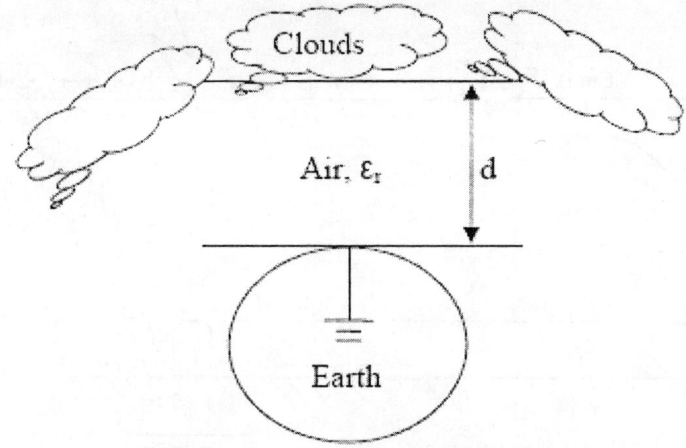

Figure 7.1: Earth: A Capacitor

increased excessively, the dielectric in between the two electrodes is bound to lose its insulating properties. A breakdown through the gap distance in the dielectric is then inevitable.

An electrical breakdown through the dielectric tends to equalize the potential between the two electrodes. The conductive breakdown channel formed through the dielectric provides a fairly low resistance path for the breakdown current to flow. Flow of charge is nothing but current. In this way, the accumulated charge in the clouds gets evacuated or discharged and injected into the ground directly or over an object, depending upon the site of lightning strike. This natural phenomenon of discharge takes care of the continuous process of building up of charge in the earth's atmosphere. The mother earth exercises its divine property of absorbing any amount of both the natural and the man made charges. It may be emphasized again that if this charge is not able to find passage to go inside the earth, it can create havocs, for example, fire, explosion, killing of living beings, damage to property, electrical installations etc. Such a situation may give rise to the development of the phenomenon of 'Ball Lightning' also (Arora, 1998; Arora, 2004).

Mechanism of Breakdown in Long Air Gaps with DC Positive Polarity Voltage

Consider a large plane and a rod electrode system in atmospheric air having a gap distance of about five meters as shown in Figure 7.2, in a laboratory.

A dc, positive polarity voltage increasing in magnitude is applied to the plane and the rod is grounded. Under these conditions, a negative polarity potential will be induced on the ground and also at the grounded electrode. Depending upon the magnitude of the applied voltage at the plane, there will be a positive maximum field intensity in the air at the plane. As the plane is a large electrode body, wide spread

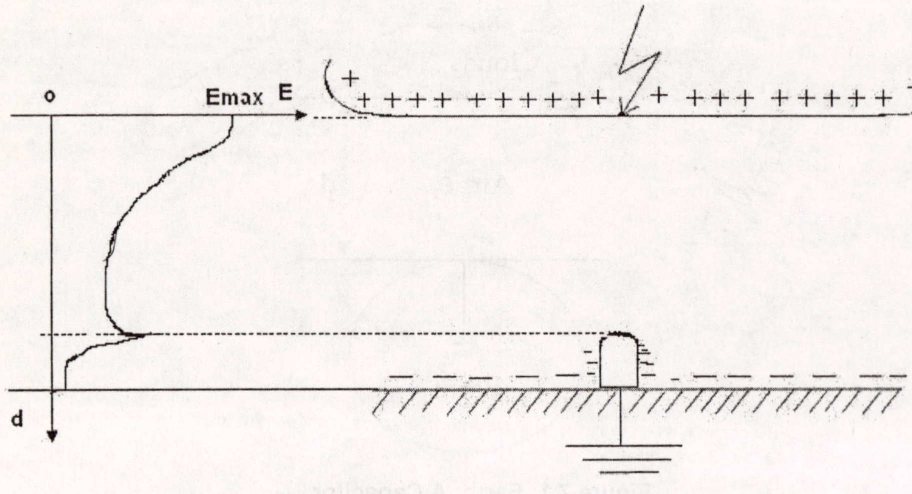

Figure 7.2: HV Plane and Grounded Rod Electrode and the Schematic of Electric Field in the Gap

and in a good depth below the plane a high field intensity will be present. It can be observed from Figure 7.2 that almost in 25 per cent gap length, a fairly high field intensity prevails. On the contrary, at the grounded rod, although a very high field intensity exists at its tip, but even a cm away from the rod the field intensity falls abruptly. The field estimation by FEM revealed that six cm away from the rod, the field intensity is as low as almost at the ground. Further examination of the situation reveals that since the polarity of the voltage induced on the ground will be opposite, the negative, it will be a negative polarity field there in the air.

The field pattern between the plane and the rod five meters away is an extremely non–uniform field configuration (Arora and Mosch, 1995). When the applied dc voltage on the plane is increased gradually, the field intensity in the gap will keep increasing as shown in Figure 7.2. Stable Partial Breakdown (PB) or Partial Discharge (PD) begins at the plane when the air below acquires the inception field intensity E_i, required for PB to begin at a voltage U_i, the PB inception voltage. In such a long air gap avalanche formation of above critical amplification are able to take place. It gives rise to a wide spread 'Streamer Corona' to take place below the plane. This streamer corona is also able to extend itself deep in the gap since the fall in field intensity in the depth is very gradual there. It is known as cathode directed streamer as shown in Figure 7.3 (a). From the Lichtenberg figures, it is well known that due to favourable space charge conditions, the cathode directed streamer is able to extend itself in the gap more as compared to the anode directed streamer (Arora and Mosch, 1995).

The situation at the rod is very different. Although a very high field intensity is present at the tip of the rod, it is confined to a very limited extent in the gap, to a few cms only. When sufficiently high voltage is applied to the plane, streamer corona at the rod may develop but to a very limited extent in the gap. The corona at the rod in this case is described as 'anode directed streamer'. At fairly advanced stage of

Figure 7.3: Development of Breakdown Mechanism Between a Plane and Rod with Positive Polarity DC Voltage

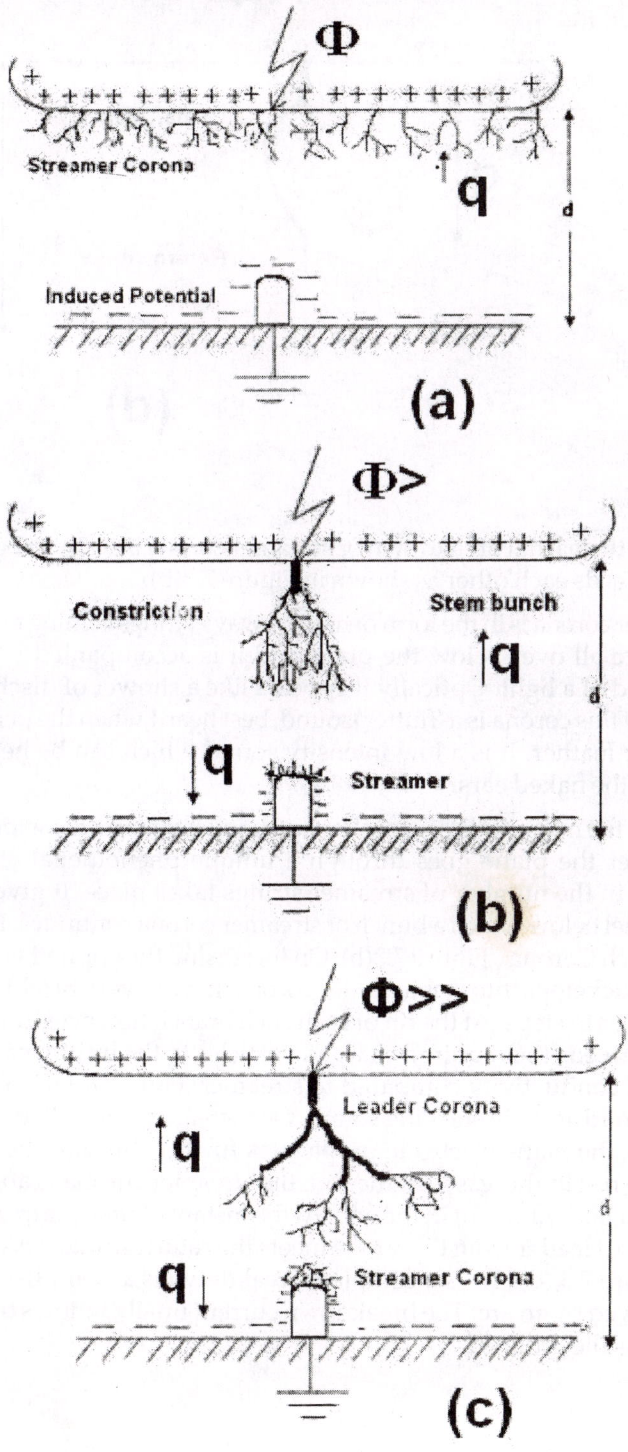

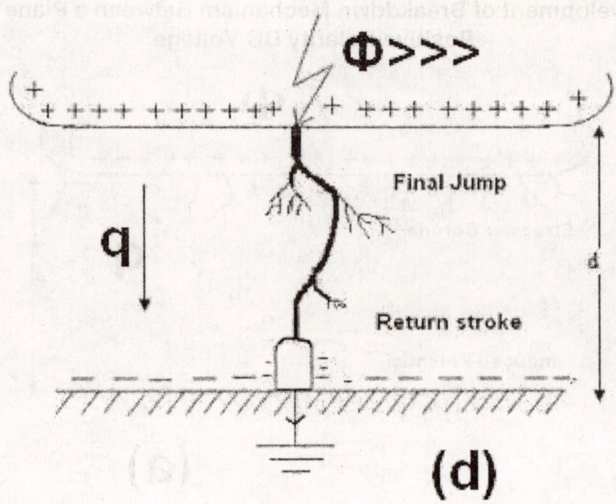

breakdown, the partial breakdown or streamer corona activity at both the electrodes develop towards each other as shown in Figure 7.3(b).

Streamer corona is in the form of narrow wavy strings coming out of the electrode. It takes place all over below the plane and it is accompanied with low intensity diffused kind of a light. Optically it appears like a shower of discharge. The sound produced by this corona is a 'flutter' sound, best heard when the peacocks dance and vibrate their feather. It is a low intensity sound which can be heard only near its source with the naked ears.

Close to the magnitude of complete breakdown voltage, the wide spread streamer corona under the plane goes through a unique phenomenal change. Suddenly constriction in the number of streamer strings takes place. It gives rise to a single bright channel below which a bunch of streamer corona continues. Hence it is known as 'Stembunch Corona', Figure 7.3(b). On increasing the applied voltage further; the stem bunch develops into stable leader corona, having very bright strings with only a few branches in steps. At the tip of each such branch however, the streamer corona continues. It feeds the required charged particles to the bright leader corona string having high conductivity compared to streamer, Figure 7.3 (c). The leader corona produces a loud audible cracking sound. On increasing the voltage, the stable leader corona from the plane electrode propagates further through the gap towards the cathode, the rod in this case. At the rod, the streamer corona is able to extend itself upwards to a limited extent in the gap. At the instant of final jump of the breakdown, the downward leader from the anode meets the return stroke developed upward at the rod Figure 7.3 (d). Thus a complete breakdown is accomplished with unstable leader followed by an arc. The breakdown current finally follows the least resistance path towards the ground.

The Mechanism of Lightning Strike

In case of lightning strike on an object on the ground, the configurational situation is quite similar to the one described in Section 4. The large plane in the laboratory simulates a big body of the cloud carrying static potential. In place of the grounded rod, it could be any metallic object at a height from the ground. The gap distance in this case could be of the order of a kilometer and above. In place of applied increasing dc voltage on the plane electrode, the rapid increase in static potential on the clouds is developed under stormy conditions due to ionization/production of charge by movement of air and the aerosols at high speed.

When the potential acquired is sufficient enough to incept partial breakdown, first a wide spread streamer corona begins to take place just below the cloud surfaces. It is followed by the phenomenon of constriction and the development of stepped leader towards the ground with streamer corona at their tips. At suitable objects on the ground, streamer partial breakdown activity may begin. The lightning strike takes place with the final jump of an unstable leader joining the return stroke from a suitable location on the ground. The exact location of the strike depends upon its height, intensity of streamer corona probability and the location of the highly charged clouds suitably coming above the site.

The whole activity develops extremely fast. Towards the advance stage of the strike, the rapid increase in potential at the clouds can be attributed to the wide scale occurrence of the streamer corona just below the clouds. This partial breakdown activity produces large amount of current/charge. Since the lower part of the air below the clouds is still in a healthy state, it still has a very high insulation resistance. Hence the charge produced due to wide scale streamer corona finds its passage back into the clouds through the discharge strings which have relatively higher conductivity or lower resistivity than the healthy air. In Figure 7.3 the arrows show the movement of charge 'q' produced in the atmosphere. An extremely rapid development of potential is achieved at the clouds by this mechanism. The phenomenon of constriction, formation of stepped leader and final jump mechanisms are followed as described. A high current of impulse waveform finally flows towards the ground through the highly conductive leader channel which provides the least resistance path.

Unlike the breakdown with high dc voltage in the laboratory, in this case, stable leader corona is not able to take place as there is an extremely rapid development in potential acquired by the clouds under stormy conditions. Hence, the constriction phenomenon of streamer corona is immediately followed by final jump with unstable leader. Depending upon the physical situation, the clouds are thus evacuated with a large amount of charge. For the lightning to repeat (cloud to cloud or cloud to ground) under such stormy conditions, it takes minutes to develop the charge/potential once again.

An Important Observation

It is true that stable streamer corona produces a flutter sound and the stable leader corona, a loud cracking sound. It was just a coincidence that the author was once in conversation on his copper wired telephone at a time when intense stormy and thunder activity was going on in the area. Suddenly, a distinct flutter sound of increasing intensity followed by a one time cracking sound could be heard on the telephone. It was revealed a while later that the lightning struck the ground only a few hundred meters away. Being of low intensity, the flutter sound produced by streamer corona is difficult to be heard with naked ears. Such ambient sound can be better heard with an amplifier. The amplifier installed on the telephone apparatus was good enough to be able to hear the sound produced by wide spread streamer corona lasting only seconds. This sound can also be described to be heard when a truck loaded with crushed stone is tilted to unload it completely. The falling crushed stone sound of increasing intensity and its abrupt discontinuation followed immediately by a cracking sound reveals the mechanism of rapid development of wide spread streamer corona activity followed quickly by the formation of unstable leader, the final jump of the lightning strike.

References

1. Alexandrov, G.N., Evanov, W.L. and Kieswetter, W.E., (1969) "Electrical breakdown strength of high voltage insulation",Energia, Leningrad in Russian.
2. Arora, R., (1998) "Traces of lightning incidences on structures", Proceedings of 24th International Conference on Lightning Protection (ICLP), Staffordshire University, Birmingham, UK.
3. Arora, R., (2004) "Ball lightning without lightning strike", Proceedings of 8th International Symposium on Ball Lightning (ISBL04)", National Central University, Chung-li, Taiwan.
4. Arora, R. and Mosch, W., (1995) "High voltage insulation engineering" New Age International Publishers Ltd, New Delhi.
5. Lemke Eberhardt, (1967) "Breakdown mechanism and characteristics of nonuniform field electrode configurations in air for switching surges", Dissertation, TU Dresden in German.
6. Pigini, A., Rizzi, G., Brambilla, R. and Garbanati, E., (1979) " Switching impulse strength of very large air gaps"' 3rd ISH, Milan No 52.15.

Chapter 8

Lightning: Its Nature and Characteristics

Chandima Gomes
University of Colombo, Sri Lanka
E-mail: gomes@phys.cmb.ac.lk, gacgomes@yahoo.com

ABSTRACT

This paper describes the origin and inception of lightning at cloud level, propagation of the stepped leader towards ground, interception of lightning flash and ground bound objects and characteristics of lightning related phenomena. The objective of the paper is to provide lightning related scientific information to non-specialized scientific community and interested general public. Therefore, the paper has been presented with non-technical terminology and most often the contents are explained with easy-to-understand and simplified models, yet not deviated from proven scientific facts.

Keywords: *Lightening, Cloud flash, Ground flash, Dart leader, Lightning physics, Lightning origin and propagation, Return stroke, Stepped leader, Thermal generation and thunder.*

Introduction

Lightning is a natural atmospheric phenomenon, which is caused by the instability of charge distribution within a cloud. It also occurs due to the charge separation in the aerosols, masses of ash and dust ejected in a volcanic eruption or a nuclear explosion. Lightning physics is the study of the various aspects of lightning such as background conditions for formation, corresponding activities, variation and distribution based on the geographical location and effects on human beings and structures.

A lightning flash originates inside a cloud, several kilometres above the ground level. Except for ball lightning, which is a very rare phenomenon, lightning is a complicated spark that electrically bridges a cloud and ground, between two clouds or between two parts of a cloud.

Thunderstorm activity in a region depends on its geographic location. In tropics and oceanic regions, thunderstorm activities are higher than that is in temperate regions and mid-country regions. Mountainous regions usually record higher thunderstorm density. Countries in Central Africa such as Nigeria, South American countries such as Brazil, and South eastern Countries such as Malaysia and Indonesia are few regions with highest lightning density in the world. However one should not forget that in many countries there are small areas which have extremely high degree of lightning occurrence, which are known a "Lightning pockets" and "Lightning belts".

In the South Asian region, lightning is predominantly observed in the inter monsoon period. In most parts of Southern India and Sri Lanka the intense lightning periods are March-May and October-November.

Initiation and Propagation of a Ground Flash

In the middle stage of formation of a convective cloud called "Cumulonimbus", strong wind turbulence takes place causing the separation of charges into several layers. The cloud charging and charge separating mechanisms are yet to be fully understood. Figure 8.1 shows the charge structure of a typical convective cloud.

In the first stage of the most common type of lightning strike, a breakdown occurs between the negative charge centre and the positive charge pocket and subsequently a channel of negative charge flows towards ground from the cloud. This channel which comes to ground with stepping in zig-zag manner is termed as "Stepped Leader". It travels at the speed of about 1×10^5 m/s. When this stepped leader is about 50-100 meters above, earthbound objects in the vicinity (eg. trees, buildings, human beings, animals etc.) start sending upward channels of opposite charge to meet the downward channel from the cloud. These upward channels are called "Positive Answering Leaders". Recent investigation by optical detection methods has revealed that the propagation speed of answering leaders is typically 10^5 m/s or less. One of these upward channels succeeds in meeting the downward channel first. Subsequently, a potential gradient wave, named the "Return Stroke" propagates

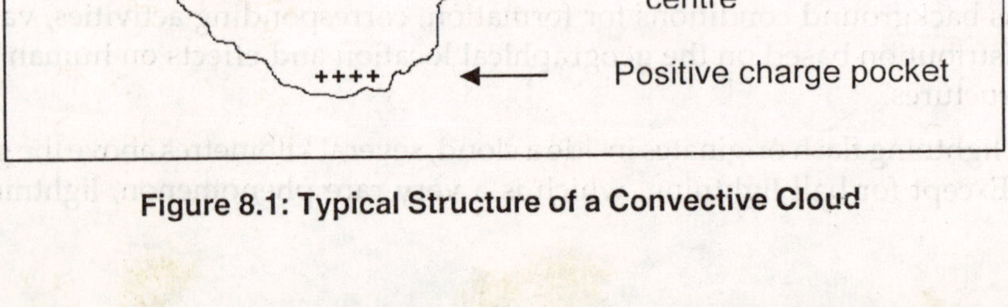

Figure 8.1: Typical Structure of a Convective Cloud

from ground to cloud at a speed of about 1 x 10^8 m/s (Cooray, 2003). The return stroke drains a large current that flows through the object, after it meets the downward stepped leader. Then we say that the object is lightning struck. If a given building is a tall protrusion in a certain landscape it may be the unfortunate object that sends the first upward channel that meets the downward leader carrying the charge from the cloud. Figure 8.2 depicts the propagation of a stepped leader towards ground and the interception with an earth bound object.

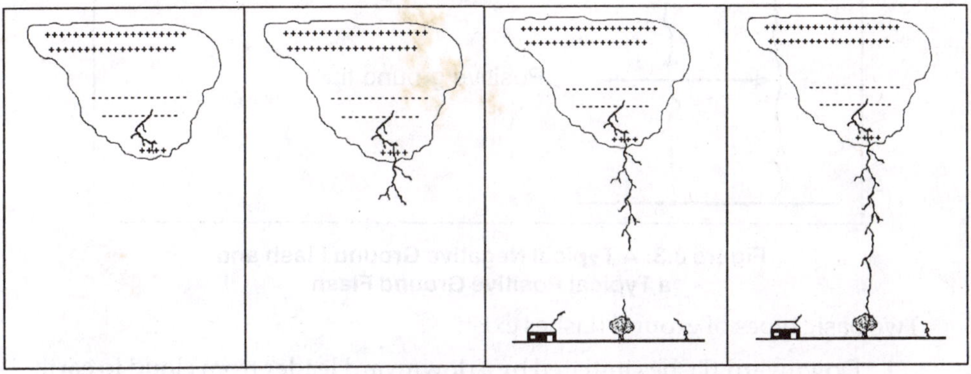

Figure 8.2: The Propagation of a Stepped Leader Towards Ground and the Interception with an Earth Bound Object

After the first return stroke draining out the negative charge cluster, another cluster may collapse into the channel tip funnelling more negative charge into the conducting path. Another leader may result coming straight away towards ground without stepping as it travels along an already formed conducting path. It is called a "Dart Leader". The dart leader will be followed by another return stroke, which is called a subsequent return stroke. There can be many dart leaders and subsequent strokes in a single lightning flash. The total number of return strokes in a single flash is termed as "Multiplicity". Typically, a negative flash has a multiplicity of 4-5, however flashes with multiplicity 18-20 have also been recorded. The combination of the stepped leader, return stroke, dart leaders and subsequent return strokes is termed as lightning flash. The total time period of a lightning flash is about half a second.

Some ground flashes, although the probability is less, may transfer positive charge into ground as well. These positive lightning is believed to emerge from positive charge source at the top level of the cloud. The percentage of positive lightning in tropics is only about 5 per cent of the total ground flashes. Typically, they are single stroked and drive much larger currents into earth than their negative counter part. Records reveal that the peak current of a positive lightning may be as high as 500 kA. They also carry long continuing currents which have values over 1kA flowing for long periods (100s of milliseconds). Such long continuing currents can be observed even in negative flashes but with much less probability (Rakov and Uman, 2007). A typical negative ground flash and a typical positive ground flash are shown in Figure 8.3. The long continuing currents are most often responsible for the triggering of forest fires and explosions due to their high energy content.

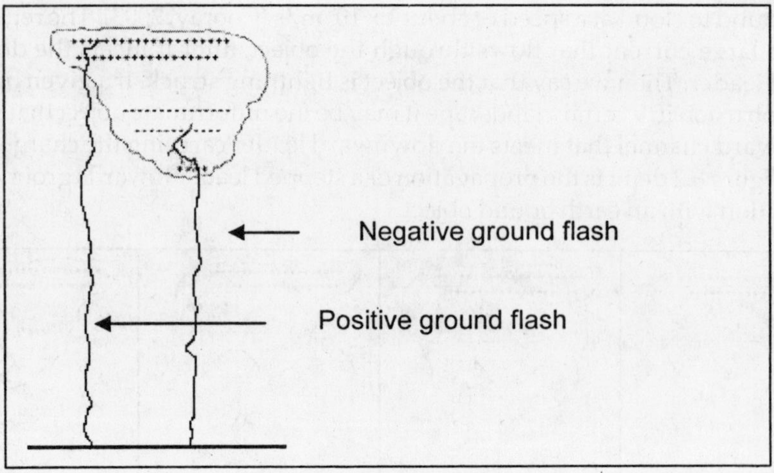

Figure 8.3: A Typical Negative Ground Flash and a Typical Positive Ground Flash

Two basic types of ground flashes exist:

1. Downward flashes initiated by a downward leader from cloud to earth
2. Upward flashes initiated by an upward leader from an earthed structure to cloud.

Majority of downward flash occur on flat territory and to lower structures, whereas for exposed and/or higher structures upward flashes become dominant. With effective height, the probability of a direct strike to the structure increases and the physical conditions change.

A lightning current consists of one or more different strokes (IEC Standards 62305-1, 2006):

1. Short strokes with duration less than 2 ms (Figure 8.4)

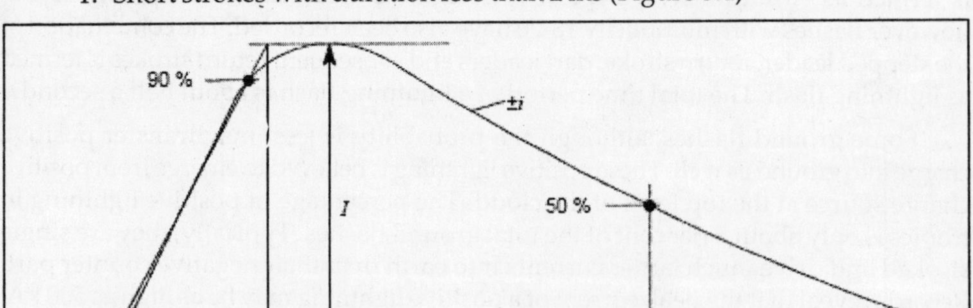

Figure 8.4: Short Strokes,
O_1: Virtual origin, I: Peak current, T_1: Front time, T_2: Time to half value

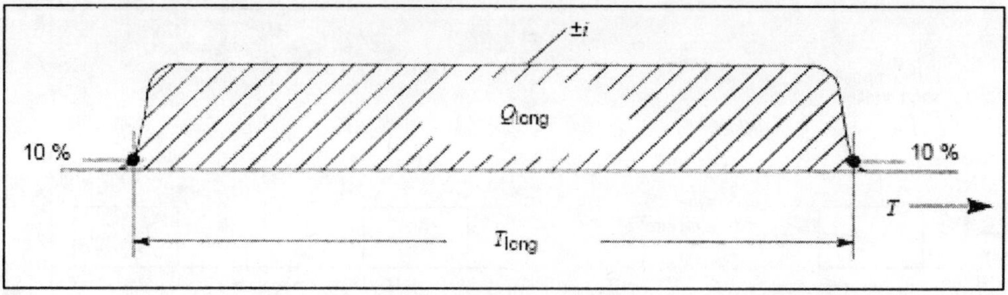

Figure 8.5: Long Strokes
T_{long}: Duration time Q_{long}: Long stroke charge (IEC Standards 62305-1, 2006)

2. Long strokes with duration longer than 2 ms and less than 1 ms (Figure 8.5).

Figure 8.6 depicts the modelled lightning currents in negative and positive flashes which are from cloud to ground. Note that multiple strokes (multiplicity greater than one) are not indicated for positive lightning.

The additional component in upward flashes is the first long stroke, which may have up to some ten of superimposed short strokes. But all short stroke parameters of

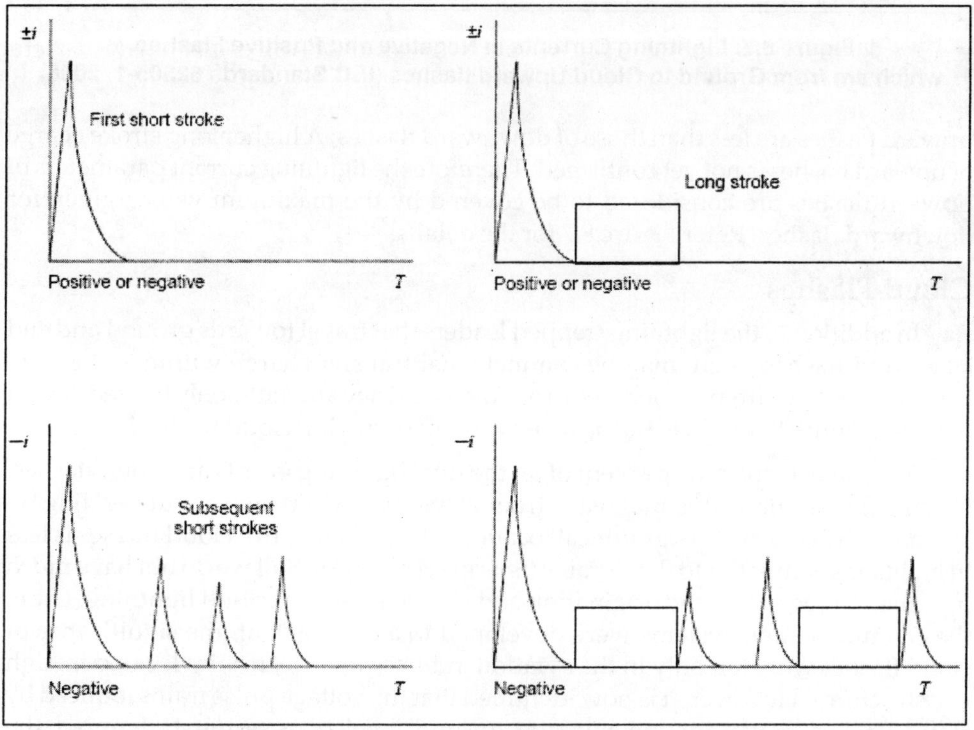

Figure 8.6: Lightning Currents in Negative and Positive Flashes, which are from Cloud to Ground

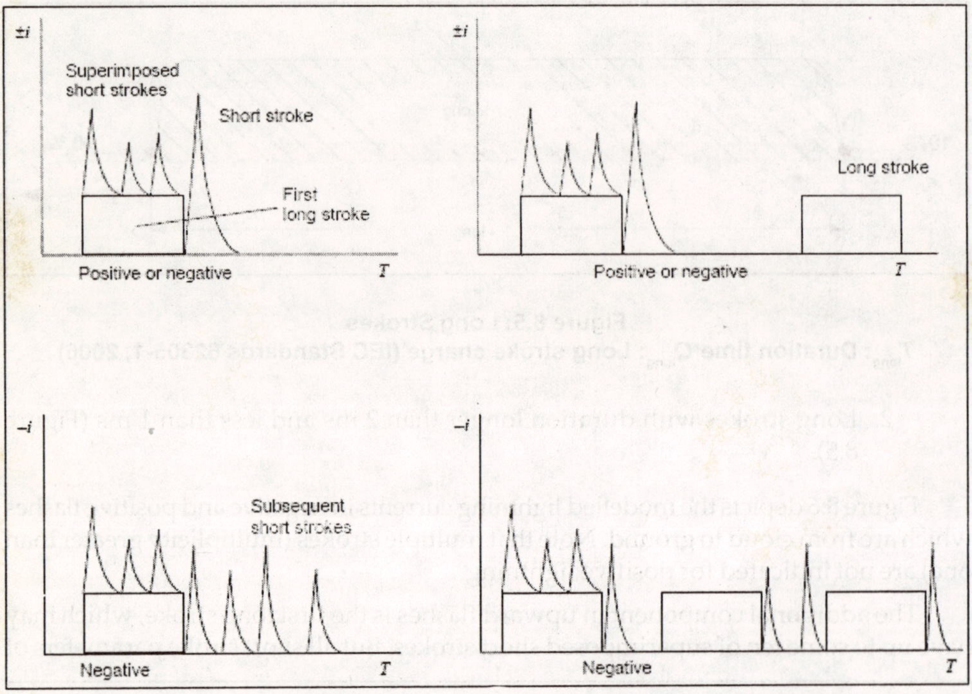

Figure 8.7: Lightning Currents in Negative and Positive Flashes, which are from Ground to Cloud Upward flashes (IEC Standards 62305-1, 2006)

upward flashes are less than those of downward flashes. A higher long stroke charge of upward flashes is not yet confirmed. Therefore the lightning current parameters of upward flashes are considered to be covered by the maximum values given for downward flashes. Refer Figure 8.7 for the details.

Cloud Flashes

In addition to the lightning stepped leaders that travel towards ground and end as ground flashes, there may be channels that transfer charge within a cloud, in between clouds or from a cloud to surrounding air. They are commonly termed "cloud flashes". Figure 8.8 depicts the possible ways of occurring cloud flashes.

In oceanic tropics, 60 per cent of all the total lightning events are cloud flashes. In temperate regions this may vary from 20 per cent to 60 per cent depending on season of the year and geographical location. The percentage of cloud flashes is less in highlands compared to flat terrains (Sharma *et al.*, 2005). Still we do not have much information regarding the origination and characteristics of cloud lightning. Until, the communication systems were developed to a great extent, the significance of cloud flashes were felt only in the aviation industry and electronics located in high rise structures. However, it is now identified that the voltage pulse trains induced by cloud flashes in conducting wires at ground level may seriously hamper the communication signal systems. Although the induced pulses are not large enough to

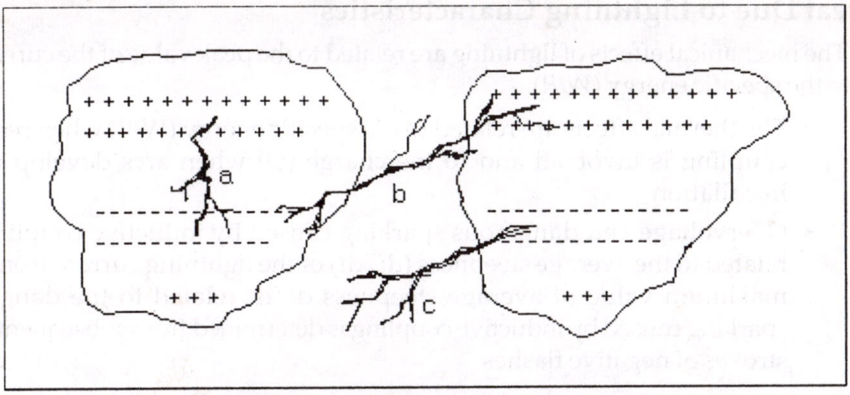

Figure 8.8: Types of Cloud Flashes

(a) Between two charge centres of the same cloud;
(b) Between the charge centres of two clouds;
(c) From a charge centre of a cloud to air

destroy the electronics, they may effect the normal operation by introducing undesired stray signals or distorting the normal signal pulses. Few pulses of a train of such induced voltage are given in Figure 8.9.

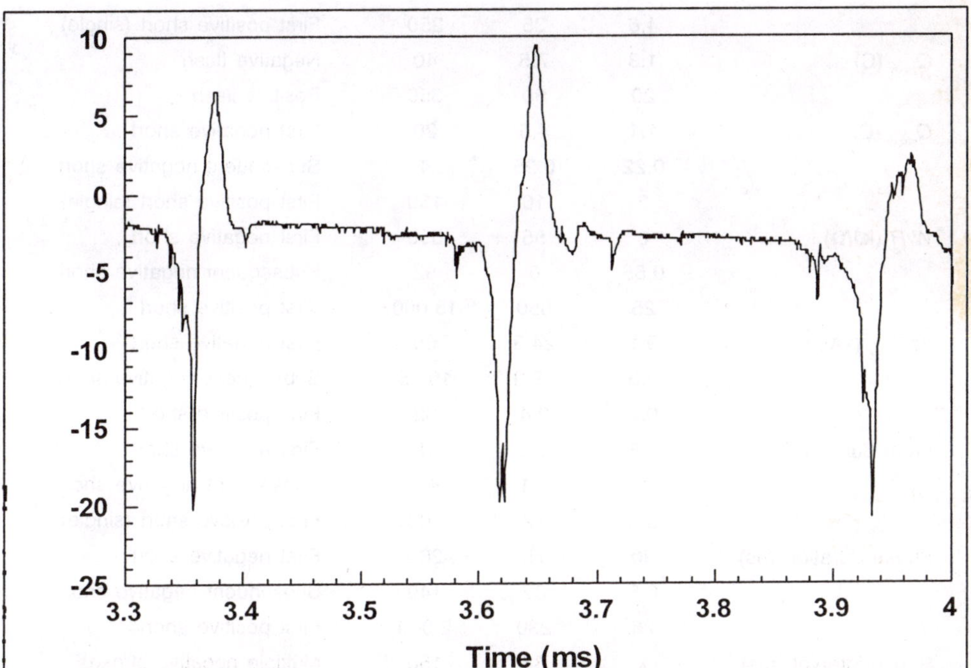

Figure 8.9: The Induced Voltage Pulses of a Cloud Flash
(Gomes and Cooray, 2001)

Threat Due to Lightning Characteristics

The mechanical effects of lightning are related to the peak value of the current (*I*), and to the specific energy (*W*/*R*).

- The thermal effects are related to the specific energy (*W*/*R*) when resistive coupling is involved and to the charge (*Q*) when arcs develop to the installation
- Overvoltage and dangerous sparking caused by inductive coupling are related to the average steepness (di/dt) of the lightning current front. The maximum value of average steepness di/dt related to the dangerous sparking caused by inductive coupling is determined from subsequent short strokes of negative flashes

Table 8.1 depicts lightning current characteristics important in engineering applications.

Table 8.1: Lightning Current Characteristics Important in Engineering Applications (IEC Standards 62305-1, 2006)

Parameter	*Values*			*Type of stroke*
	95%	*50%*	*5%*	
I (kA)	4	20	90	First negative short
	4,9	11.8	28.6	Subsequent negative short
	4,6	35	250	First positive short (single)
Q_{flash} (C)	1.3	7.5	40	Negative flash
	20	80	350	Positive flash
Q_{short} (C)	1,1	4,5	20	First negative short
	0.22	0.95	4	Subsequent negative short
	2	16	150	First positive short (single)
W/*R* (kJ/Ω)	6	55	550	First negative short
	0.55	6	52	Subsequent negative short
	25	650	15 000	First positive short
di/dt_{max} (kA/μs)	9.1	24.3	65	First negative short
	9.9	39.9	161.5	Subsequent negative short
	0.2	2.4	32	First positive short
Front duration (μs)	1,8	5.5	18	First negative short
	0.22	1.1	4.5	Subsequent negative short
	3,5	22	200	First positive short (single)
Stroke duration (μs)	30	75	200	First negative short
	6,5	32	140	Subsequent negative short
	25	230	2 000	First positive short
Stroke interval (ms)	7	33	150	Multiple negative strokes
Total flash duration (ms)	0,15	13	1 100	Negative flash (all)
	31	180	900	Negative flash (without single)
	14	85	500	Positive flash

The Lightning short current is modelled for the purpose of analysis by the following equation

The following equation is the mathematical model used to represent the lightning short current by IEC and BS EN Standards

$$i(0,t) = \frac{I_0}{k} \frac{(t/\tau_1)^{10}}{\left[(t/\tau_1)^{10} + 1\right]} e^{(-t/\tau_2)}$$

where,

I_0 is the peak current, k is the correction factor for the peak current, t is the time, τ_1 is the front time constant and τ_2 is the tail time constant.

The following set of expressions, in cylindrical co-ordinates, can be applied to calculate the electric and magnetic fields at any point in space (Master *et al.*, 1983). Figure 8.10 shows the geometrical parameters of the equation.

$$dE(r,\phi,z,t) = \frac{dz'}{4\pi\varepsilon_0}\left\{\left[\frac{3r(z-z')}{R^5}\int_0^t i(z',\tau - R/c)d\tau + \frac{3r(z-z')}{cR^4} i(z',t-R/c) + \frac{3r(z-z')}{c^2R^3}\frac{\partial i(z',t-R/c)}{\partial t}\right]a_r + \left[\frac{2(z-z')^2 - r^2}{R^5}\int_0^t i(z',\tau - R/c)d\tau + \frac{2(z-z')^2 - r^2}{cR^4} i(z',t-R/c) - \frac{r^2}{c^2R^3}\frac{\partial i(z',t-R/c)}{\partial t}\right]a_z\right\}$$

$$dB(r,\phi,z,t) = \frac{\mu_0 dz'}{4\pi}\left[\frac{r}{R^3} i(z',t-R/c) - \frac{r}{cR^2}\frac{\partial i(z',t-R/c)}{\partial t}\right]a_\phi$$

Thermal Generation and Thunder

One meter of lightning channel dissipates about 40,000 Joules on an average. This is enough to lift a ton of water to a 4 meter height. Lightning channel could be upto 5 km long and dissipate about 200 million Joules. This total energy is dissipated in about 100 microseconds. Each second about 100 lightning flashes strike the Earth. The total power dissipated by lightning is about 20 billion watts. Each year lightning dissipates about 175 TWh. If we divide the total power equally around the globe each square kilometer will receive 40 watts.

The flow of current through the leader heats the air to a very high value. The maximum temperature of the lightning channel reaches to about 40,000 K. The

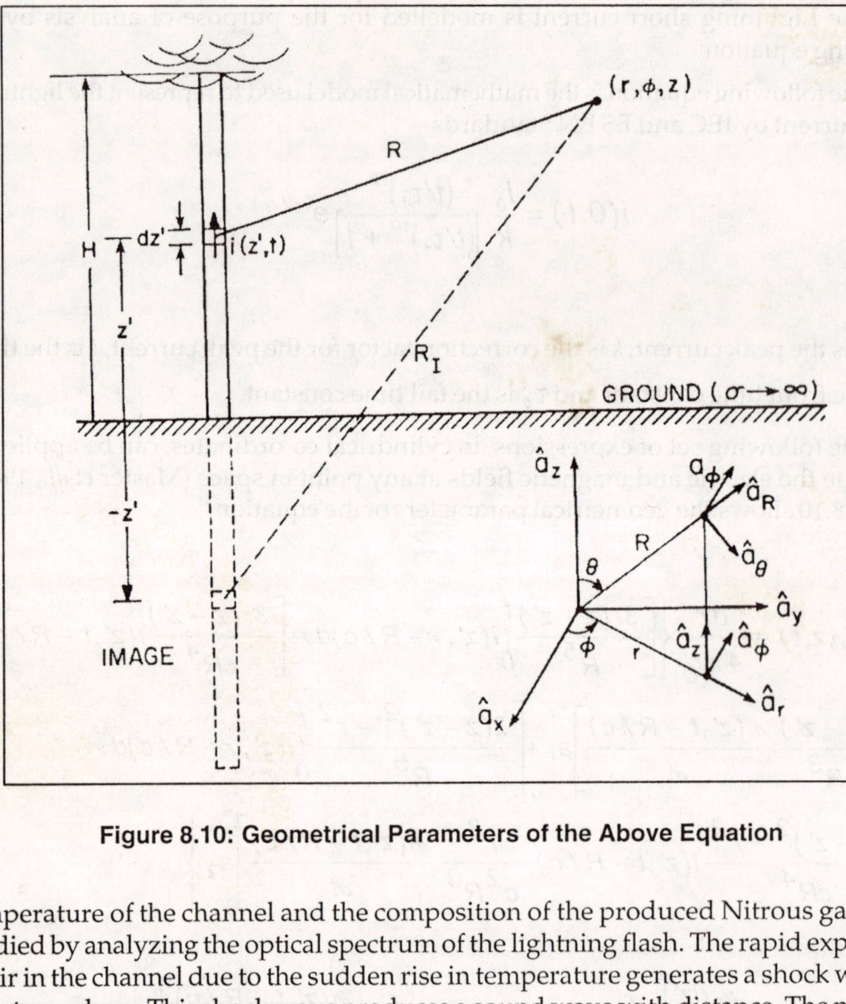

Figure 8.10: Geometrical Parameters of the Above Equation

temperature of the channel and the composition of the produced Nitrous gases are studied by analyzing the optical spectrum of the lightning flash. The rapid expansion of air in the channel due to the sudden rise in temperature generates a shock wave in the atmosphere. This shock wave produces a sound wave with distance. The number of seconds between the light and the thunder, divided by 3 is approximately equal to the distance to lightning in km.

As the lightning strikes the Earth and courses downward through the sand, the sand is instantly super heated (*i.e.*, melted and fused). After cooling, glass-like hollow tubes (Fulgurites) can sometimes be located beneath the surface of the sand.

Step Potential

When lightning strikes a certain point at ground the potential at the point of strike rises to a very high value with respect to distant ground. The potential at the point of strike and the time dependent potential gradient away from that point is a function of the earth resistivity profile and the lightning frequency spectrum. The step potential is dangerous to both living beings and electronic/electrical equipment. As the potential gradient may increase to over several kilo volts per meter, a person or animal with large span of body parts along the potential gradient may be subjected to a partial current that will be very hazardous.

References

1. Cooray, V., 2003. The lightning flash, published by the Institute of Electrical and Electronic Engineers, England.

2. Gomes, C. and Cooray, V., 2001. Characteristics of cloud flashes, 14th International Symposium on EMC, Zurich, Switzerland.

3. IEC Standards 62305-1, 2006. Protection Against Lighting; Part-1: General Principles, International Electrotechnical Commission.

4. Master, M. J., Uman, M. A., Lin, Y. T., and Standler, R. B., 1981. "Calculation of lightning return stroke electric and magnetic fields above ground," *J.Geophys. Res.*, vol. 86, pp. 12 127–12 132.

5. Rakov, A.R. and Uman, M. A., 2007. Lightning: Physics and Effects, Cambridge University Press, London.

6. Sharma, S., Fernando, M., Gomes, C., 2005. Signatures of electric field pulses generated by cloud flashes, Journal of Atmospheric Solar-Terrestrial Physics, Volume 67, Issue 4, Pages 413-422, March.

Chapter 9

Lightning Detection System in Malaysia

Wan Mohd Nazri Wan Daud
Malaysian Meteorological Department,
Selangor, Malaysia
E-mail: klia@met.gov.my, wnazari@met.gov.my

ABSTRACT

In Malaysia, thunderstorms are a common phenomenon occurring all the year round, frequently during the afternoon and early evening. Thunderstorms occur throughout the year but are most likely to happen in the inter monsoon periods, namely April to May and October to November. Over land, thunderstorms frequently develop in the afternoon and evening hours while over the sea, thunderstorms are more frequent at night (mostly due to CCN size).

In order to meet the need for the development of automization in atmospheric condition detection and sensing, standardization of the establishment of operation of National Lightning Detection Network (NLDN) and expansion of its applications, Malaysian Meteorological Department (MMD) operates the SAFIR lightning detection system in Peninsular Malaysia. Eight lightning detection sensors detect lightning activities anywhere in the peninsular and its surrounding waters to enable MMD to issue early thunderstorm advisories and warnings to the users, such as, airlines and power utilities. Nested in this network is Precision Lightning Warning System (PLWS) at Kuala Lumpur International Airport (KLIA) for precise location of lightning activity, its development and movement in order to enhance flight safety and operation.

Introduction

A thunder storm is one of nature's most spectacular phenomenons. The lightning and thunder has fascinated and frightened mankind all throughout. Till today the mystery of lightning and its atmospheric implication is yet to be fully understood. Early scientists did discover resemblance between electricity and lightning. Benjamin Franklin in his kite experiment confirmed the electrical characteristics of lightning. Clouds are negatively and positively charged forming a giant electric dipole floating around in our atmosphere.

Malaysia is one of the hot spots of global lightning activity, being located in the tropics that produce the largest amount of lightning. Deaths and injuries to people, livestock and other animals, thousands of forest and bush fires, as well as millions of dollars of damage to buildings, communication systems, power lines, and electrical systems are also the result of lightning. The threat of lightning causes interruption of power supply and loss of production.

Lightning data is important to understand the variability of lightning activity in the tropics and may help understand our complicated climatic system. The convective storms and resultant lightning activity is characterized as short but intensive with a strong rise in cloud-to-ground lightning. Information on thunderstorms, ranging from accurate localization and characterization of lightning strikes to early detection and warning is vital for preventing thunderstorm hazards. Intra-cloud lightning activity significantly anticipates the cloud to ground lightning phase as well as other severe weather phenomena (intense precipitation, severe turbulences, tornadoes and downburst).

How Lightning is Formed

Lightning is the primary way for the atmosphere to relieve the excess of charge formation. Lightning comes from the parent cumulonimbus cloud that may reach up to level colder than freezing point. Flashes which do not strike the ground are intra-cloud lightning that travel from one part of the cloud to another or cloud to air. Lightning flash originates in the mixed water vapour and iced region. Electrical property of liquid water and ice that causes the separation of electrical charges builds up until there is a lightning discharge.

Types of Lightning

There are several types of lightning and some lightning strikes take on particular characteristics. Certain type of cloud-to-ground lightning are called bead lightning or ribbon lightning. Ball lightning is described as a *floating*, illuminated *ball* that occurs during thunderstorms. The main types of lightning are intra-cloud and inter-cloud which are not hazardous except for aircraft. The most dangerous is cloud to ground that can kill or injure people by direct or indirect strikes.

Lightning Detection System in Malaysia

The Lightning Detection System in Malaysia consists of:

- Wide Area Lightning Localization (SAFIR) which consists of eight lightning detection stations located in the Peninsula of Malaysia.
- Precision Lightning Warning System (PLWS), which consist of three Electric Field measurement equipment, located at the runways of KLIA.

Wide Area Lightning Localization (SAFIR)

The SAFIR system consists of a network of 8 detection stations. Each station has a VHF (Very High Frequency) interferometric array and an LF (Low Frequency) sensor for the localization and characterization of total lightning activity (intra-cloud and cloud to ground). The SAFIR Interferometric array uses different phase measurements of electromagnetic waves produced by lightning for long range finding direction of lightning activity. The SAFIR LF discrimination sensor is a wide-band electric antenna capable of identifying cloud to ground lightning characteristics (peak current, polarity, rise/decay time). All data is GPS synchronized and transmitted in real time to the Central Processing System, which computes the location of lightning discharges by triangulation technique.

Precision Lightning Warning System (PLWS)

The PLWS System consists of 3 Electric Field measurement equipment that measure the atmospheric electric field intensity at the runways of KLIA. The Electric Field Mill creates a high rate of change of alternating electrical field by using a motor-driven rotor stator arrangement. When a thunderstorm builds above its location, the electric field increases steadily. The charges from the electrical field are sampled, amplified and transmitted to the Precision Lightning Warning Console. When the electrical field reaches a predefined threshold, lightning hazard potential warning are sent to the Remote Alarm Displays located in the vicinity of the KLIA. An accurate measurement of the electric field provides information that helps to assess the probability of lightning strike.

Lightning Data for Meteorological Application

The SAFIR provides complete information on thunderstorms and characterization of lightning strikes. This enables efficient early detection of storm cells, accurate tracking information and advance warning of imminent thunderstorm hazards.

The PLWS system provides advance warning and the risk of local lightning on the basis of observations of atmospheric electric field and lightning impulse signal activity. Warning of the local risk of lightning activity based on simultaneous observations of the ambient atmospheric electric field are needed to enable lightning sensitive operations to be closed down and personnel are protected.

Monitor of Total Lightning Activity

Mapping the details of all lightning discharges and their time of occurrence provides monitoring of lightning rate of occurrence in user specified areas.

Monitor of Total Lightning Density and Tracking of Thunderstorms

The intensity of the storm is displayed by the density of electrical discharges. Inter-cloud and/or cloud to ground types of discharges can be selected. The most active and hazardous areas prone to thunderstorms can be identified through total lightning density. By determining the contours of thunderstorm cells the most hazardous areas can be displayed.

Prediction of Lightning Activity

The PLWS is able to predict the occurrence of lightning within the user-defined area. Early warning of lightning (or potential lightning) in close proximity allows appropriate safety measures to be implemented by those involved in a diverse range of activities. The warning system allows people in an exposed position to seek shelter. This includes people engaged in outdoor recreational activity, as well as people working in the open in exposed situations. Early warning also allows for precautionary actions to be taken in respect of critical plant processes or activities.

To Improve Short-term Forecasting

Lightning measurements can be used to improve short-term weather forecasting. Analysis of lightning data provides short-term forecasts (nowcasting) of convective and severe weather hazards. The assimilation of lightning data into numerical models provides weather prediction. Relationship between clouds to ground lightning activity suggests that real time lightning data is useful in the nowcasting of severe local storms. Lightning data should be incorporated into radar data in order to give a more accurate and timely picture of the current convective weather. By combining the two, a more accurate map of convective hazards can be obtained.

To Improve Rainfall Estimation

The correlation between total lightning activity and precipitation intensity conducted on statistical basis can provide estimation of rainfall. The intensity correlation, as well as the anticipation of total lightning versus precipitation can be used to improve flash-flood nowcasting.

To Distinguish Clouds of Convective/Stratiform

Lightning observations can be considered for convective/stratiform identification of clouds in the atmosphere. High radar reflectivity areas obtained through conventional radar are not systematically associated with electrical activity. Microburst is often associated with convective clouds which are preceded by intense intra-cloud lightning activity. By integrating radar data with lightning data meteorologist can improve the nowcasting of microburst phenomena.

Lightning Data for Industrial Use

Utilizations of lightning detection data and the provision of information on thunderstorms in advance can result in significant savings in infrastructure planning, protection and maintenance. Lightning information is used by electric power systems, aviation, nautical safety and tourism, protection of telecommunications and computer systems, insurance companies, construction, agriculture, mining, oil and gas exploration and, increasingly, early detection of forest fires which are, at times also caused by lightning.

Aviation

Aviation hazards include lightning, turbulences, hail, icing and downburst. Thunderstorms are one of the predominant meteorological phenomena affecting air traffic and airport operations. Mapping of intra-cloud lightning provided by the

Lightning Detection System, which provides information about the most active and convective zones in the storm, reflects the areas that produces air traffic disturbance. This information is valuable for improving air traffic management and flight safety.

All kinds of ground-support services, including aircraft refuelling, baggage handling, catering and aircraft and facility maintenance are affected by impending or actual severe storm conditions. Lightning is costly for the aviation industry and inconvenient for passengers. The Remote Alarm System can minimize these impacts, by triggering an alarm to notify the operators, and confirm when the risk has passed.

Power Plants

The anticipation of lightning strikes in specific area of the power network allows to identify risk areas, and this information can be applied to optimize the location of power transmission lines. Knowledge of the lightning activity helps power plant operators to define the areas in the power network where power outages and over voltages are likely to occur. Warning can be issued to industrial customers having equipment or activities that are sensitive to this phenomenon. The real time localization of lightning strikes on sensitive equipment and power networks provide immediate information for fault analysis and decision in systems operation and maintenance.

Statistical analysis of lightning data enables characterizing lightning activity impact on the power network and also defines the technical specifications of lightning protection and over voltage protection equipment for the power network and power plants. Analysis of lightning data can contribute to site selection of power lines and power plants to avoid the most exposed areas to lightning strikes.

Lightning Protection

Dynamic lightning protection for sensitive installations and for protection of personnel can improve safety, efficiency as well as quality of system operation. Having a properly designed lightning protection system is very important. Manufacturer of lightning protection system can improve the quality of their products such as Air Terminals (lightning rods), Conductors, Surge Arrestors and Suppressors. Protection strategies and designs for the equipments can also be further enhanced.

Lightning data is utilized to calculate the risk of direct and indirect lightning strikes to structures; evaluate the need for a lightning protection system; understand how electric and magnetic fields penetrate buildings; select appropriate transient protection technology and to identify where to install surge protection devices.

Lightning Warning for Recreational Activities

People participating in outdoor recreational events especially golf courses and large sport events, are vulnerable to lightning strikes. Real-time warning system can be broadcast through the cellular networks to inform and warn of approaching lightning danger.

Conclusion

The Lightning Detection System provides early warning and information to system users allowing maximum time for effective human or automated responses to minimize damage to lives and property. The usage of this system results in a significant saving of lives and a widespread reduction of injuries. The Lightning Detection System plays a vital role to provide valuable information on the lightning activity. This system should be extended further to East Malaysia.

The Lightning Warning System should be installed at all airports, power plants and other sensitive plants or activities in the country. Implementation of this System can virtually eliminate random decision-making whenever a lightning occurs and provide more efficient operation and reduction in operating cost and increased safety.

References

1. Chubb, John and Harbour, John. A system for the advance warning of risk of lightning. John Chubb Instrumentation, Unit 30, Lansdown Industrial Estate, Gloucester Road, Cheltenham, GL51 8PL
2. Lightning Detection System by Vaisala (Brochure)
3. The Relationship between Severe Storm Reports and Cloud-to-Ground Lightning Polarity in the Contiguous United States from 1989-98

Chapter 10

Lightning Detection and Warning Systems

Mahendra Fernando and Chandima Gomes

University of Colombo, Sri Lanka

ABSTRACT

Lightning detection and warning methods are based on several techniques. Different techniques employ different characteristics of lightning generated waveforms. Most techniques sense various frequency bands of electromagnetic waves between VLF to microwaves emitted during the lightning flash. We discuss these techniques and the accuracy of each technique in locating the ground lightning. The applications of these detection techniques to issue lightning warning signals have also been discussed.

Keywords: *Flash counters, Lightning detection system, Lightning mapping, Locating systems, Lightening warning systems.*

Introduction

Lightning detection and mapping systems can be used to minimize the harmful effects of lightning by providing early warnings of such hazards. These systems can also be used to determine how much lightning actually occurs within a given region and the statistics of discharge parameters that are important in research and in the designing of lightning protection systems.

It will be useful to list out some characteristics of lightning which are employed in direction finding systems (David *et al.*, 2005):

- The field spectrum of lightning vary from 1 Hz to near 300 MHz
- The peak of the spectrum is in the range of 5–10 kHz
- From the peak to 10 MHz the amplitude varies with (frequency)-1

- 10 MHz to 10 GHz amplitude varies with (frequency)-2
- Radiation up to 300 GHz may detect from lightning

The type of information used to detect lightning depends on the frequency of the radiation detected by the system. Using Very-Low-Frequency (3–30 kHz) and LF (30–300 kHz), one can forecast the approximate ground striking point of ground flashes. The best system can obtain an accuracy of about few hundred meters. VLF systems that operate in narrow bands have higher uncertainties (tens to hundred km). The accuracy of location of the systems, which depends upon the measurements of change of the peak amplitudes, does not depend on the bandwidth. VHF–UHF systems can be used in lightning imaging with an accuracy of few tens to hundred meters. Accuracy of lightning detectors can be increased by having number of stations. Single station detectors are usually used to count lightning flashes within a certain region. Lightning detection systems based on electrostatic field measurement are used as early warning systems. Electric and magnetic fields generated by lightning are widely used in lightning flash counters.

Lightning Detection Systems have the following applications:

- Widely used for scientific studies to understand the phenomenon of lightning
- Lightning warning/locating systems are very useful for public safety
- Data provided by systems may be used to get information about lightning activity and thunderstorms (long term and short term), which are very useful for public safety and better protecting system
- Can be used to track the movements of thunderstorm–to switch off sensitive instruments, keep the maintenance crews on alert, to stop high risk activities such as refuelling of aircrafts, take off of flights, warn people to stay away from vulnerable places etc.
- Evaluation of the credibility of insurance claims on lightning damages
- Evaluation of the lightning risks–lightning density, number of thunderstorm days, and lightning currents can be used to evaluate the lightning risk
- Improvement in the lightning protection systems
- Improvement in the lightning protection standards and codes
- Identification of the high lightning activity areas–to improve the protection level, avoid establishing industries in areas that are highly vulnerable to lightning

Types of Lightning Detectors

- Warning Systems
- Flash Counters
- Locating systems

Lightning Warning Systems

They are capable of warning the user about possible lightning strikes within a certain distance in advance. They are widely used at airports and places where the lightning is a major threat. Lightning locating systems may also be used as a lightning warning system. Warning systems are mainly based on static or slow electric field variation associated with thunder clouds (1 Hz–1 kHz). Some systems use lightning generated optical and thunder signals or HF variation of radiation field associated with lightning. However, almost all the lightning warning systems use electrostatic field variation associated with thunderclouds measured using electric field mils (EFM). They differ from one another by the analysis algorithms (some are patented) and software used by them. They can warn few seconds before a possible lightning flash (ground or cloud). They are not expected to give the exact location of lightning strikes but can warn about approaching thunderstorm. Approach of a possible thunderstorm can be detected in advance, giving the time to avoid activities highly vulnerable for lightning (such as refuelling of aircrafts etc).

Lightning Flash Counters (LFC)

The first antenna based LFC was developed in 1895. Most commonly used types are the CIGRE-500Hz, CIGRE-10KHz, and CGR1 flash counters. They can count and record the lightning activities within a certain range with a fairly good efficiency–CIGRE 500 Hz was found to be able to detect ground flashes within 37 km and ground flashes within 17 km. CIGRE 10 kHz was found to be able to detect ground flashes 20 km and cloud flashes within 6 km. Using inbuilt filters LFCs can distinguish ground and cloud flashes with fairly good accuracy (Lojou *et al.*, 2007). This information is used to identify the cloud/ground flash ratio to estimate lightning density.

Lightning Locating Systems

There are four basic methods of locating lightning activity:

- Magnetic Direction Finders
- Time of Arrival Systems
- Interferometry Systems
- Satellite Observation

Magnetic Direction Finders

These are the most well-known and common type of detectors. First generation of DF systems was based on detection of magnetic fields generated by lightning flashes. They could detect only cloud to ground strikes and their location accuracy was not very good. They have higher detection efficiency but the surrounding structures may effect on the accuracy on the direction.

Time of Arrival Systems

Time-of-Arrival Sensor provides the time at which some portion of the lightning electromagnetic field signals are received. Very short and short baseline systems operate at VHF (30–300 MHz) region. Long baseline systems operate at VLF and LF region (3–300 kHz). Generally, VHF signals are associated with the air breakdown processes. VLF is generated due to the current flow in already existing lightning channel. Short-baseline systems are used to image the lightning channel. They can provide the spatial and temporal development of a lightning channel. Long-baseline systems are used to locate the ground striking point.

Interferometry Lightning Locating Systems

Lightning produces noise-like bursts of electromagnetic radiation lasting from tens to hundreds milliseconds. These bursts are difficult to identify using TOA systems since it is difficult to identify individual pulses. In interferometry there is no need of identifying individual pulses. Interferometer measures only the phase difference between narrow band signals corresponding to those noises like burst. Two or more closely placed sensors are used to obtain the phase difference. If there are two identical receivers as in TOA systems, phase difference gives a plane on which the VHF source lies. If there are three identical sensor systems, one can obtain the azimuth and the elevation of the VLF source. If two or more sets of three sensor systems are located about 10 km apart, one can obtain the exact location of the source (Serghei and Sangkasaad, 1999). The first interferometer was designed in 1979, which operated at 34.3 MHz with 3.4 MHz bandwidth. Advanced version of interferometer was used in New Mexico, which operate at 274 MHz with 6 MHz bandwidth. Commercial version is available at a centre frequency between 110 and 118 MHz with a bandwidth of 1 MHz.

Satellite Observations

Earth orbiting satellites can be used to detect lightning using light or radio frequencies. This method can cover a large area. The method can also be used to locate both cloud to ground and cloud-to-cloud flashes. However at present, satellite observation cannot be used to distinguish cloud and ground flashes.

References

1. David M. S., Los Alamos, N. M., Wiens, K. C., and Jacobson, A., 2005. VHF lightning detection and storm tracking from GPS orbit, 12th Conference on Aviation Range and Aerospace Meteorology, USA.
2. Lojou, Murphy, B., Demetriades C., and Cummins, D., 2007. Comparison of LF and VHF lightning detection methods for thunderstorm warning and nowcasting applications, Geophysical Research Abstracts, Vol. 9, 05137.
3. Serghei, F., Sangkasaad, S., 1999. Computer based lightning detection and photonic location, Electric Power Engineering, PowerTech Budapest 99. International Conference on Volume, Hungaria.

Part IV

Lightning Protection, Safety and Suppression

Chapter 11

Culture of Safety Against Lightning: Indian Perspective

C. Lakshmi Narasimhan* and D.V.S. Bhagavanulu

Centre for Disaster Mitigation and Management,
VIT University, Vellore – 632 014, Tamil Nadu, India
**E-Mail: clakshminarasimhan@vit.ac.in*

ABSTRACT

Thunderstorms and Lightning are climate related, highly localized phenomena in nature known for devastating consequences. Many scientific experiments have culminated in inventions for lightning safety, yet the mystery behind lightning is still unresolved and lightning as a phenomena is not completely understood The technology of lightning protection have registered steady improvements but even with all the known precautions, complete safety is still beyond our grasp.

Creating awareness among the general people could go a long way in mitigating lightning threats. Asian countries like India, Sri Lanka, Bangladesh, Nepal and Bhutan have started Lightning Awareness Centres and one of their objectives is to spread awareness among the people. The High Powered Committee of the Government of India on Disaster Management too has identified Thunderstorms and Lightning as natural hazards of great concern. The Bureau of Indian Standards purveys lightning protection guidance for structures and the builders are advised to adhere to the prescribed code. Research and Development programmes are being supported on lightning protection and many leading Indian institutes and Laboratories are working on lightning safety. The paper lays stress on spreading the culture of safety against lightning. It deals with the issues, Indian standards and methods of lightning protection, and introduces ongoing awareness programmes and research and development needs for lightning safety in the Indian context.

Keywords: *Lightning protection, Standards, Awareness, Mitigation, Research.*

Lightning: An Underrated Disaster

Lightning is a natural phenomenon where the charge generated due to cloud/ air movement and other turbulent atmospheric conditions get down to the earth through a conductive path with disastrous direct and indirect effects. The direct effect being the high current (in the range of several thousands of kilo amperes) passing through structures or equipment or humans and the indirect effects being temporary rise of equipment voltages for a very short duration, known as surges.

The amount of loss of human life and properties due to lightning is significantly high. It is found in the recent years that lightning kills more people each year than tornadoes or hurricanes globally. Based on cases documented by the US National Lightning Safety Institute, in the United States, over the past 30 years, an average of 73 people are killed by lightning each year and hundred or more are injured, some suffering devastating neurological injuries that persist for the rest of their lives. According to estimation more than 500 people die every year in South Asia and that to 1000 people die per year in SAARC countries, in Sri Lanka about 50 people die per year (Ahmad and Gomes, 2007). Apart from human lives, economical resources like cultivated fields, buildings, infrastructures, communication networks, power plants, trees and farm lands etc are often destructed by lightning events.

The inevitable questions will rise in one's mind. When the statistics above are so alarming, why little attention is being paid to Lightning Safety as compared to other disasters like flood, hurricane and tornado? Why lightning disasters receive little media attention? Because, the lightning disaster incidents are infrequent and mostly sporadic as compared to other natural disasters. Also without graphic property destruction, it garners less media attention. Moreover lightning is highly a localized phenomenon and hence its total impact is not as evident as other disasters.

Then why it is important to worry about the lighting? It is necessary to pay the highest attention to lightning because the vast majority of the lightning disasters can be easily, efficiently and inexpensively avoided. The US agencies like National Institute of Lightning Safety (NLSI) and National Oceanic and Atmospheric Administration (NOAA) are actively involved in creating Lightning Awareness among the US Nationals. Although notable efforts have been taken by the scientific and disaster management community of South Asian countries to educate the public about lightning safety and minimize the number of deaths, still the fatalities and property damages due to lightning are high in these countries.

Thunderstorms in India

The High Powered Committee on Disaster Management (HPC), India, constituted in August 1999 with an aim towards a systematic, comprehensive and holistic approach towards disasters had identified thirty odd disasters of which Thunder and Lightning was one.

Thunderstorms occur in different parts of India during different seasons, but widespread thunderstorms activity all over the country occurs during the hot weather period, also known as the Pre-monsoon period, from March to May, every year. Some parts of the country experience thunderstorms during the monsoon season also from

June to September. During the post monsoon season *i.e.* October and November, thunderstorms occur in association with cyclonic storms and depressions mostly over peninsular India.

In India, the thunderstorms sometimes produce hailstorms which vary from less than a centimetre to about 5 cm or more in diameter. A series of thunderstorms along a line often extending hundreds of kilometre is called a 'Squall Line'. The squall lines are more severe convective phenomena than isolated thunderstorms. Thunderstorms lead to other convective phenomena called tornado. Tornadoes are extremely severe vortices of very small dimensions occurring in association with intense and large cumulonimbus clouds or cyclonic storms. When thunderstorms occur all over India, the most probable regions of tornado occurrence are Assam and adjoining regions, West Bengal, Orissa and Gangetic plains, Punjab and Haryana.

Lightning Strike on Major Indian Cities

The average numbers of thunderstorm days (ATD) in a year for the important major cities of India are given below. The map showing average number of thunderstorm days in a year in India is given in Figure 11.1 (BIS, 2005).

City	*ATD*
Delhi	30
Mumbai	18
Kolkata	70
Chennai	47
Ahmedabad	11

Depending up on the Average number of Thunderstorm Days (ATD) in a year (as per the details provided in IS 2309), the places in India can be classified as follows:

ATD	*Hazard Rating*	*Count of Locations Threatened*
< 10	Very Low hazard	23
10-30	Low Hazard	61
30-50	Moderate Hazard	57
50-80	High Hazard	34
≥80	Very High Hazard	05

Damages Due to Lightning in India

The number of deaths, injuries and damages to properties due to lightning is high in India. It is a major concern that several fatalities are being reported due to lightning from its North Eastern states every year.

According to the National Crime Record Bureau, India in the year 2001 around 1507 persons died because of lightning. In Orissa alone, about 277 persons were

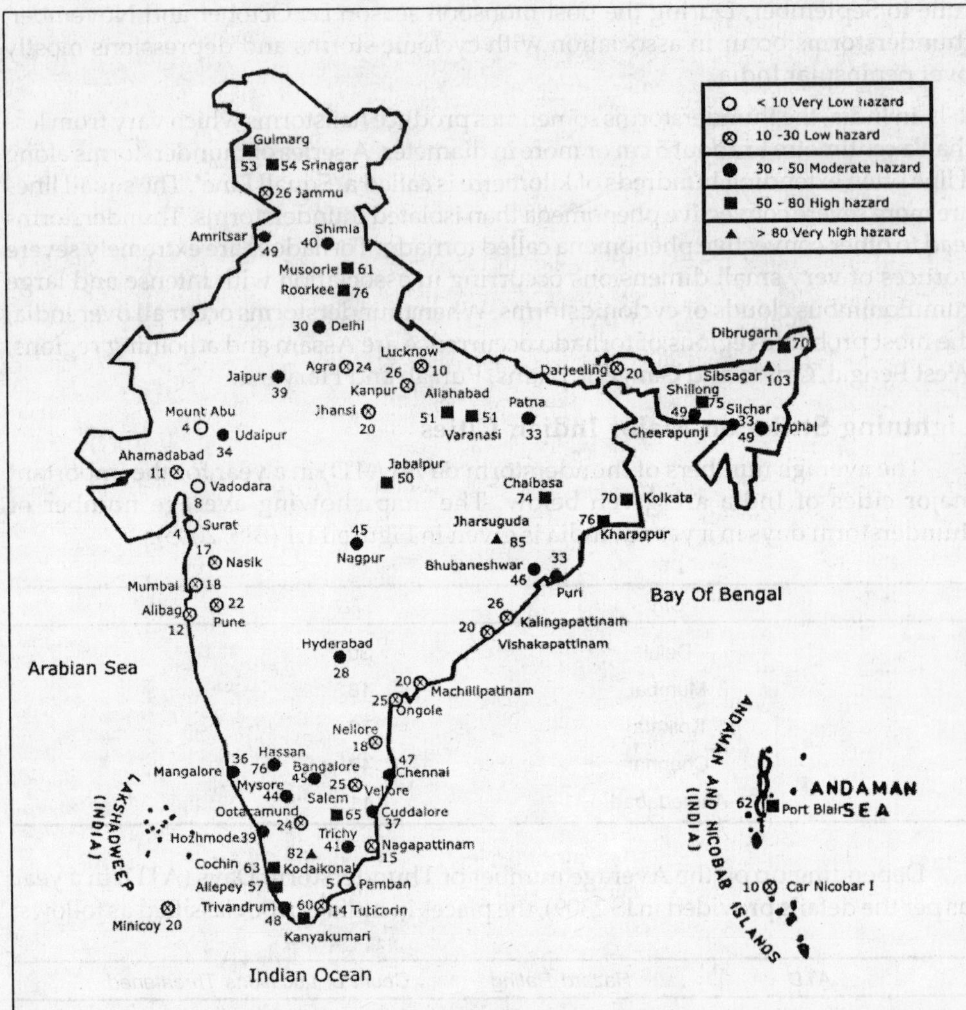

Figure 11.1: Average Number of Thunderstorm Days (ATD) in a Year in Some Places in India (IS 2309:1989)

killed by lightning in 2004 and also, it is reported by the state government in Orissa that during 2001-2004, around 900 persons were killed only due to thunderstorms.

At least 279 people were killed, and an estimated 200,000 made homeless, in severe floods in the southern Indian state of Tamil Nadu, in November, 2006. The flooding was caused by torrential rain over four weeks in October and early November, and was compounded by more monsoonal storms which hit the region between November 21 and 24. These monsoonal storms were associated with strong thunderstorms; however the deaths due to them were not reported separately.

69 persons were reported to be killed by lightning from various parts of Maharashtra state in the same period. Around 11 persons were killed and 100 were injured in lightning incidents in Madhya Pradesh state and 11 persons were killed in Jharkhand state during April and May, 2006.

Electrical equipments worth Rs. 2 lakhs were damaged, when lightning struck the house of Volga Crasta at Kallianpur, Karnataka in October, 2006.

In the year 2005, The Mumbai floods were caused by the eighth heaviest ever recorded 24-hour rainfall figure of 944 mm which lashed the metropolis on 26th July, 2005 and intermittently continued for the next day. 644 mm (25.4 inches) was received within the 12-hr period between 8am and 8pm. It is reported that the floods caused a direct loss of about Rs. 450 crores. Within in three days about 406 persons were reported to be killed by these unprecedented floods. However, unfortunately, there was no report made separately on lightning incidents and deaths though some sporadic incidents of lightning were reported from other places like Satara, Kolhapur and Pune districts of Maharashtra State, India.

This year the monsoon is yet to set and bring the torrential rains, but within the period from March and April, 2007 around 53 persons were killed and 10 were reported to be injured (source: various dailies) by lightning strikes that were associated with heavy to moderate pre-monsoonal rains.

The telecommunication network in Kangra district, Himachal Pradesh was paralyzed after lightning struck the main telephone exchange at Jassur on 2 March, 2007. The lightning damaged telecommunication equipments worth lakhs of rupees in the main telephone exchange. 15000 telephone lines out of 24, 000 lines were out of gear and 29 telephone exchanges of Kangra district remained suspended with headquarters at Dharamsala. These statistics indicate the severity of lightning strikes.

Protection Against Lightning

Since the lightning cannot be avoided, the logical way to avert the risks of lightning strike is to find a protection for personal and structural safety. As explained earlier the current passes through the structures or equipments or living beings could be fatal. The protection and safety against lightning can be achieved in two ways

- Safety through Lightning Protection Systems
- Safety through Public Awareness and Education

Safety Through Lightning Protection Systems

Since 1970, after the Franklin's invention of Lightning protection rod, there is a remarkable advancement in the science of Lightning Protection. The scientific and technological world has put its entire effort on bringing systems for the protection of valuable infrastructures and equipments against lightning.

Lightning Protection to Structures

Direct and Indirect Strikes

A Lightning bolt may bring 300 kA of electricity to the ground in just a few milliseconds. It heats the air in the core of the bolt to around 30,000° C-five times hotter than the surface of the Sun. The enormous current associated with the lightning flash often destroys the power and communication networks in an area where it strikes. The lightning may directly hit a structure (direct strike) or a part of a lightning flash that hit another structure may affect the near proximity (side flash). The direct lightning or side flashes cause damages at a rapid speed so that once the structure is struck by a lightning; it is difficult to prevent any electrical damages or human injuries and prevent fire from spreading to other structures close to the affected structure.

The high lightning discharge currents in the lightning bolt induces high voltage on other electric circuits. Once a lightning is struck on a nearby object at even 500 m distance, the whole structure would be under a strong dose of electromagnetic induction. When this radiation passes through electronic equipments such as computers and sophisticated medical and defence instruments etc. their components may get damaged. This may happen even when the equipments are unplugged from their service lines. However, the chances of ordinary electrical equipments getting damaged by such induced voltages are very less.

Surges and Hazards

Potential surges are momentary increase in the normal working voltage of a system. Sometimes referred to as 'spikes', 'over-voltages' or 'transients', these surges can affect power cables, data/telephone cables and instrumentation wiring, causing anything from data loss to the total destruction of equipment. These are indirect effects of lightning that destroy sophisticated equipment, especially the sensitive electronic equipment. The effects of these surges and transients are not always visible. Burnt/charred Printed Circuit Boards (PCBs) or malfunctioning software, etc. are indications of the effect of surge/transients. It is estimated that 70 to 85 per cent of all transients are generated internally within one's own facility mainly due to switching. However, 15-30 per cent transient over voltages may be caused due to travelling waves caused by lightning. The lightning protection standards provide methodology to protect structures and buildings from lightning strikes.

Standards on Lightning Protection

The following standards are being followed in India for lightning protection and safety.

The Indian code of practice: Indian standard: IS 2309: 1989; Protection of Buildings and Allied Structures against Lightning-Code of Practice (Reaffirmed in 2005)

This Code outlines the general technical aspects of lightning, illustrating its principal electrical, thermal and mechanical effects. Guidance is given on how to assess the risk of being struck and it offers a method of compiling an index figure as an aid in deciding if a particular structure is in need of protection.

The Code also offers guidance on good engineering practice and the selection of suitable materials. Recommendations are made for special cases such as explosives stores and temporary structures, for example, cranes, spectator stands constructed of metal scaffolding. Where current carrying conductors are directly associated with structures coming within the scope of this Code, certain recommendations relating to them are included.

International Standards

- British Standard 6651 (1999): Code of Practice for Protection of Structures against Lightning (This code will be replaced by BS EN 62305 (Parts 1-4) in August 2008)
- American Petroleum Institute (API) Recommended Practice 2003-Protection Against Ignitions Arising Out of Static, Lightning and Stray Currents. The Chapter 5 discusses direct and indirect effects of lightning as well as protection of specific equipments.
- National Fire Protection Association NFPA- 780: Standard for the Installation of Lightning Protection Systems. It describes minimum standard to residential, commercial and industrial facilities.
- Oil Industry Safety Directorate (OISD) 180

Assessment of Lightning Risk and Need of Protection

Indian Standard on Lightning Protection (IS 2309) provides the methodology to assess the lightning protection requirement for structures and buildings.

Estimation of Exposure Risk

The probability of a structure being struck by lightning in a year is a product of 'Lightning Flash Density' (N_g) and the 'Effective Collection Area' (A_c). The Lightning Flash Density (N_g) is the number of flashes (to ground) per square kilometre. The Annual Thunderstorm days per year of a location can be translated in terms of estimated average annual density (N_g). The relationship between thunderstorm days per year (ATD) and lightning flashes per square kilometre per year ($N_{g)}$ are given in IS 2309.

The effective collection area (A_c) of a structure is the area on the plan of the structure extended in all directions to take account of its height. For ex. for a simple rectangular building with a length of L, width of W and Height H meters, the effective collection area would be having length (L+2H) and width (W+2H) meters and four rounded corners formed by quarter circles with a radius of 'H' metres.

Therefore, $Ac = (LXW) + 2(LXH) + 2(WXH) + \pi H^2$

The probable number of strikes per year (P) is the product of N_g and $A_{c.}$ The acceptable risk figure accepted by IS 2309 is 10^{-5}, *i.e.* 1 in 100,000 per year.

Overall Assessment of Risk

After finding the probable number of strikes on the structure (P), next step is to find overall assessment of risk based on the following 5 weighing factors.

- Use of structure
- Type and Nature of Construction
- Value of its contents
- Degree of Isolation
- Type of Terrain

IS 2309 elaborately explains the weighing factors and values for each factor is given in the code. The overall factor is calculated by multiplying the above 5 factors. The final risk assessment is the product of probable number of strike to the structure (P) and overall multiplying factor. If it exceeds 10^{-5}, lightning protection is necessary.

'Furse StrikeRisk 2.0' is a lightning Risk Assessment tool developed by M/S. Furse (Lightning Protection manufacturers) engineers based on BS 6651.This simple tool enables the user to carry out the lightning protection risk assessment.

Functioning of Lightning Protection Systems

When a downward leader propagates from the cloud, the air termination sends a streamer upwards. Thus the lightning is attracted towards the air termination rod (or to the metallic mesh).

The leader a highly conductive channel, established between the cloud and the air terminal allows the lightning current safely pass into the earth through the rest of the system. Thus, instead of repelling, a lightning protection system attracts a lightning strike.

The system is called the "Franklin Rod System", named after Benjamin Franklin who first proposed lightning rods in 1750.

Selection and Design of Lightning Protection System

The essential guidelines that are outlined in IS 2309 are given below.

Air Termination (Vertical, horizontal)

The structures may be protected from lightning by either channelling the current along the outside of the building and into the ground or by shielding the building against damage from transient currents and voltages caused by a strike. The method constrains the path of lightning currents and voltages through use of lightning rods, or air terminals, and conductors that route the current down into a grounding system, as shown in the Figure 11.2 When a lightning leader comes near the building, the lightning rod initiates a discharge that travels upward and connects with it, thus controlling the point of attachment of lightning to the building. A lightning rod functions only when a lightning strike in the immediate vicinity is already imminent and so does not attract significantly more lightning to the building. An air termination networks consists of vertical or horizontal conductors or combination of both.

Protective Angle

In simple terms, zone of protection is the volume within which a lightning conductor gives protection against a direct lightning strike by giving direction to the strike. For a vertical conductor rising from ground, the zone has been defined as a cone with its apex at the tip of the conductor terminal with its base on the ground. For a horizontal conductor the zone has been defined as the volume generated by the cone with its apex on the horizontal conductor moving from one end to the other.

However, for practical purpose of providing an acceptable degree of protection to a structure, the protective angle for any single component of an air termination network, vertical or horizontal, is considered to be 45° (Figure 11.3). Overhead

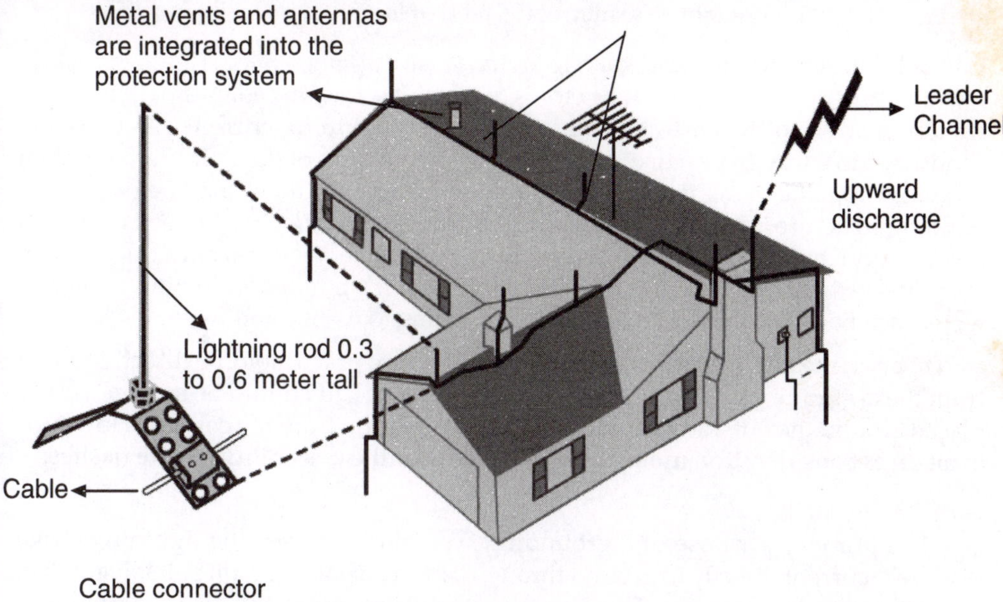

Figure 11.2: Lightning Rod Protection System for a Residential Building (Encyclopaedia Britannica, 1999)

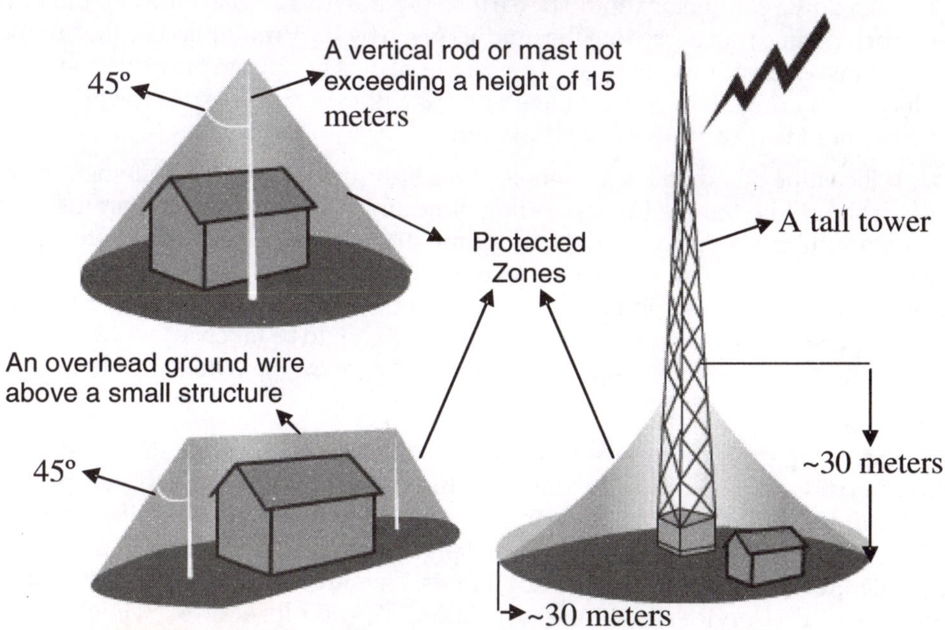

Figure 11.3: Protection Angle for Vertical Air Terminal (Encyclopaedia Britannica, 1999)

conductors and grounded vertical air terminal may also be used to provide a cone-shaped area of lightning protection, as shown in the Figure 11.3. Such systems are effective when their height is 30 metres (98 feet) or lower.

Down Conductors (Number and Routing to Avert Side Flashing)

The function of a down conductor is to provide a low impedance path from the air termination to the earth electrode so that the lightning current can be safely conducted to earth. In practice, depending upon the form of the building, it is often necessary to have many down conductors, some or all of them may be part of the building structure itself. For example, a steel framed building might need no added down conductors. The framework itself provides efficient natural network of many paths to earth. However, structure made entirely from non-conducting materials would need down conductors deployed according to its size and form.

In brief, the down conductor system must, where practicable, be directly routed from the air terminal to the earth termination network. It should be symmetrically placed around the outside walls of the structure starting from the corners. However, in all cases consideration must always be made for the possibility of side flashes.

Earth Terminations

The primary purpose of a grounding system is to divert the lightning strike discharge current directly to ground through a low resistance circuit suitably rated to carry the impulse currents. This has the effect of reducing the strike period to a minimum, and reducing or eliminating the problem of side strikes as the charge is able to follow the least resistance path to the ground.

Each down conductor should be earthed separately. Each earthing should have value of resistance not exceeding the product given by 10 W multiplied by the number of earthing electrodes provided. The whole of the lightning protective system, including any ring earth, should have a combined resistance to earth not exceeding 10 W without taking into account the bonding.

If the value obtained for the whole of the lightning protective systems exceeds 10W, it should be reduced by extending or adding the electrodes in parallel or by interconnecting the individual earth terminations of the down conductors by a conductor installed below the ground level, sometimes referred to as a ring conductor. Buried ring conductors laid in the manner described above are considered to be an integral part of the earth termination network and should be taken into consideration when assessing the overall value of resistance to earth of the whole installation.

Surge Protection

Lightning protection rods and down conductors, can protect structures from direct strikes and from side flashes. But the service lines such as power, telecommunication etc in the buildings can be affected by the lightning currents. Special devices used for preventing such dangerous current induction from entering are called surge diverters or surge suppressors. The surge diverter is connected at the entrance of the service line to the installation. A good level of protection can be obtained if these are connected to the power socket of electrical or electronic equipment as well. In case of a lightning strike it provides a convenient path for the induced voltage to divert to the earth without permitting it entering into the equipment. Surge/ diverters suppressors, which have to be connected to protect power lines, communication lines and data lines, are different from one another.

Electromagnetic Compatibility (EMC)

Electromagnetic radiation is associated with lightning and can cause damages to the sophisticated electronics in a building. Prevention of such intrusion of undesired electromagnetic impulses through both radiation and conduction is termed Electro Magnetic Compatibility (EMC). "Faraday Cage" (Figure 11.4) is the usual method of radiation prevention, in which building is screened with the conductive materials so that the structure behaves like cage. This method of protection is provided to the part of the building where sophisticated electronic equipment is installed (such as computer rooms, medical theatres and scanning rooms, control chambers of power plants, airports, military bases, and communication bases etc.).

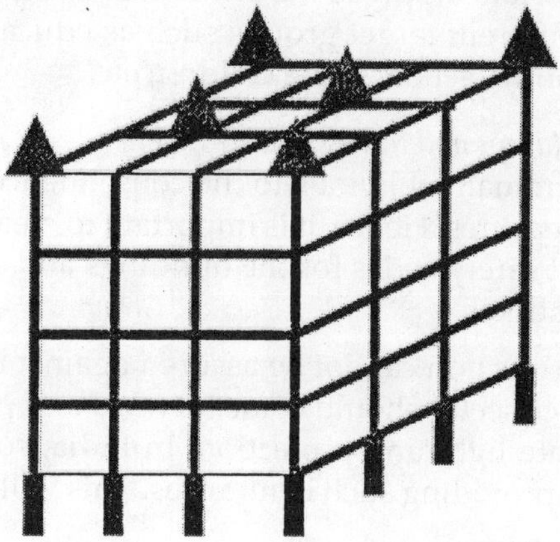

Figure 11.4: Faraday Cage Type Lightning Protection

Maintenance of Lightning Protection System

No lightning protection system is maintenance-free. Every type of LP system whether it is surge diverters installed on power lines or Franklin rods on the top of buildings or surge protection devices installed to protect electronic equipment, needs to be maintained based on applicable standards. Monitoring the surge counter reading gives an idea of the local lightning activity in an area. Earthing plays an important role in the efficiency of lightning protection system.

Following regular tests can ensure an effective lightning protection system:

- Tests on earthing system
- Inspection of air terminations
- Down conductors
- Checking on Surge diverters and suppressers

Safety Through Public Awareness and Education

Another way to mitigate with the hazards of lightning strikes is by creating awareness and dissemination of knowledge about lightning and possible protection mechanism to the public and administrators.

Creating Public Awareness

Creating Awareness for Personal Safety

Lightning strikes occur in India every year during the two monsoon seasons, as well as pre and post monsoon periods. Due to their sporadic occurrences, the common people really do not have concern over the danger associated with lightning strikes. It is a common sight in India people out doors watching thunder and lightning, continuing their work in paddy fields, the fishermen going to sea during lightning etc. It leads to lightning casualties and deaths leading to the poor people to lose their family members. It is important to spread the awareness on lightning protection and personal safety among different target groups such as educated and uneducated people, villagers, rural youths, school going children etc.

Creating Awareness for Buildings and Infrastructure Safety

The masses in India remain oblivious to the consequence of lightning strikes and its technical safety measures. Hence, it is important to create awareness among the public about different safety codes for the buildings and structures to prevent damage due to lightning strikes.

It is true that total protection cannot be assured against lightning. Hence it is required that the insurance sector should come forward and provide insurance for buildings having adequate lightning protection. In India, some of the insurance companies like ICICI are providing such insurances. This will encourage people to adopt safety measures.

Enforcement of Lightning Protection Standards

Role of Builders and Building Companies

If a common man does not know about building standards and the required lightning protection, he may be forgivable, but if a builder or building company does not follow the code, it is an offence. They are supposed to know about the building codes and should carry out Risk Assessment for each disaster probable in their area of construction and should take appropriate mitigation measures. If they are unaware, they should be given adequate knowledge and the probable disaster. The Certificating Authority also should ensure that all necessary precautionary measures are taken for such a disaster probable in that area.

Apart from the personal buildings, public structures like flyovers, bridges, airports, ports/dockyards and archaeological monuments are also prone to lightning strikes. Hence it is important to adopt proper safety and mitigation measures.

Involvement of Technical People in Lightning Protection

Telecommunication, Electricity and Power supply are the major public sectors suffering huge losses and asset damages due to Lightning strikes and Surges. It is important that technical people working in these sectors should be given adequate training on Lightning Protection. Telecommunication systems, including mobile phone services, should be forced to take precautionary measures.

Awareness Programmes on Lightning Safety in Schools

Catching them young will help in many ways for the country. Children are the future of country. If they are trained when they are young, they would be very useful in dissemination of awareness for other target groups such as rural mass, uneducated men and women in the villages.

Each school should have a lightning disaster management programme. They should follow the Building standards and codes. Authorities should enforce every school to have lightning protection and safety measures. Dos and Don'ts and Personal Safety during Lightning should be taught to every child and mock drills for fire should be periodically rehearsed.

Lightning Awareness Programmes in India

Lightning awareness workshops were conducted by UNESCO, New Delhi in India with the aim to disseminate lightning protection awareness in India and surrounding regions. The participants were mostly from educational sectors who were encouraged to involve actively in the awareness promotion programmes.

With support from South Asian Lightning Information and Resource Centre (SARI)/Energy Small Grants program and UNESCO, New Delhi the South Asian Lightning Awareness Program (SALAP) has been launched to provide much needed awareness and expertise in this region on lightning protection and safety.

A 'Lightning Awareness Cell' was formed under the umbrella of 'Regional Energy Centre', Kerala (Non profit organization under the Travancore Cochin Literary, Scientific and Charitable Societies Act-XII of 1995) in June 2005. It is promoting lightning protection awareness by conducting Lightning Workshops for local and technical people.

The Lightning Awareness Cell, Guwahati has been formed under The Energy and Resources Institute (TERI) in August 2005. The cell is promoting Lightning Awareness among school and college teachers, Panchayat Members and villagers, Media Professionals in different regions of the country. It had organized two days workshop on lightning in Guwahati in April, 2006. Some of the planned programmes under the cell are, entrepreneurship development programmes involving participants from all the states, mapping of lightning affected areas in India.

Centre for Innovation in Science and Social Action (CISSA), Thiruvananthapuram, Kerala is a nonprofit, non governmental organization of scientists and citizens promoting rigorous scientific analysis, innovative policy development and effective citizen advocacy to build a cleaner, safer and healthier world. It has joined hands with The Lightning Awareness Cell, Regional Energy Centre, Kerala and South Asian Lightning Information and Resource Centre and conducted a one day workshop on Lightning protection for academicians and professionals from various industries, for example, telecommunications, aviation, military, hydrology and meteorology sectors in October, 2006 at Thiruvananthapuram.

Centre for Disaster Mitigation and Management (CDMM), VIT University, Vellore, India

One of the areas of major thrust at CDMM is innovative education and training on Disaster Mitigation and Management. CDMM has produced a number of knowledge products in this area and conducted seminars, discussion meetings and Roundtable Conferences on natural disasters. As part of the Safety and Awareness Programme to mitigate lighting disasters, the tips for lightning safety are being disseminated. The activities of this centre can be viewed at www.vitcdmm.org

Lightning Research Programmes in India

In India, some of the leading academic and research institutions have been carrying out R&D programmes relating to thunderstorms and lightning. The research areas and testing facilities developed in two of such institutions are briefly mentioned in the following.

Department of High Voltage Engineering, Indian Institute of Science, Bangalore

The Department of High Voltage Engineering at Indian Institute of Science, Bangalore is one of the leading research institute involved in research on Electromagnetics and Lightning. Their current research programmes are on electromagnetic field theory, electrostatic field theory in complex geometries and space charge phenomenon, transient field in composite lossy dielectrics and machine windings, field associated with lightning and lightning induced voltages, etc. They have designed and built lightning protection systems for the satellite Launch Pad at Sriharikota, India. They provide lightning test facility for aircrafts *e.g.*, lightning protection for HANSA aircraft etc. Their Research and Development projects involve; development of high voltage and high current facilities for lightning, aircraft interaction analysis, development of sensors for the measurements of lightning currents in strokes intercepted by the lightning protection systems.

The Atmospheric Science Division, Centre for Earth Sciences Studies (CESS), Thiruvanathapuram, Kerala

The Atmospheric Science Division, CESS is conducting combined research in Atmospheric Electricity, Lightning and related Instrumentation. They have undertaken studies on lightning hazards in Kerala. The summary of the work is given below:

To understand the lightning activity in Kerala, lightning data for the past 17 years (1986-2002) was collected. Reports of casualties from newspapers, records of lightning accidents available from village revenue records and other sources like telecom department are used for this study. These data sets were screened to eliminate duplicate incidents. Then it was analysed for spatial and temporal distribution of lightning occurrence. Data on cumulonimbus (Cb) cloud observations were collected from India Meteorology Department for the stations Thiruvananthapuram, Alapuzha, Kochi, Kozhikode and Kannur for the same period. This data was used to study the occurrence of thunderclouds. From the beginning of northeast monsoon to the occurrence of the next southwest monsoon season is a period in which lightning activity is seen to be high in Kerala. The lightning occurrence data when posted on a physical map of Kerala clearly shows that midland regions of Kerala are more affected than the coastal plains and highland regions. The Palakkad gap region experiences the least strikes. This indicates that the Western Ghats play an important role in influencing the formation of Cb clouds (Murali Das *et al.*, 2007)

Along with the above study, an electric field meter is being used to monitor atmospheric electric field. The movement of thunderclouds and their effect on electric field is being studied with this data. The lightning events as recorded by the meter and the actual region where lightning struck are being studied to evaluate the usefulness of the electric field data.

Apart from the research work, the CESS scientists are involved in awareness camps that are conducted in areas of high lightning strike frequency and disseminating knowledge on lightning protection.

Conclusions

Though lightning incidents are low, whenever they strike, they cause severe damage to life and properties. Casualties due to lightning can be easily, efficiently and inexpensively avoided. Lightning safety can be achieved mainly by creating public awareness, technical education on Lightning Protection, educating people on lightning and surge protection. Stringent steps to ensure adherence of building standards and codes wherever necessary and promoting research and development on lightning protection are essential. There is a need to give lightning its due attention as one of the natural disaster. It should be given a priority to be included in National Disaster Management Programmes.

Tips for Personal Safety from Lightning

Your life is precious. Please spend a few minutes of your time to go through this message from CDMM carefully, and free yourselves from the fear of thunderstorms and lightning for all times. It is unfortunate that people are either killed or disabled by lightning just because they keep watching the beauty of rain, thunder and lightning outdoors or take a shelter under a tree or continue with boating, swimming, fishing, climbing, playing, golfing or talking over telephone, unmindful of the damage lightning could inflict.

Remember, no place on the earth is safe against thunder storms and lightning, especially when you are outdoors. All thunder storms are dangerous despite their usually small area of coverage (typically 24 km in diameter). Lightning could strike all exposed objects including buildings, water tanks, hill tops, vehicles, electrical poles, animals and people. There are no exceptions or exemptions. Here are a few tips for your safety:

1. When you see lightning and hear thunder of a storm even before you could count 30, it is a sure warning signal that you should rush indoors to protect yourselves.
2. If no shelter is available in the neighbourhood of where you are, then seek protection by getting in to a hard topped vehicle with windows closed. You are much safer inside a car than outside because the closed metallic body of the vehicle usually provides protection, if you are careful not to touch metal.
3. Keep distance from vulnerable locations like isolated trees or isolated tall structures. Lightning can strike the same place twice and can spread out nearly 20m after striking the ground.
4. If you get a tingling sensation or standing hair experience, it is to be considered as a premonition of impending threat of lightning. In such a situation, quickly acquire the lowest profile by crouching down the knees of your feet but never make a mistake to lie flat on the ground.
5. Lightning can affect a building in three ways (a) direct hit (b) through external wires and pipes, and (c) through the ground. Lightning current can also travel through reinforcement in concrete walls, floor surface etc. Beware.
6. Do not use wired phones. Mobile phones are also prone to attract lightning.
7. Lightning can strike through external doors and windows. Porches and staircases outside the building may not also be safe.
8. Unplug all the electrical and electronic equipment as soon as the thunder and lightning seem likely. Do not forget to disconnect radios and TVs from external antennas.
9. Avoid contact with all sorts of pipes and avoid taking a shower during thunder and lightning.
10. Monitor thunder storms and lightning from indoors. You should go out only after ensuring lull for at least 30 minutes since the last thunder.
11. No rain does not mean no danger of lightning. Lightning may occur as far as 15 km from the nearest rainfall area. Be alert.
12. Do not be under the false impression that the rubber shoes you wear and the rubber tyres of your car will protect you from lightning to strike upon.
13. If someone is struck by lightning, at once come to his or her rescue. It is a very wrong notion that those struck by lightning carry an electrical charge.
14. A lightning protection system may be present; still the lightning can always strike. A lightning protection system, however, ensures a low resistance path for discharge of lightning energy. Good systems of protection carry lightning charge through lightning rods and cables from the building to the ground, and dissipate the charge. Ensure that the building is well protected.
15. If any part of a building is hit by lightning, call fire department immediately. Check whether any body is hurt.

16. The immediate cause of death due to lightning in most cases is cardiac arrest. It is important therefore to check whether the victim is still breathing and has a pulse. Act accordingly.
17. Loss of memory, dizziness, fatigue, chronic headache or difficulty in sleeping could be the consequences of any sad lightning experience.

Acknowledgements

The authors are grateful to the Vice Chancellor, VIT University, Vellore and Director, NAM S&T Centre, New Delhi for the opportunity to present this paper. Thanks are due to Dr. R.K.Bhandari, Chairman, Centre for Disaster Mitigation and Management at the VIT University and Dr TVSR Appa Rao, Advisor, CDMM for their valuable guidance.

References

1. Ahmed, M., and Gomes, C., 2007. Lightning Safety Awareness Programme Especially in South Asia to Minimize Loss of Human Lives and Properties. Presented in the International Roundtable: Lessons from Natural Disasters-Policy Issues and Mitigation Strategies, held at VIT University during 8 to12 January.
2. Bhagavanulu, D. V. S., 2007. Lessons from Flood Disasters in India–An Overview. Presented in the International Roundtable: Lessons from Natural Disasters-Policy Issues and Mitigation Strategies, held at VIT University during 8 January to 12 January.
3. Bhandari, R. K., 2006. Disaster Management in India: A New Awakening. Disaster and Development, Vol.1, pages 1-26.
4. Gomes, C., Kithil, R., and Ahmed, M. Developing a Lightning Awareness program model for Third world based on American-South Asian experience.
5. High Powered Committee on Disaster Management, India, Report.
6. http://www.lightningsafety.com/nlsi_pls/American_model_for_ asia.pdf.
7. Indian Standard: IS 2309: 1989; Protection of Buildings and Allied Structures against Lightning-Code of Practice (Reaffirmed in 2005)
8. Murali Das, S., Sampath, S., and Mohankumar, G., 2007. Lightning Hazard in Kerala. J. Mar. Atmos. Res. Vol. 3, No. 1, Jan., 111-117.
9. Sreejith, P. G., 2003. Lightning and Surges: Myths and Facts. Monthly E-Newsletter to 'Manage your risks profitably' from Cholamdandalam M S Risk services Limited, Risk Note 1, April.

Chapter 12

Human Safety Against Lightning

Chandima Gomes

University of Colombo, Sri Lanka

E-mail: gomes@phys.cmb.ac.lk, gacgomes@yahoo.com

ABSTRACT

In this paper we discuss the mechanisms through which lightning may affect human beings, the health hazards that may caused by the exposure to lightning currents, and the safety and protection measures that should be taken against the deleterious effects of lightning. We also emphasize the importance of educating the general public and community workers in the safety and protection against lightning.

Keywords: *Natural hazards, Injuries, Lightning, Lightning protection, Human safety, awareness, Health hazards, Step potential, Thunderstorm, Touch potential.*

Introduction

Lightning is a natural hazard that causes serious economical losses and personal injuries and deaths in many parts of the world. Most importantly lightning cause human casualties. When lightning strikes a human being he may be killed, badly injured or saved with few skin burns and long standing psychological trauma. Lightning ignites fires that may bring an entire building or a house down to ashes, thus causing economical losses as well as hazards to human beings through secondary effects (exposure to fire, explosions, falling material etc.). At a lower degree of damage, the lightning current may destroy electrical, electronic and communication equipment. This may also cause human causalities indirectly, especially if the damaged equipment and devices are used for vital medical applications. Many of these damage and losses could be minimized by educating the engineering and general public in lightning protection and safety awareness.

In the world over 20,000 people are affected by lightning and succumbed to their injuries every year (Kithil, 2007). The number of people who survive with life-time injuries, temporary disabilities and psychological trauma may be several times more than that. In the South Asian region the lightning caused deaths and injuries are much larger than it has been estimated before (Gomes *et al.*, 2006a). The objective of this paper is to provide public awareness in the essential facts of human safety against lightning. Therefore the paper has been documented with information presented in an easy-to-understand format.

Effects on Human Beings

Lightning may injure or kill human beings and animals, basically in five primary ways:

1. Direct strikes: The entire lightning current may pass through or over the body as a result of the lightning being attracted by the body (*e.g.* A person in an open field may be the subject of a direct lightning strike).
2. Side flashes: The entire lightning current or a part of the lightning current may pass through the human body due to the transfer of flash from a lightning struck object to a body in proximity. (*e.g.* A person underneath a large tree or inside a tent on wooden pole may be subjected to a side flash if the tree or the tent is hit by lightning)
3. Step potential: A partial current may pass through the body if two parts of the body on the ground fall in the direction of the potential gradient developed due to nearby lightning strike current injection into the ground. (*e.g.* two feet of a person separated in the direction of increasing potential)
4. Touch potential: A partial current may pass through the body if part of a body comes in contact with a higher elevation of the lightning struck object while the other part remains in contact with ground. (*e.g.* a person touching a flag pole by hand while standing on ground)
5. Proximity to the strike: The shock wave generated by the lightning current leader due to sudden expansion of air may damage the skin or ear drums when a person is very close to the point where lightning strikes.

There are several secondary effects, such as falling from higher elevations due to the momentary shock, falling of heavy materials from structures (detached due to lightning strike) on the person, burns due to volatile materials in the surrounding catching fire, psychological trauma etc.

The passage of current inside the body may lead the person into ventricular fibrillation (unsynchronized muscle operation of the heart), respiratory arrest (inability to breath), burning of vital organs such as brain, liver, kidneys etc and internal bleeding due to bursting of blood vessels. The person may also suffer from nervous system damage, broken bones and loss of hearing or eyesight. Lightning injuries can lead to permanent disabilities or death. On an average, 20 per cent of strike victims die and 70 per cent of survivors suffer life-long from severe injury and disability (Brown and Gaasch, 1992). These injuries are primarily neurological, with a wide range of symptoms, and are sometimes difficult to cure.

A person struck by lightning does not carry any current or charge, hence he should be attended immediately and given first aid. Almost 90 per cent of the lightning related deaths due to primary causes could have been avoided if the deceased had been attended within a short time period (Andrews *et al.*, 1996).

The vast majority of lightning casualties can be easily, quickly and cheaply avoided if the proper measures are followed. People need increased awareness of the lightning hazard and knowledge of lightning safety.

Sheltering Under Thunderstorm Conditions

It should be noted that for a random atmospheric phenomenon such as lightning, no place is 100 per cent safe, however, some places are safer than others.

One of the safest locations during a thunderstorm is inside a sturdy metallic enclosure such as an abandoned cargo container, a car or a train. In the absence of such enclosures, one may seek shelter in a large, enclosed and substantially constructed building, preferably with steel reinforcement (concrete slabs and pillars reinforced with steel), plumbing and electrical wiring. Such structures are shopping malls, cinema halls, schools, office buildings, and private residences made with brick, concrete etc. If lightning strikes the building, the steel bars, plumbing and wiring will conduct the electricity more efficiently than a human body. If no such buildings are available, then an enclosed metal vehicle such as a car, van or bus makes a good alternative. However, convertible vehicles offer no safety from lightning, even if the top is covered with the foldable cover. Other unsafe vehicles during lightning storms are those which have exposed parts such as open cabs, golf carts, tractors, trailers, three wheelers, motorcycles, agricultural vehicles, construction equipment and open boats.

Any structure made of flimsy non-metallic materials or having large exposed areas is not safe during a thunderstorm. These include beach shacks, thatched huts, picnic shelters and camp tents, sports pavilions, carports, rooftop terraces, houses made of wood, paper pulp etc. It should also be noted that structures with metal roofs are very much likely to attract lightning. If the roof is fixed on a structure which is not properly earthed, the occupants will be at a great risk of getting side flashes. One should never sleep on floor, especially inside a risky building, when thunder is roaring around.

Once inside a sturdy building, one should stay away from electrical appliances and plumbing fixtures. Once lightning strikes a structure, the current is most likely to flow along metal parts such as railings, fences etc. Therefore, touching or staying very close to such parts should be avoided. As an added safety measure, the person should stay in an interior room, preferably sitting on a chair or a bed. Lightning can travel great distances through power lines, especially in rural areas. When the lightning is striking around, electrical appliances, especially corded telephones and wired microphones should not be used unless it is an emergency. However, there is no additional lightning threat of using mobile phones, codeless phones or FM microphones. Nevertheless, it should be noted that the person who handles the electronics of the public addressing system is at a risk of getting a shock if the system is connected to the electricity service. If the trip switch gets off under thunderstorm condition it should be kept at off-position until the storm is over.

Working on computers is also dangerous if they are connected to phone and electrical cords. The repairing of electrical system, telephone system or leakage in the roof during thunderstorm periods should strictly be avoided. One should also not take a shower or bath or use a hot tub during an intense thunderstorm.

Inside a vehicle, one should roll the windows up, and avoid contact with any conducting paths leading to the outside or connected to the body of the vehicle (*e.g.* radios, body-fixed telephones and key in the keyhole etc.). One should also avoid leaning against vehicles and should get off bicycles and motorcycles.

Outdoor Safety Measures

Under thunderstorm conditions people should not stay at open areas such as playgrounds, outdoor recreational areas, paddy fields and other agricultural fields, beaches, river banks, open roads etc. One should also avoid higher elevations such as mountain tops, roof tops etc. Hiking is obviously an activity to be avoided. One of the most important rules of outdoor lightning safety is to avoid seeking shelter under large trees during thunderstorm periods. Once a tree is subjected to a lightning strike the large current that flowing along the tree trunk may jump to the bodies of the people who gather around the tree. One should also avoid taking bath in open pools, streams, rivers, lakes etc, under thunderstorm conditions. A person may be drowned to death if he falls unconscious in an unattended environment while he is taking a bath or swim in a pool (even if the water is only a couple of feet high). Therefore one better avoid being even in an indoor pool, especially when you are alone.

In many countries such as USA the lightning safety plans essentially include the 30/30 Rule. The 30/30 Rule states that people should seek shelter if the "Flash-To-Bang" time delay (length of time in seconds between the vision of the lightning flash and the subsequent hearing of thunder) is 30 seconds or less and that they remain under cover until 30 minutes after the final sound of thunder. A 30 second lead-time is necessary prior to a storm's arrival because of the possibility of distant strikes. A 30-minute wait, after the last thunder is heard, is necessary because the trailing storm clouds carry a lingering charge. This charge can and does occasionally produce lightning on the back edge of a storm, several minutes after the rain has ended.

Several studies have revealed that most people struck by lightning are struck not at the height of a thunderstorm but before and after the storm peak (Gaber *et al.*, 1996; Holle *et al.*, 1995, John *et al.*, 2006). This can be scientifically explained as in many cumulonimbus clouds that produce lightning, the anvil of the cloud from which lightning can be emanated, is several tens of kilometers shifted from the rain base. This shows that many people are unaware of how far lightning can strike from its parent thunderstorm. Therefore, one should not wait for the rain to start seeking shelter and should not leave shelter just because the rain has ended.

Figure 12.1: Safety Position in the Event of a Severe Thunderstorm (if you are caught outdoor). For the purpose of convenience. Wear boots or rubber slippers if it is possible.

Safety Position

If one can not go elsewhere and compelled to stay outdoors in a severe thunderstorm (as he may be far away from a proper shelter), he should move to the safest location available (away from open fields, higher elevations, water etc.) and adopt the safety position described below.

The person should crouch down, put the feet together and place hands over ears to minimize hearing damage from thunder and duck the head as much as possible (refer Figure 12.1). Each person in a group, in safety position, should at least be 3 m away from one another. A minimum of 30 minutes should be elapsed from the last observed lightning or thunder before resuming normal activities.

In the event of very close thunder activities, one should not use earphones and headsets. All removable metallic parts on the body such as backpacks, caps with metal tips, wrist watches, metallic badges etc and any metallic item such as golf clubs, fishing rods, agricultural tools, tennis rackets, umbrella etc should be removed or dropped aside. The reason of dropping such metal objects is to avoid getting side flashes and also to prevent heat being trapped into a single point in the event of a lightning strike to an unfortunate person. It is useful to wear shoes or slippers made of insulation material (such as rubber, clothes, leather, plastic, etc.), as that will avoid the person being subjected to step potential. Studies that have been done in Bangladesh reveal that step potential may lead to the death of people more often than one would think.

If lightning is imminent, it sometimes gives a few seconds of warning. These warnings include, hair standing-up on end, tingling of skin, vibration of light metal objects and hearing of a crackling sound. If this happens and if the person is alone, he should just drop down in a crouching position. If it is a group, people should quickly spread out so that there are several body lengths between each person before dropping down to the crouching position. Then if one unlucky person is struck, the others are protected and can provide first aid to the victim.

Lightning Safety Awareness

Several of the states in India and other countries in South Asia (Sri Lanka, Bangladesh, Bhutan, Maldives, Nepal Northern parts of Pakistan are subjected to lightning hazards. The situation is even worse in several central African, far east Asian and South American countries. Therefore proper dissemination of knowledge on lightning protection and safety measures is essential to curb the death toll and other hazards to the human beings and live stock. Although a notable effort is made by the scientific community during the last several years to educate the public in the prevention of lightning hazards, still the number of deaths and injuries in these countries due to lightning is undesirably high. According to the National Crime Record Bureau, India 1507 persons died in India during 2001 because of lightning, which is about 1 per cent of the natural and unnatural accidental deaths in the country. In Orissa (a state in Eastern India) alone, about 300 persons were struck by lightning and subsequently died in 2004. The educators and community workers in developing countries are at a distinct disadvantage as they do not get opportunities to access up-to-date knowledge or training in lightning safety measures (*Gomes et al.*, 2006b). Web based lightning safety guidance and training which has shown fruitful results in developed countries such as USA and Canada, the same is not a very successful technique of educating public in the third world at present (*Gomes et al.*, 2006b). Therefore it is proposed to establish lightning awareness centres in each developing country. The lightning awareness centre in each country should develop modalities to take the message of lightning safety to the public. In different regions these modalities may be different. For examples awareness programs conducted for children at secondary school level were very successful in Sri Lanka while folk songs and street dramas on lightning safety became a very powerful awareness promotion tool in Bangladesh.

References

1. Andrews, G., Berger, N., Floret, T., Ishikawa, N., Kitagawa, and Ohashi, M., 1996. International safety and rescue guide against lightning hazards, Proceedings of the 23rd International Conference on Lightning Protection, September 23-27, Florence, Italy, 738-743.
2. Browne B. J., Gaasch, W. R., 1992. Electrical Injuries and Lightning, Emergency Clinics of North America, 10: 211-226.

3. Gomes, C., Kithil, R. and Ahmed, M., 2006. Developing a lightning awareness program model third world based on American experience, Proceedings of the 28th International Conference on Lightning Protection (ICLP), Kanasawa, Japan, September.

4. Gomes, C., Abeysinghe, K. R. and Ahmed, M., 2006. Lightning incidents and awareness in South Asia: Experience in Sri Lanka and Bangladesh, Proceedings of the 28th International Conference on Lightning Protection (ICLP), Kanasawa, Japan, September.

5. Graber J, Ummenhofer, W., Herion, H., 1996. Lightning Accident with Eight Victims: Case Report and Brief Review of Literature, The Journal of Trauma, 40: 288-290.

6. Holle, R. L., Lopez, R. E. and Howard, K. W., 1995. Safety in the Presence of Lightning. Seminars in Neurology, 15: 375-379.

7. John O. S., Connaughton, D. P., Pittman, A.T., 2006. Risk Management in Sport and Recreation, Human Kinetics, Chapter-5: lightning Safety.

8. Kithil, R. Jr., 2007. Personal Communication on Lightning Safety, National Lightning Safety Institution, USA.

Chapter 13

Lightning Protection of Power Network in Mauritius: A Review

Prabhakar Sembhoo
Central Electricity Board,
Curepipe, Mauritius
E-mail: prabhakar.sembhoo@ceb.intnet.mu

ABSTRACT

There is always an utmost necessity for providing power transmission and distribution networks with protection against over voltages. The search for increasingly effective means of protecting very expensive power system equipment and improving system reliability have thus resulted in a great evolution in surge protection technology from a simple spark gap in the early fifties to the gapless metal oxide arrestor.

The aim of this report is therefore to provide an overview of the Lightning Protection Studies conducted by the Central Electricity Board of the Republic Mauritius. It also gives a general view on the various lightning protective measures applied in practice so as to enhance our mitigation capabilities.

Keywords: Lightning stroke, Back flashover, Induced surges, Basic insulation level, Surge arrestors, Shielding and gapless.

Introduction

Lightning is one of the most beautiful phenomenons in nature. Beyond its powerful beauty it is universally known as the major enemy of the power industry because it is the main cause of most disturbances on all electrical installations. These disturbances include major power failures, transient features impacting the quality of the power supply and equipment damages resulting in long interruptions affecting greatly the system reliability.

Ever since the dawn of the electric power industry, utilities have studied lightning with hopes of mitigating its negative effects on the system. Despite considerable improvements in lightning protection technology, it continues to wreak considerable havoc on power transmission and distribution system. That is why it is one of the major concerns for everyone in the power sector.

The study on the effects of lightning comprises two steps as follows:

- To anticipate what could happen in a given installation and come out with recommendations for improvements. This is possible now using dedicated software which can simulate installation reaction.
- Carry out an engineering and cost study on insulation coordination, taking into account the cost of installations, maintenance and loss of revenue resulting from outages.

About the Central Electricity Board

The Central Electricity Board (CEB) is a parastatal body wholly owned by the Government of Mauritius and reporting to the Ministry of Public Utilities. Established in 1952 and empowered by the *Central Electricity Board Act* of 25 January 1964, CEB's business is to "prepare and carry out development schemes with the general objective of promoting, coordinating and improving the generation, transmission, distribution and consumption of electricity" in Mauritius.

In 2006, the total production for the island was 2,091 GWhr of energy. The CEB produced about 51.5 per cent (1,075 GWhr) of the country's requirements with its four thermal power and seven hydroelectric plants, which have a combined installed capacity of 377 MW. The remaining 48.5 per cent of energy requirements was procured from independent power producers. CEB employs approximately 1,700 persons and delivers electricity to nearly 360,000 customers through 7,300 km of distribution network.

Demand for electricity is expected to grow @ 5 per cent annually in the foreseeable future.

Table 13.1: Details of Generation, Transmission and Distribution

	Generation	
1.	Number of CEB Power Stations	3 Diesel, 1 Gas Turbine and 7 Hydro
2.	Number of IPP Stations	Four
3.	Number of IC Engine Units	Nineteen
4.	Number of Gas Turbine Units	Three
5.	Number of Coal/Bagasse Units	Seven Coal/Bagasse and 7 Bagasse only
6.	Number of Hydro Units	Thirteen
7.	Total available capacity	460 MW
8.	Maximum system demand (Historical peak)	347.3 MW
9.	Energy generated (FY 2006)	2,091 GWhr

Contd...

Table 13.1–Contd...

	Transmission	
10.	Transmission voltage	66 kV
11.	Type of system	3 phase, 3 wire, 50 Hz
12.	Length of overhead lines (As on July 2005, includes both Tower Lines and lines on Concrete Poles)	215
13.	Length of underground cable (As on July 2005, mostly XLPE with some Oil Filled)	14
14.	Approximate number of segments *i.e.* point-to-point feeders in Transmission network	61
15.	Number of Major Sub-stations	28
16.	Typical configuration of Major Sub-station	Single split bus with multiple Power Transformers
17.	Number of Power Transformers	101 incl Sugar Estates
18.	Total Power Transformer installed capacity	1,858,000
19.	Typical characteristics of Power Transformers	OF, YY, 66/22 kV and 22/6.6 kV, LV Neutral earthed through resistor/reactor, OLTC on HV
20.	Number of energy import points (import from both IPPs and Own Generation)	31
	Primary Distribution	
21.	Primary Distribution voltage	Usually 22 kV with some 6.6 kV
22.	Type of system	3 phase, 3 wire, 50 Hz
23.	Length of overhead lines (As on July 2005, mostly on Wood or Concrete Poles)	2270
24.	Length of underground cable (As on July 2005, mostly XLPE with some PILC)	220
25.	Approximate number of primary distribution point-to-point feeders	150
26.	Number of Distribution Sub-stations	24
27.	Typical configuration of Distribution Sub-station	Mostly pole mounted, some ground level indoors/outdoors, HRC fuse on HV and LV
28.	Number of Distribution Transformers	4350
29.	Total Distribution Transformer installed capacity	963000 kava
30.	Typical characteristics of Distribution Transformers	ON, DY11, 22/0.4 kV, LV 3 phase, 4 wire, Neutral earthed, Fixed tap

CEB Lightning Protection Study

In the mid 1990, the Central Electricity Board of Mauritius experienced many lightning-caused outages. In many areas of the island, lightning was a major source of power failures, sub-station switchgear damages, nuisance of fuse operations, damaged cable terminations, faults in distribution transformers and overhead line equipment failures. Furthermore, the issue of power quality was gathering momentum and this led to increased emphasis to reduce lightning-caused momentary outages and every effort was geared towards improvement of system design to reduce the vulnerability to lightning. A crucial part of the efforts to tackle these problems was better understanding of the phenomenon of lightning.

In the late nineties, the Central Electricity Board of Mauritius called for the services of the consulting firm TAP (Trans-Africa Projects Limited) to carry out studies on Lightning Protection of its system which was conducted in two phases. The first phase of this study dealt essentially with the evaluation of the need while the second phase mainly involved with investigation of the lightning protection schemes carried out on digital simulation.

Insulation Coordination and Lightning

Insulation coordination is the design of appropriate electric withstands strengths of equipment with respect to the over-voltage stresses that appear in the system. It takes into account the ability of available protective devices to reduce the probability of voltage stresses, which may damage the equipment or withstand to continue the power supply.

Lightning generated over voltages are developed by three ways:

- Back flashovers resulting from direct strikes on the tower ground wires
- Direct strikes on the phase conductors
- Induced surges resulting from nearby strikes to ground.

There are a number of factors that affect the frequency of lightning strike on overhead power lines. These include:

- Overall level of lightning activity for the area
- Physical dimensions of the line, particularly tower height
- Presence of naturally shielding objects, such as tall trees or buildings in the vicinity of the line.

Lightning Protection Study: Phase 1

In this phase of the study all major sub-stations were visited for the generic audit of the present lightning protection schemes. It deals mainly with the following:

- An audit of the existing lightning protection schemes
- An evaluation of present practice followed a major 66 kV sub-stations for shielding against direct lightning strike.

In its report TAP outlines the methodology followed in this study and discusses the effectiveness of the present shielding arrangements, with recommendations where necessary, as well as the findings of the lightning protection audit.

Figure 13.1: Map of Mauritius Showing the Transmission Lines and Power Plants

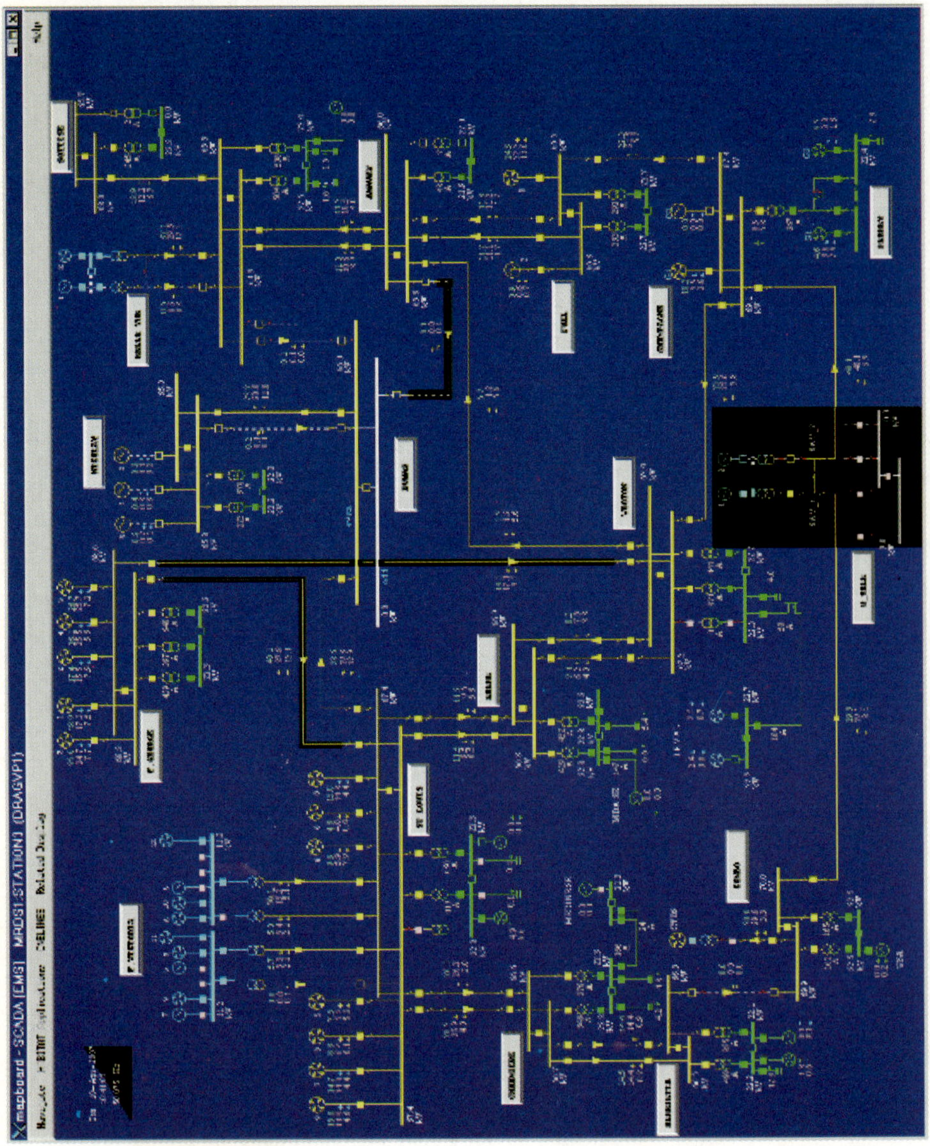

Figure 13.2: Schematic Diagram of the National Grid

Lightning Performance of Substations and Methodology of Protection

Over voltage stresses caused by lightning normally come to the substation via the overhead lines. Such overvoltages may cause flashover and serious damage to equipment and thereby jeopardize the supply of power to customers. It is essential to prevent this by proper co-ordination of protective devices with the equipment insulation strength.

Installation of surge arrestor at the entrance of a feeder at the sub-station offers the first line of protection to equipment such as voltage transformers, current transformers, breakers and the general busbar arrangement. Due to the multiple reflections of the travelling waves that take place under the various substation operating configurations, additional surge arrestors should be used to protect power transformers due to their strategic importance and cost.

If the overhead shielding of the substation is not optimal, direct strikes to the substation area could result in flashovers on the substation equipment. The voltage rise, determined by the stroke current and the surge impedance of the phase conductor, occurs and it could cause an insulation failure. Proper location of overhead shield wires or masts ensures a low shielding failure rate by intercepting the strokes and diverting them to ground.

Within this framework of evaluation this phase of the study report deals only with the impact of lightning on high voltage equipment excluding the electromagnetic interference on secondary systems.

It is required that surge arrestors be installed as close as possible to the equipment they are to protect. Due to the travelling wave nature of the impinging surge the protected equipment experiences a higher voltage than the arrestor residual voltage because of the reflection occurring at the equipment terminal of the incoming voltage

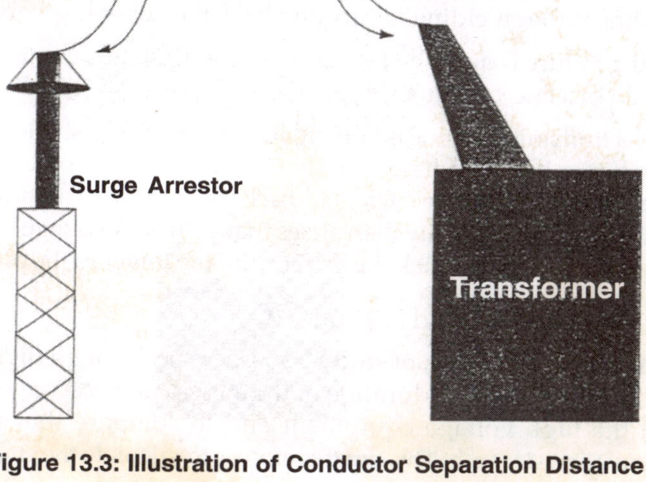

Figure 13.3: Illustration of Conductor Separation Distance

wave. Consequently the arrestor has a limited protective range within which the equipment is protected.

In its study, TAP used the following equation as a simplified approach to calculate the maximum allowable conductor separation distance.

$$L_{max} = \frac{v\left\{\frac{BIL}{1+M_p} - U_{res}\right\}}{2 \times S} (H_{arrestor} + H_{structure})$$

where:

Lmax: maximum allowable conductor separation distance (m)

$H_{arrestor}$: Height of arrestor (m)

$H_{structure}$: Height of structure (m)

v: velocity of wave propagation (m/µs)::::: 300 m/µs for overhead lines and 150 m/µs for cables

BIL: Basic Insulation Level of equipment to be protected (kV)

M_p: Protective margin required: Minimum IEC recommendation = 20 per cent

U_{res}: Residual voltage of the arrestor (kV)

S: Steepness of incoming wave (kV/µs)::::: 2000 kV/µs

Extracts from TAP report pertaining to the assessment made for various and Saint Louis major sub-stations.

Lightning Performance of Transmission Lines

The primary effect of lightning discharges on power lines is the introduction of transient overvoltages on the system. Depending upon the line insulation withstand characteristics, this may or may not lead to an equipment failure and hence the outage. The two common ways whereby lightning discharge interact with transmission line is the shielding failure and back flashover mechanism.

A shielding failure is described when a ground flash terminates directly on the phase conductor of a line, even in the presence of an overhead shielding ground wire.

Provided a transmission line is sufficiently and properly shielded, the majority of ground flashes in its immediate vicinity should terminate on the shield wire or supporting towers. As the stroke current is discharged to the earth through the tower footing impedance, the possibility then arises that sufficient voltage may build up on the tower crossarm to cause a back flashover from the tower to the phase conductor.

Lightning Protection Study: Phase 2

The emphasis of this phase of study is to ascertain through digital simulation, the magnitude, waveform and duration of the anticipated voltage stress caused by lightning on the high voltage equipment and to compare this stress with the equipment insulation strength. The aim therefore is to calculate the stresses developed in the substation and especially at the connected Power Transformer due to lightning backlash over and shielding failure events on the connected transmission lines.

Of main interest are the stresses at the transformers because steep fronted wave impulses create an extremely non-linear voltage distribution along the high voltage windings.

The following part of this report outlines the methodology followed in the study and discusses the effectiveness of the present surge arrestor protections with recommendations where necessary.

Methodology and Model

The aim of this phase of the study is to study with the help of an Electromagnetic Transient Programme (EMTP) the magnitude and wave shape of impinging lightning surge derived from a backflash over the 66 kV transmission lines and its effect on the connected substation.

As a sample study, Wooton 66 kV substation was used. A particular severe contingency was considered consisting of only the Rose-Hill double circuit incoming lines. These lines were connected to the two busbars with the bus-coupler breaker in closed position. One of the busbar was connected to a 20 MVA transformer and the other open ended busbar, due to be connected to transformer number 2 through breaker.

A schematic representation of the complete three-phase double circuit line and substation model as used in the study is shown in Figure 13.4.

The method employed requires the representation of the main system by a computer model, which could be tested using the simulation for the most severe

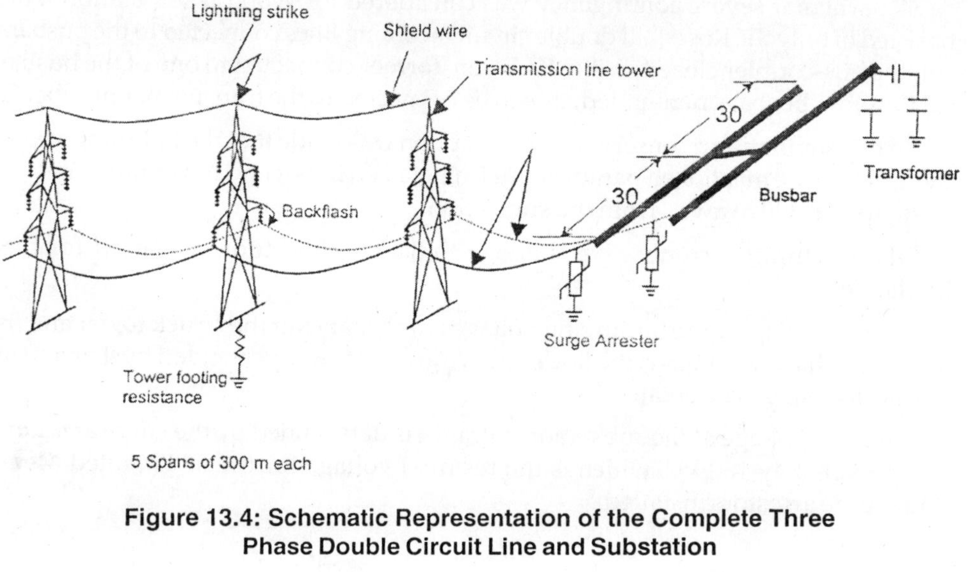

Figure 13.4: Schematic Representation of the Complete Three Phase Double Circuit Line and Substation

lightning event the station could experience within its lifetime. The simulation follows the outline given in CIGRE technical brochure 63 "*Guide to procedures for estimating the lightning performance of transmission lines*".

Measured lightning current surges display a concave wave front with an exponential decaying tail. In this study the injected lightning surge simulates these characteristics. The correlation between amplitude, front time and steepness are derived from the log-normal distributions as given in Electra No 69.

As described the lightning current injected into the shield wire results in a voltage developing across the insulator strings that may lead to a flashover. This breakdown process is simulated using a leader progression model that is accepted to best represent this process.

Metal oxide arrestors and other equipment were modelled using the voltage-current characteristics and component values typical of 66 kV equipment respectively.

Results

Two amplitude values for the lightning stroke current were selected; with their associated steepness and front time derived from the log-normal distributions as given in Electra No 69.

Amplitude kA	*Probability of Exceeding Amplitude %*	*Maximum Steepness kA/μs*	*Front Time μs*
30	52	25.32	2.31
100	4.5	49.1	4.8

Case Study 1-A

A particular severe contingency was considered for Wooton sub-station. This consisted of only the Rose-Hill double circuit incoming lines connected to the busbars with the bus-coupler closed. A 20 MVA transformer connected to one of the busbar and the other busbar open-ended, due to be connected to the transformer number 2.

In this simulation a conservative assumption was made that the lightning stroke having the above mentioned parameters terminated on the second tower from Wooton substation *i.e.* 300 m away from the substation.

The lightning current wave shape with 30 kA amplitude was used for this simulation.

From the display the impinging voltage wave shapes at the struck tower and its associated phase conductor, the line entrance arrestor, the open ended busbar and at the transformer can be obtained.

The overvoltage at the substation entrance is determined by the surge arrestors to approximately 160 kV, which is the residual voltage for the 60 kV rated Metal Oxide surge arrestors installed.

In another display the multiple reflections at the open ended busbars, due to the open transformer and two breakers can be seen. The high frequency transient overvoltage is the stress that is being applied across the phase to earth insulation of the open circuit breaker.

Case Study 1-B

This is an identical case as 1-A regarding the lightning stroke current, the stroke position and the substation configuration. However, in this case an additional set of lightning arrestors are placed close to the power transformer.

The simulation results showed that this provides much better improvement in the overvoltage control for the transformer.

Due to the substantial reduction in the voltage stress and the difficulty in assessing the Lightning Impulse withstand limits for the insulation in aged transformers, TAP has recommended replacing all arcing horns on power transformers by Metal Oxide gapless technology arrestors.

Summary of Recommendations

- Remove all spark gaps on transmission lines.
- Replace arcing horns by MO arrestors on power transformers.
- Get rid of the old technology surge arrestors.
- To increase the substation failure rate periods due to lightning discharges to an acceptable level it was recommended to erect lightning masts.
- In order to reduce the outages on transmission lines due to back flashovers, ensure that the tower footing resistance is kept lesser than 25 ohms.

Other Areas of Consideration

For the lightning mitigation programme to be effective, the utility must take additional measures beyond installing lightning arrestors. The Central Electricity Board has identified the following guidelines to make our programme more effective and consistent.

- Maintenance: Replaced all damaged or aged arrestors in a timely manner. At times failed arrestors have gone unnoticed and replacements have been delayed. It is to be noted that the integrity of the system is compromised for each arrestor not in service.
- Grounding: Earthing resistance measurement of substations and Transmission towers to be conducted regularly. Install ground rods as needed when the new arrestors are installed. If this step is overlooked or not considered, arrestor performance is likely to be much not effective.
- Replacement of all non-linear resistor type surge arrestors by metal oxide units.
- With the purchase of the 'Leakage Current Monitor Equipment', we have embarked on a predictive maintenance programme. The measurement of the resistive component of the continuous leakage current provides us the

most accurate techniques for the condition monitoring of our ZnO arrestors in service.

General Conclusion

As we are all aware, lightning phenomenon is a very complex issue and the scientific/engineering community is more aware of the problems caused to the power system performance. Hence a study for better lightning protection of the equipment is an ongoing process.

This conference will serve as an opportunity to all of us to keep abreast of the recent trends in this domain.

References

1. Britten, A.C., 1992. Insulation co-ordination of power lines. Chapter 8 of courses on Lightning Protection organised by Eskom.
2. Merwe, W.C. Van Der, 1992. Insulation co-ordination of terminal equipment Chapter 4 of courses on Lightning Protection organised by Eskom.
3. Merwe, W.C.Van Der, 2001. Lightning Protection Investigation for Central Electricity Board–Mauritius .
4. Metz-Noblat, Benoit de. Cahiers techniques from Merlin Gerin. Lightning and electrical installations.

Chapter 14

Suppression of the Lightning Activity by the Anti Hail Rockets Fired into Thunder Cloud

Mladjen Ćurić
Institute of Meteorology,
University of Belgrade, Serbia
E-mail: curic@ff.bg.ac.yu

ABSTRACT

The objective of this paper is to review activity in Serbia that lead to lightning reduction. The review is focused on the organization of monitoring of thundercloud in Serbia. A radar network in so called hail suppression polygons is described. The rocket firing station network and rockets characteristics as a delivering system as seeding agents into target areas of thundercloud are also discussed. Special attention is devoted to the statistical estimation of the changes in the lightning activity in Serbia based on data at meteorological stations having professional observers. Two separate series of data are considered, the seeded and the unseeded periods. Two methodologies were applied for the selection of this series. The ratio of the average lightning frequency during the seeding activities in the area of the station and the average frequency before these activities are considered. The ratio for both methodologies shows a significant reduction in the lightning activity, even up to 50 per cent.

Introduction

Agricultural crop protection from hail is being carried out in Serbia for more than four decades. Cloud rocket seeding technology has been gradually improved and became the most effective among others methodologies (Ćurić, 1990; Radinović, 1972). Hail suppression system covers about six million hectares of agricultural surface. This is one of the largest areas in the world protected by such a system.

Although this hail suppression project is considered operational, many of the activities are still under investigation.

The basis for artificial modification of hail clouds was established in 1935 and 1938 when Tor Bergeron and Watter Findeisen advanced a theory of rain based on the coexistence of ice crystals and supercooled droplets in the Cb cloud and the rapid transfer of vapour from droplets to the crystals (Bergeron, 1935). At about this time a thriving business in cloud seeding started. Research groups in cloud physics were established in different countries. Commercial cloud seeding was also initiated in these countries (Bojkov, 2003).

Organization of Rocket Firing into Thundercloud in Serbia

The operational nonrandomized hail suppression project in Serbia is being carried out by the Meteorological Service since 1967. All protected areas are organized in so called hail suppression polygons (Figure 14.1). Each polygon has a radius of approximately 30 km. This program is designed to operate all 24 hours a day during the summer months (15th April to 15th October). All thunderstorms (hailstorms) drifting over the polygon are monitored by S band (10 cm wave length) radar located at the centre of the polygon (Figure 14.2). The radars are conventional, Doppler and polarized. Their technical characteristics are as follows: transmitting power 600 kW,

Figure 14.1: The Network of Radar Centres in Serbia

Figure 14.2: Meteorological Radar on Samosh Polygon

pulse length 1/2μs, wavelength 10 cm, beam width 1.1°, antenna gain 42.3 dB and antenna reflector 6.1 m.

When a monitored thundercloud development meets specific criteria based on radar reflectivity, the level of the significant temperatures and the ratio of the depths of cold and warm parts of cloud, the clouds are seeded with glaciogenic seeding agents (silver iodide particles). The seeding agents are delivered into target area of the thundercloud by rockets fired from the ground based network of firing stations separated by about 5 km (Figure 14.3).

The firing stations are manned by the trained volunteers. The responsibilities of the observer, apart from firing the rockets, are to observe and report days with lightning, thunder, hail and others precipitation type (ranged in nine classes). Such dense network of the firing stations has special mesometeorological network.

With the help of a large number of ground measurements and observations, standard meteorological and radar data have been collected so far. The other data, such as the number and type of rockets fired into each cloud are also collected. All such information is available in the annual reports, "The Hailstorm Data Series".

The rockets are fired from the ground based rocket launcher (Figure 14.4). Each launch site needs at least one arsenal for storing the rockets. It is notable that personnel requirements are very intensive as there must be trained staff whenever storms are forecast.

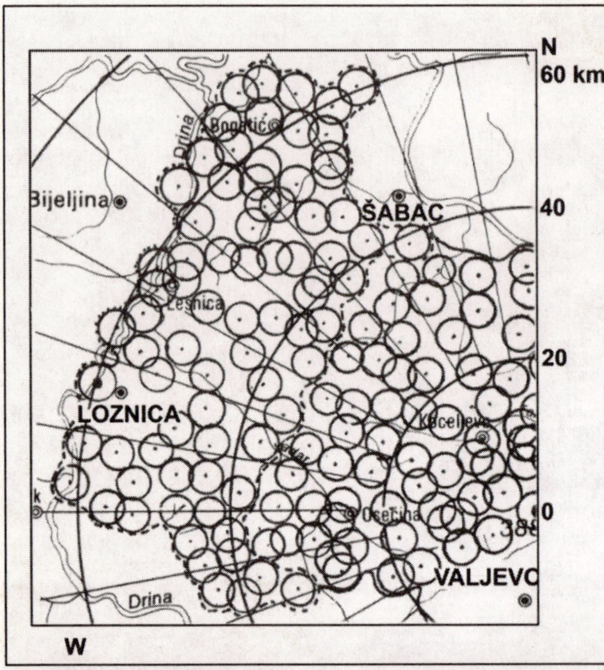

Figure 14.3: The Network of Ground Based Rocket Stations for Polygon Valjevo

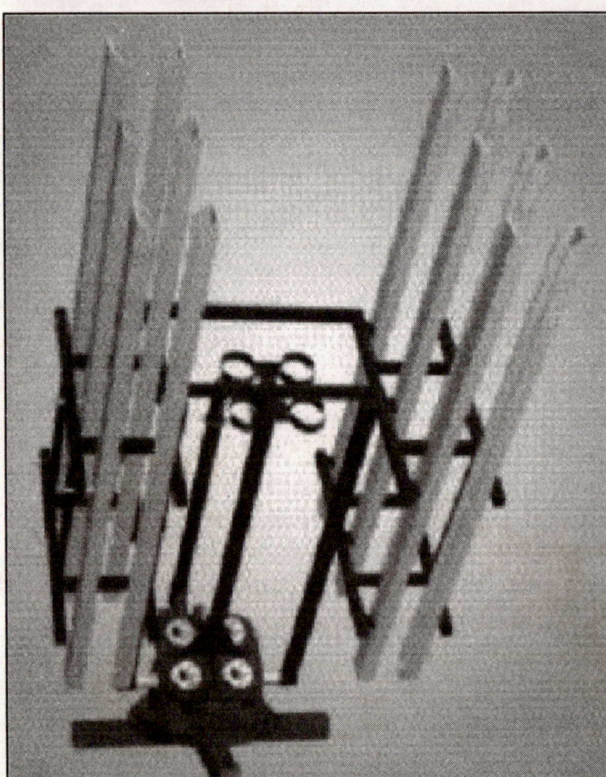

Figure 14.4: The Ground Based Rocket Launcher

The rockets in use are designed to release a plume of nucleating material along a trajectory in thundercloud (Figures 14.5 and 14.6). Launching crew receives details about the necessary elevation and azimuth angles from the radar operators. The targeting may be automated by telemetry of aiming and firing instructions to the launcher. The greatest advantage of the rocket system is its ability to reach any region of the thundercloud in a very short time. Rockets reach the seeding zone in several seconds and the entire trajectory is completed in less than one minute. This permits an almost immediate response to a hail threat.

Evaluation of Lightning Suppression by Rocket System

Although no planned project of the diversion of lightning is conducted so far in Serbia, the seeding of thunderclouds for hail suppression actually lead to the diversion of lightning. This diversion provided protection from lightning over large area for an extended period of time. Obviously, it is more efficient than lightning protection system for individual sites ranging from cow barns to missile silos, front shelters to high- rise building systems. Lightning can strike anywhere on the earth (Figure 14.7). Lightning is responsible for more outdoor deaths and property loss than many other

Figure 14.5: The Hail Rocket

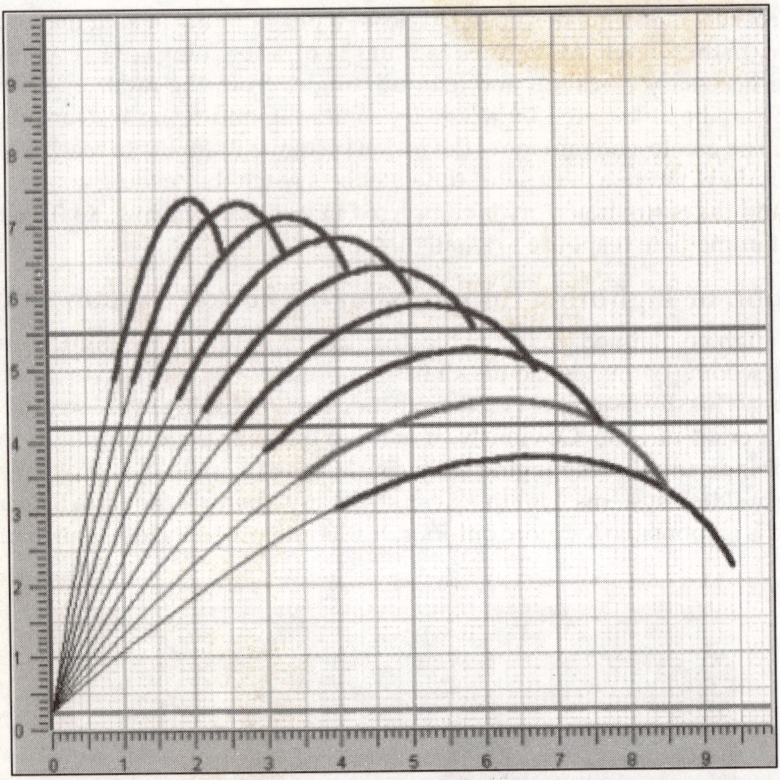

Figure 14.6: The Trajectories of Rocket Depending on the Launching Elevation Angles

Figure 14.7: Lightning Strokes Travelling Along Branched Paths from Cloud-base to Ground over Belgrade in May 1999. Some branches apparently terminate in the air without reaching the ground.

violent forces of the nature. Due to this reason the areal protection is much more efficient than the only protection of individual objects.

There are two major reasons for the reduction of lightning activity while conducting the hail suppression project. The seeding of thundercloud with silver iodide produces an excess of ice crystals, which cause numerous corona discharges within thunderstorm and reduce the need for the flash to reach the ground. The theory predicts that lightning can be triggered even with a small and inexpensive rocket fired into a thundercloud. The anti-hail rockets with a length of about 1m and 10 cm in diameter (*see* Figure 14.5) fired from ground reach a peak height up to 8 km. On the way, the rockets pass through the lower negative and upper positive poles of a cloud in a very short time. Each of them triggers lightning discharges in small area and certain time period. Ten to hundred such rockets are fired in every hailstorm. Since the beginning of hail suppression project in Serbia, until now, about 400,000 rockets are fired.

In order to show that the rocket firing reduces the lightning we have considered the observed data of lightning and first precipitation at the site Loznica a first order meteorological station (*see* Figure 14.3). In the hail suppression project the rockets are fired before the first precipitation on the ground. If we show that the lightning precedes the precipitation we would be able to show that rockets trigger lightning before its natural occurrence.

Table 14.1: Absolute Frequencies of Rain Shower Occurrences Per Time Intervals (in min.) and Years. The first number refers to the frequency when the shower occurred after and the second one before the discharge.

Year	*Time Int. (Min.)*												
	0-1	*1-2*	*2-3*	*3-4*	*4-5*	*5-6*	*6-7*	*7-8*	*8-9*	*9-10*	*10-15*	*15-20*	*>20*
1951	4/0		1/0		1/1		2/0	1/0		3/0	1/1	1/0	1/0
52	2/1	3/3	0/1	1/0	3/0			1/0	1/0	0/1	4/0		2/0
53	6/0	0/1	1/0	1/0	4/2		1/0	1/0		3/0	4/0	4/0	
54	7/0		2/0	2/0	5/1		1/0	1/0		4/0	6/0	3/0	1/1
55	2/0		0/1		4/1	1/0				4/0	1/0	2/0	1/0
56	5/1	1/1	1/0	1/0	5/0	2/0	1/0	3/0	2/0	4/0	1/0	2/0	1/0
57	4/0		5/1	0/2	6/3		1/0	1/1	2/0	2/0	5/2	3/0	
58	4/0	1/0			2/0	2/0					4/0	1/0	1/0
59	1/0	1/0	1/0		2/1					1/0	2/0	0/1	1/0
1960	3/0	3/0	2/0		3/1		2/0	1/0		2/0	2/0	1/0	1/0
61	3/0	2/1			5/1		1/1			2/0	1/0	1/0	1/1
62	2/0				4/0		1/0	0/1				2/0	3/0
63			2/0		1/0		0/1			3/1	1/0	2/0	1/0
64		2/0			4/0					0/1	1/0	1/0	1/0
1965					1/1	1/0					1/0		
Σ	43/2	13/6	15/3	5/2	50/12	6/0	10/2	9/2	5/0	28/3	34/3	23/1	15/2

The first occurrence of rain is observed by professional observers and simultaneously rain is recorded in a continuous manner. Time delay for the first precipitation after the lightning is measured by an observer with the help of a stopwatch. Absolute frequencies of precipitation occurrences per year are shown in Table 14.1. The time delay is considered in multiple of 1-minute intervals (Curić and Vukovic, 2005; Vukovic and Curić, 2005).

Analysis of data shows that in about 90 per cent of the cases the lightning preceded the first precipitation and only in 10 per cent of the cases the first precipitation occurred before the lightning. It can also be seen that in more than 50 per cent of the cases the first precipitation occurred within the interval of 5 minutes after the discharge.

Results and Conclusions

Special attention is paid to the statistical estimation of the changes in the lightning frequency in Serbia based on data at meteorological stations having professional observers. Two separate series of data are considered, the seeded and the unseeded period. The first year for which lightning frequency data is taken was in 1951. We have considered 15 year long period before the beginning of hail suppression project. The equally long seeded period has been taken from 1975-1984.

The ratio of the average lightning frequency during the seeding activities in the area covered by the station and the average frequency before these activities shows a reduction in the lightning activity by about 40 per cent.

In our analysis we have used a special methodology for selecting the same number of days from seeded and unseeded period, which have the same natural potential for lightning. The ratio of the lightning frequency in this case is greater than earlier. The lightning reduction is up to 50 per cent.

This preliminary statistical analysis indicates that thundercloud seeding due to the hail suppression can be considered as a field experiment, which significantly reduced the lightning. This is in good agreement with result of field test of triggering lightning by rockets conducted in New Mexico (Kasemir, 1974). For complete analysis we must use an aeroplane equipped with cylindrical field measuring instruments to record the reduction in electrical field after firing of rockets.

Acknowledgments

The authors would like to gratefully acknowledge the Hydrometeorological Service of Serbia for providing necessary data and Mr. Dragomir Bulatovic for his help in preparing the figures.

References

1. Bergeron, T., 1935: On the physics of clouds and precipitation. Proc. 5th Assembly UGGI, Lisbon, 2, 156-161.

2. Bojkov, R., 2003: Brief review of current status of hail suppression, WMO, Report Series No. 41, Report No. 6, 49-55.

3. Curić, M.,1990: One evidence of the hail suppression efficient derived from radar measurements. J. Wea. Mod.,19, 79-81.

4. Curić, M., and Z. Vukovic, 2005: The influence of lightning on precipitation revealed by mesoscale numerical model. IAMAS Abstracts, Beijing, China, G2.

5. Kasemir, H. K., 1974: Lightning suppression by chaff seeding and triggered lightning (In: Weather and climate modification, Ed. Hess,W.N.). A Wiley publication, London, 612-629.

6. Radinović, D., 1972: Hail Control–Operative and scientific research project. U.S. Department of Commerce and National Science Foundation, Washington, p. 124.

7. Vukovic, Z., and M. Curić, 2005: The influence of the acoustic-electric coalescence on phase and mass transfer of supercooled drops. Pure Appl. Geophys,162, 1-25.

Chapter 15

An ICT Perspective on Lightning and Earthing in South Africa

Abednego Maliwa Ngcobo
Telekom College,
Olifantsfontein 1665, South Africa
E-mail: ngcoboam@telkom.co.za

ABSTRACT

Lightning and surge is one of those unpredictable, dangerous and damaging incidents that can be avoided if protection is installed correctly. The most common mistake is that people believe that only external structural protection is necessary for the safety of the structure and house hold.

The danger of lightning is exacerbated by the ignorance about the conductor used for installation and the supplier who are not able to supply correct material for the specific problem. We must take into consideration the principles of electricity, because lightning is an electrical phenomenon. There are direct strikes of lightning acting as primary source and produce the electromagnetic field which could cover a distance of up to 10 km. It induces in all conducting materials the secondary effects. This is more dangerous than direct strikes some times.

The lightning flash (strike) research and determination of soil resistivity could provide an accurate method and suitable materials required for a perfect protection.

What is a Surge?

A surge is a sudden and temporary increase in electrical current or voltage.

The most well known and visible source of surges is lightning. Lightning is not necessarily the main or highest occurring source of surges in a particular area.

Electrostatic Induction

An electrostatically charged cloud would cause a potential difference to everything on the ground. Similarly, a potential difference may occur between clouds of opposite charged polarities.

When a lightning discharge takes place between clouds or between clouds and earth, the electric field collapses momentarily, causing sharp fronted current pulses injected in all conducting materials at the point of lightning strike.

Electromagnetic Induction

A lightning discharge along a conductor induces current pulses into nearby power or telephone circuits due to induced magnetic field around the conductor.

Earthing

Earthing can be described as a conductor a system which, at all times, by means of one or more earth electrodes provides a low impedance path for the immediate discharge of electrical energy, without causing danger, to the general mass of earth.

Gas Arrestor

A gas arrestor is a voltage limiting protection device made up of two electrodes, contained in a gastight glass or ceramic housing, filled with Argon or Neon gas. In its normal state the resistance between the electrodes is very high and the characteristic of the subscriber's line is in no way affected. It is well known as spark gap protector as it provides a conducting path for the current above a certain voltage.

Earth Electrode

The following types of earth electrode systems are used. A single earth spike (rod) or a combination of the spike and trench method would constitute a low impedance path sufficient to withstand a longer duration of discharge.

Introduction

In undisturbed fine weather, the earth carries a negative charge with the corresponding positive charge in the upper atmosphere. By convection, this result in a positive (downward) field.

Within the cloud, static electricity builds up to an extent where neutralizing discharges or flashes occur. These flashes can be in the form of an inter-cloud (cloud-to-cloud), intra-cloud (within cloud) or cloud-to-ground flash.

The dramatic cloud-to-ground flash is of most concern. This dynamic phase of lightning commences in the form of a luminescent downward leader from the base of the cloud, which proceeds in a series of steps and branches toward the ground.

Fields of high magnitude can lead to point discharges taking place at sharp objects such as the tips of radio masts and flag poles. These objects are essentially conductors producing an intense field concentration at the tip. Natural objects can also promote point discharges, particularly in mountainous areas where physical elevation further intensifies the field. (Golde, 1973)

Lightning strike is a form of visible electric discharge between rain clouds, and between a rain cloud and earth, the phenomenon of this incident is clearly illustrated by the following figures:

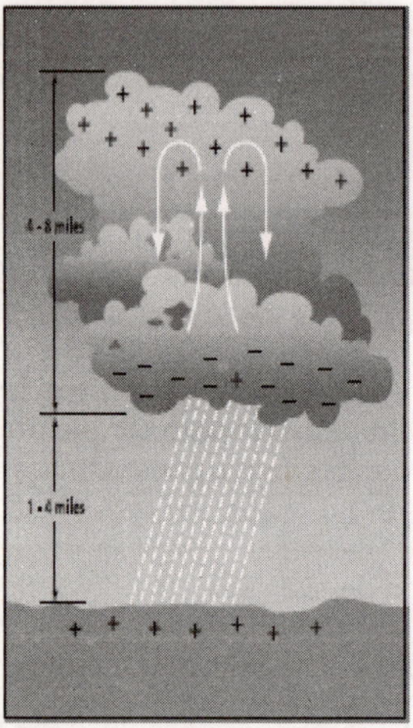

Figure 15.1: Electric Discharge Between Rain Clouds

Figure 15.2: Electric Discharge Between Rain Clouds and Earth

Figure 15.3: Lightning Incidence

Integrated Approach for Lightning Protection and Structural Protective System

To provide a perfect lightning protection in general is a demanding exercise. The problem should be analysed and clearly defined to provide solution. There are five important points to be considered when planning comprehensive lightning protection (Eriksson, Strauss and van Niekerk).

- Structural lightning protective system
- Earth electrode system
- Grounding arrangement practice
- Interference minimisation practice
- Electronic protection practice

The Structural protective system is employed to protect industrial, public and domestic structures (Electrical Route, Satellite Tower, Microwave Mast, and Telecommunication Outdoor Plant). The effectiveness of this structure protection could be attained by employing the following six point plan protective system (http//www.erico.com,; Golde, 1973; Eriksson *et al.*, 1978).

- Capture the lightning strike
- Safely convey the energy to ground
- Dissipate the energy into the ground system
- Bond all ground points together
- Protect incoming AC feeder
- Protect Low voltage circuits

The pivotal conductor standing above the structure (Air terminal) attracts the lightning as this is the initial point of discharge. It is important that lightning is connected to the low impedance path with the help of a well designed down conductor. The energy then is dissipated into the ground which is a major exercise. Capturing the lightning takes place mostly when the structure experiences direct strike. In the proximity of the building, other services that feed the structure, experience induced surge. This problem dictates the protection and equipotential bonding of all affected circuits to the structural protection system. (http//www.erico.com,; Golde, 1973; Eriksson *et al.*, 1978).

Design of Earth Electrode

The protection of lightning depends upon a number of factors. If any of them is omitted or ignored, it renders the whole system to be ineffective. Correct product for the system installed by professionally competent person is very important to obtain quality lightning protection system (Clark, 1989).

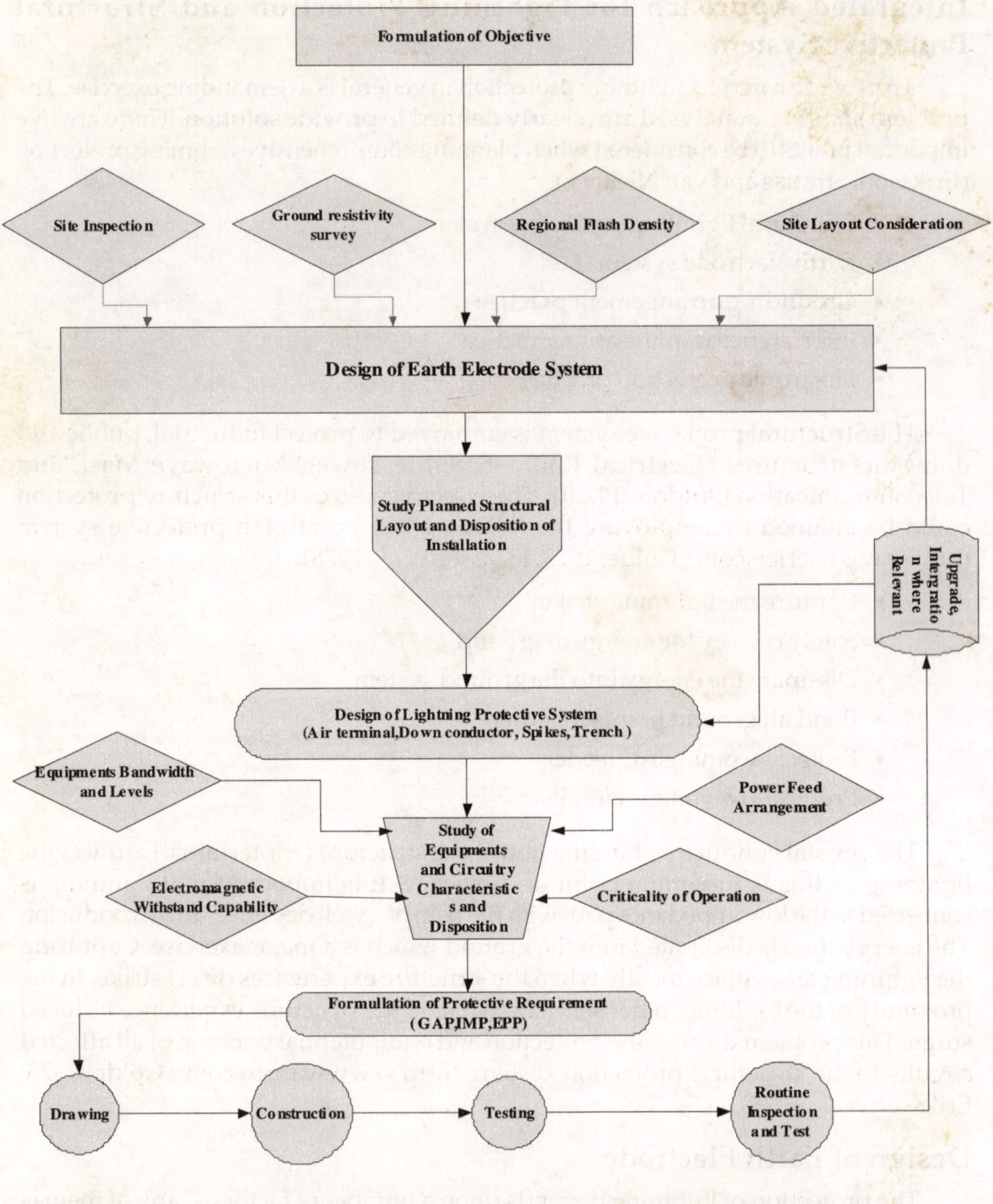

Figure 15.4: Comprehensive Approach Towards Providing Effective Lightning Protection for the Structure Including Power Feed and Data Circuits

The soil resistivity, regional flash density and site layout are the key factors in determining the type of earth electrode suitable for the area. Normally the flash density map is available from the weather bureau of each country. The suitable electrode system can be determined by ground testing (vibroground) null balance ohmmeter.

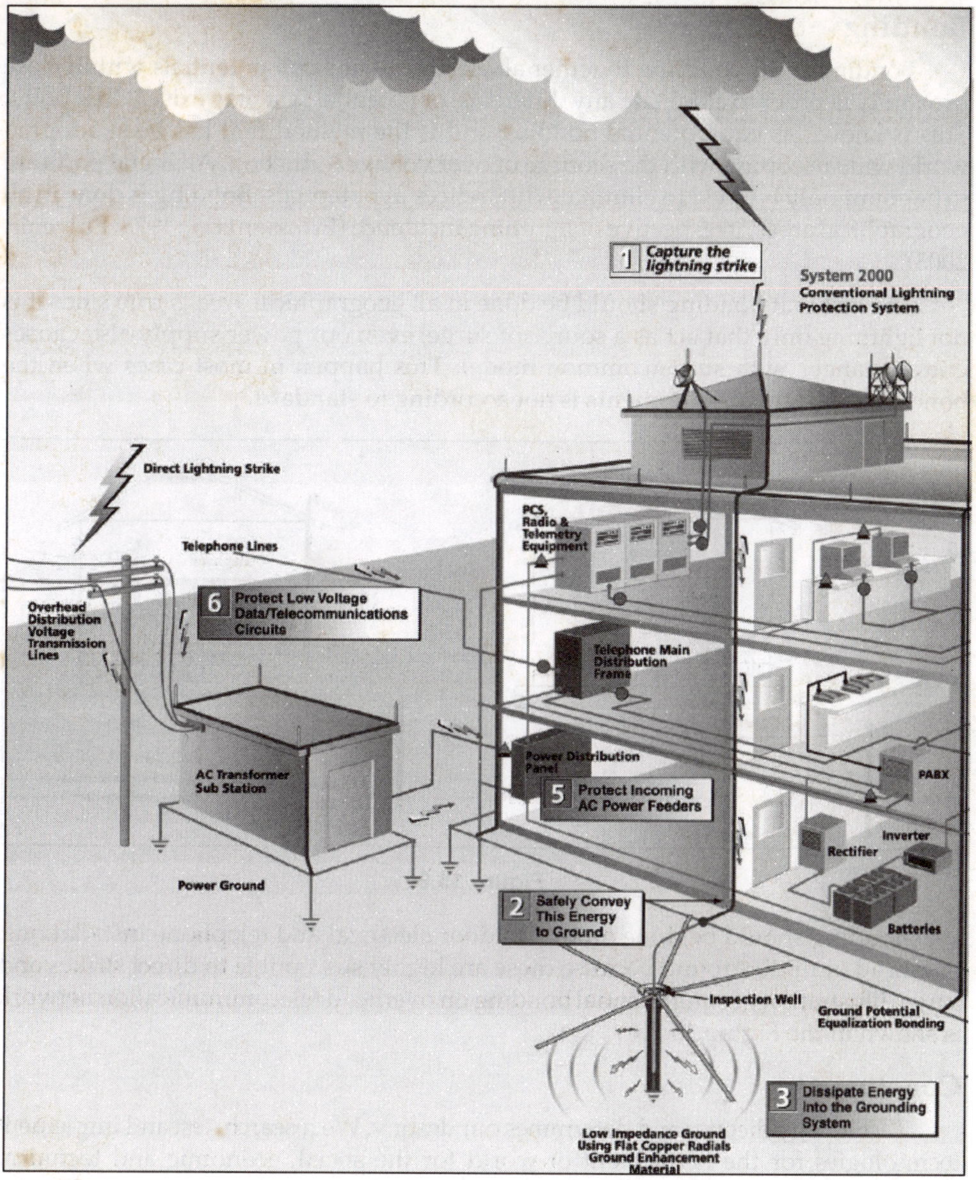

Figure 15.5: Illustration of the Structural Protective System Employing Six Point Plan

This illustration is based on the principles of WENNER called four electrode method of testing soil resistivity. Variety of soil resistivity is a result of, soil type, texture, compactness, chemical composition, moisture content and the temperature. The measurement of soil resistivity guide us to make a decision on the impedance of the electrode and the type(Mesh grid, Spikes, Trench) (Golde, 1973; Erikssonet *al.*, 1978).

Bonding

Bonding is the coupling together all electrodes at earth potentials within close proximity in order to eliminate any difference of potential that may exist at that point. This is known as equipotential bonding and is the method that has been adopted world wide in coping with the scourge of over voltage induction. All metal parts are to be commonly bonded to eliminate differences in potentials. Bonding is done in all geographical areas, irrespective of lightning incidence (Eriksson *et al.*, 1978; Pulvenis, 2003).

The fact that bonding should be done in all geographical area is true since it is not lightning only that act as a source of surge, even our power supply also causes critical danger with surge(common mode). This happen in most cases when the bonding of electrical equipments is not according to standard.

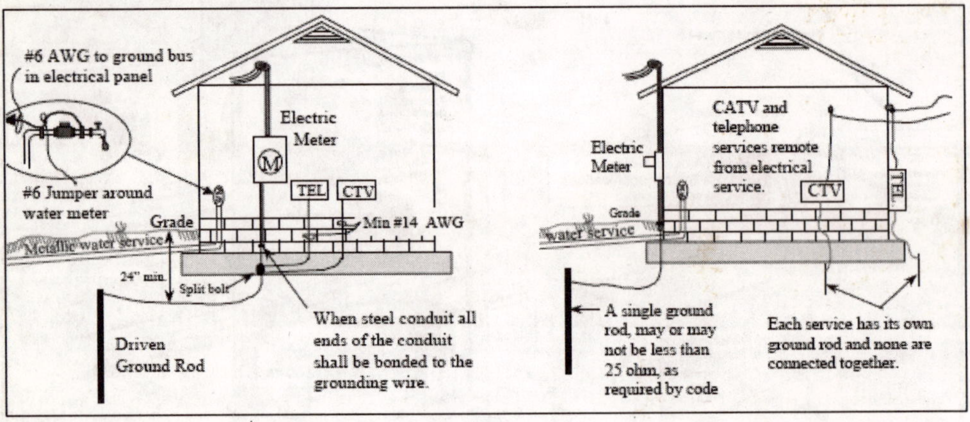

Figure 15.6

Bonding should be done on the outdoor electrical and telephone installations, overhead or underground because these are highly susceptible to direct strikes and surge. Illustration of equipotential bonding on overhead telecommunication network is shown in the Figure 15.7.

Conclusion

Technology dictates and determines our destiny. We research, test and implement technologies for the betterment of world for the social, economic and technical standards. The necessity to protect electronic appliances that are connected to the electrical network has become a worldwide phenomenon.

This challenge goes to all suppliers of electrical equipments to legislate agreement and provide a common point for each other ensuring safety of the personnel, property and the equipment self. This exercise will enable the owner to claim for guarantees and insurance in the event of the damage. Moreover it will save the owner from high maintenance bills for his/her equipments even if it is the supplier's fault.